"*Taming Your Crocodiles* is a daring and important addition to the field of leadership development. It's personal, provocative, and practical. It challenges us to become radically honest with ourselves about who we really are and how our learned crocodilian fears are holding us back from who we can be. And it provides an inspiring, well-structured path to help us coach ourselves and others to let go of our crocodiles and lead from a place that realizes much more of our true potential."

—Vijay Govindarajan, Coxe Distinguished Professor, Dartmouth College's Tuck School of Business; Marvin Bower Fellow 2015–16, Harvard Business School; *New York Times*, *Wall Street Journal* best-selling author

"In this simple but transformative book, you have everything—absolutely everything—you need to go on life's greatest journey to grow as a leader, not by changing yourself but rather by discovering who you are becoming."

—Chris Ernst, Director, Learning & Organization Effectiveness, Bill & Melinda Gates Foundation; author of *Boundary Spanning Leadership*

"I do believe that the issue of fear is personal and that is why it is buried in the workplace. *Taming Your Crocodiles* is groundbreaking not only because of its structured methodology, but also for its courage in calling out the issue itself. I am deeply impacted by *Taming Your Crocodiles*. I can speak personally and freely on this topic because this work has liberated me to lead more fearlessly at Microsoft and beyond."

—Toni Townes-Whitley, Corporate Vice President, Microsoft Worldwide Public Sector and Industry

"Inspiring, thought-provoking, and comprehensive. *Taming Your Crocodiles* offers a compelling combination of process, stories, and practice. It invites us to reflect on who we are and how to lead ourselves and others from an authentic place. Including lessons from the great leaders of our time, it helps readers to evolve by becoming more conscious of their inherent strengths and more free from self-limiting mind-sets and behaviors. A must-read for anyone who wishes to grow their leadership to the next level!"

—Joel Brockner, Phillip Hettleman Professor of Business, Columbia Business School

"In *Taming Your Crocodiles*, Hylke brings his life's work to the page to help readers explore what makes them come alive and to show how self-discovery can serve as a road map to a fulfilling life. Hylke writes as he lives—an endlessly curious observer who leads with vulnerability and an eagerness to explore connectedness. If treated as a book to be read and retired, *Taming Your Crocodiles* is a collection of compelling and creative ways to unlock our individual consciousness and power. If, however, it is treated as a travel companion through the leadership journey, it can serve as a guide to lifelong learning and reflection. Drawing from his own experiences and the teaching of his mentors/heroes, Hylke offers questions and perspective to empower us to write our story alongside him. In this way, *Taming Your Crocodiles* can double as the story of who we will choose to be and how we will choose to evolve as leaders and citizens."

—Kyle Angelo, Vice President & Executive Director, City Year Seattle/King County

"For your business to grow successfully, your people must grow continuously. To better enable that growth, they must be coached and, in turn, learn to coach others. This deeply thoughtful book goes well beyond Coaching 101 to the powerful 'art of coaching' that will guide and inspire you to a 'coaching culture' that becomes part of your organizational DNA."

—Ron Bergamini, CEO,
Action Environmental Group

"*Taming Your Crocodiles* presents a compelling and clear view into why individuals act and keep acting within growth-limiting barriers, offering simple alternatives that allow us to flourish and, along the way, enjoy the fascinating ride. Every time I sit to read this book, I learn more about me and how I become true to myself in front of my team. Highly recommendable."

—Augusto Muench, President,
Boehringer Ingelheim South America

"I have read many books and attended various courses on leadership during my career. For sure, *Taming Your Crocodiles* is among the top on my list, since it provides profound lessons on self-development as a foundation for coaching others and reinforces the need of having a personal purpose-driven path to keep growing into a better leader."

—Gioji Okuhara, Board Member & CEO,
Brazilian consumer goods companies

"We often wish we could get rid of the fears that prevent us from growing. What if we could learn to grow through them instead? *Taming Your Crocodiles* helps us reconcile with ourselves. Rediscover our true nature through an introspective journey made of questions and testimonials. Change perspective, so fears no longer drive our decisions. How would it feel to lead our life the way we truly want to and be able to inspire the people we care for? *Taming Your Crocodiles* helps us to become masters of ourselves first, so we become more effective in coaching the people we care for."

—Sebastien Arrivault, Strategy Director,
AKQA Portland

"*Taming Your Crocodiles* is helping me and our organization build a learning culture in which we keep enhancing our performance. Self-awareness, self-reflection, and helping each other grow are becoming an integral part in the way we work. This journey of bringing our fearful crocodiles under the aegis of our wise owls is deeply fulfilling. And it works, as we work the tools together: I am seeing a profound and positive impact in our organization. It helps us grow as individuals, as teams, and as an organization. And, above all, it's a never-ending story. When you are ambitious, want to perform better, and are also curious to get to know yourself better, you sign up for lifelong learning. And the rewards are magnificent: you are getting wiser."

—Bert van der Hoek, CEO,
De Friesland Zorgverzekeraar

"*Taming Your Crocodiles* touches the heart of leadership. It helps us to become aware of our greatness and what holds us back from it. And it invites us to touch the depths within ourselves, providing an inspiring path that compels us to keep growing and to encourage others to do the same. I recommend this enjoyable guide to anyone who wishes to get to know themselves better as a leader and as a human being."

—Simon King, Senior Human Resources Executive,
Life Sciences Company

TAMING
YOUR
CROCODILES

YOUR
CROCODILES

Unlearn Fear & Become
a True Leader

HYLKE FABER

Foreword by
Toni Townes-Whitley
Corporate Vice President, Microsoft

ixia
PRESS

Mineola, New York

Bibliographical Note

Taming Your Crocodiles: Unlearn Fear & Become a True Leader is a new work, first published by Ixia Press in 2018.

International Standard Book Number

ISBN-13: 978-0-486-82084-2
ISBN-10: 0-486-82084-X

Ixia Press
An imprint of Dover Publications, Inc.

Manufactured in the United States by LSC Communications
82084X01   2018
www.doverpublications.com/ixiapress

For Tante Durkje.
You taught me love.

Since there is no obscuration of mind,
there is no fear.
—Heart Sutra

We shall not cease from all exploration
and the end of all exploring will be to arrive
where we started and know the place for the first time.
—T. S. Eliot

Contents

Foreword

For God hath not given us the spirit of fear; but of power, and of love, and of a sound mind. —2 Timothy 1:7 (KJV)

LEADERSHIP LITERATURE IS RIPE with prescriptive profiles of success and formulas for understanding markets, building teams, leveraging assets, and driving growth. Across this continuum is a focus on the leadership characteristics necessary and the environmental conditions within which to apply them. Hylke Faber, in this critical addition to the leadership discourse, has refocused us on the root cause of not only leadership challenges but the deeper human condition: fear and its debilitating effects. *Taming Your Crocodiles* extends beyond a treatise on the role fear plays in limiting leadership, but prescriptively outlines a path toward authenticity with all the requisite benefits for leaders and their organizations.

I first met Hylke while working with my leadership team at Microsoft. New to the organization, I had assessed quickly that my team did not feel empowered, focused their energy internally, and operated suboptimally, with fear of making mistakes or being ridiculed. Together, we initiated a "fear study" leveraging a *Circumplex* assessment tool to determine the level of aggressive, passive, and constructive activity in my corporate and field organizations. As a result, we were able to establish the baseline of significantly passive-aggressive cultural characteristics that dwarfed constructive behaviors. More important, we changed the narrative by identifying "fear" as our critical leadership challenge, in an unlikely corporate environment. Having named our crocodiles, we set forth a path to tame them, collectively creating a roadmap to be "fearless" and shift our energy from internal concerns to external combat with our competitors. With Hylke's support, we outlined the path toward authenticity and personal growth necessary to reshape our team culture and lead the way for other teams within Microsoft.

Herbert McCabe, quoted in "Why Go to Church," stated that "the root of all sin is fear: the very deep fear that we are nothing; the compulsion, therefore, to make something of ourselves, to construct a self-flattering image of ourselves we can worship, to believe in ourselves—our fantasy selves." Leaders across all industries and public institutions are prone to lead with their "fantasy selves." The positions we hold and their ability to influence our daily existence drive us to refine our external image. In truth, we often lead from that place, unable to distinguish the difference between "what we do" and "who we are." *Taming Your Crocodiles* provides each of us a mirrored path to our true selves and our leadership truth: that only in our authentic, transparent selves can we transform the world around us. With equal parts inspiration (*why* we face our fears), direction (*what* we should focus on), and instruction (*how* we establish an authentic environment for ourselves and our teams), *Taming Your Crocodiles* provides us the rare opportunity to *see* ourselves and *free* ourselves as leaders in a safe context. From only this beginning can we fully adopt and deploy the multitude of leadership tools and methodologies available in this and other publications.

"Fierce, Fearless & Forgiving" is the personal narrative that Hylke helped me to develop with the knowledge of how to tame my crocodiles and lead an iconic, complex global organization through its most transformative season. I invite you to read, record, and review all aspects of this important book as you look to operate in authenticity and lead fearless teams.

Toni Townes-Whitley
Corporate Vice President, Worldwide Industry
Microsoft Corporation
January 2018

Introduction

"Every man's life represents a road toward himself."
—Hermann Hesse

AUTHENTIC OR BORROWED LEADERSHIP?

WHO AM I, TRULY? This question may be the most important question we ever ask. Consider this: Who do you look at first when you see a picture of family and friends with you in it? Yes, admit it, it's you. We are wired to look at ourselves. We want to get to know ourselves.

The more we know ourselves, the more we understand what makes us great and what mental blocks we have put in our way. The more we know ourselves, the more adaptable, and fearless, we become as we learn to rely on our true selves, no matter what happens around us. Our true self is untethered to circumstances. "Know Thyself" was inscribed over the gate of the oracle in Delphi. This motto helped thousands of people in ancient Greece face their greatest challenges.

What happens when we ignore the question: Who am I? Unconsciously, we may lead our lives from a borrowed set of ideas about who we are, such as "I should be safe, liked, productive, special, and in control." We may have picked these beliefs up from our families, friends, colleagues, our culture, or from other sources of conditioning. For a while our borrowed ideas may help us lead full lives . . . until they don't. Fixation on any idea tends to become a limitation. Attachment to safety may lead to fearfulness; a focus on being liked may lead to our betraying our own ideals; needing to excel can result in putting excessive pressure on ourselves and others; emphasizing control induces isolation and rigidity; and the need to be special can cause arrogance and judgment of our own self and others. Do we want to lead ourselves, and the people we care for, from a set of borrowed ideas? Or, do we wish to live and lead from a place that reflects who we truly are, no matter what others may have taught us?

Living based on borrowed ideas can seem unavoidable. We learn a set of values from our primary caregivers, then we go to school and learn about how to fit into the external world, and then we get a job where we are influenced by our organization's culture. Meanwhile advertising is continuously instructing us how to lead our lives at every step of the way. If we are not conscious, we can spend a whole life living someone else's ideas. That's the bad news.

GROWTH LEADERSHIP— TRANSFORMING CROCODILES INTO OWLS

There is also plenty of good news. Rather than living from borrowed values, we can choose to approach life and leadership from a different vantage point, as a great adventure to learn who we really are and live from that increasingly authentic place. We call this being Growth Leaders. Growth Leaders approach every moment as an opportunity for self-discovery, contribution, and excellence. The word "leadership" comes from the Middle English word "leith," which means "to die." When we commit ourselves to Growth Leadership, we are willing to let die—to let go of—those parts that are not us, our borrowed selves, and grow more into who we truly are every day and serve from that place, to the best of our abilities.

Why do we hold on to our borrowed selves, such as being perfect, liked, the best, in control, and special, even when they constrain us? We will explore this question deeply in this book, but in short, these limiting inner dynamics are fear-based. Part of our nervous system, the primitive reptilian bit, is a major fear producer, and generates these inhibiting thoughts and behaviors we will call our "crocodiles." From this perspective, growing into our authentic selves is unlearning fear—taming our inner crocodiles and bringing them under the aegis of the wiser parts of ourselves, which we will call our "owls."

As we go on this growth journey to tame our crocodiles and develop our owls, we tap into an endless source of fulfillment, innovation, and connection. When Gallup surveyed thousands of managers about how to retain their most talented employees, they found that half of the factors are about providing a culture that fosters learning and development. We love to learn—and when we make ourselves our primary field of study, we guarantee ourselves a course of discoveries that lasts a lifetime. Self-discovery motivates. Self-discovery is not a destination. It's an endless journey. We are never done discovering who we really are, and how to serve from that place.

INTRODUCING THE QUESTION "HOW AM I GROWING?"

We practice Growth Leadership by staying curious about this question: *Who is driving my behaviors right now, my borrowed fear-based thinking or my authentic, wise self?* Or in other words, *who is talking now, the owl or the crocodile?* To approach this inquiry as a journey, we can add another question: *How am I growing?* This question may invoke a sense of ongoing exploration and fascination.

"How are we growing?" is different from a question that we ask routinely: "How are you doing?" To that we tend to answer "Fine," "Busy," "Great," or maybe nothing at all. "How are you doing?" has lost meaningfulness for most of us.

Notice what happens when you ask yourself "How am I growing?" instead. How am I growing by giving in less to my fearful crocodilian urges? How am I growing by acting more from my wise owl, even if it's not comfortable yet for me to do so? How am I growing in wisdom when I look at a current challenge I have with the eyes of the owl rather than giving into my fear-based reactions? How am I growing when I think about who I wish to become less impeded by crocodilian thinking? You may find that at first, you don't know the answers. Maybe, when you sit with these questions as a patient, kind detective, you discover some nuggets of learning. When you allow yourself to spend some time asking these new questions, you may tap into some unexpected sources of fascination and inspiration.

THE BENEFITS OF GROWTH LEADERSHIP

I have found tremendous joy by asking the question "How I am growing?" over and over again. It has given me permission to keep discovering more of what is true about myself and my world, without judgment or regret. In asking myself "How am I growing?" I have started to see life as a process of growth. In that is tremendous forgiveness for our mistakes. I no longer worry about my destination; knowing that there is growth in the journey has led to the lessening of my self-judgment. If I make a misstep, or do something that I previously would have punished myself for, I don't dwell on it. I learn the lesson from it and move on. I don't hold on to anything. Another way of looking at forgiveness is to see that to forgive is to refuse to hold onto the pain of the past. When I am not holding onto past errors, I am available in the present moment and can give all my faculties to it—now.

"How are you growing?" We have found that this question provides guidance and strength without fail. And when we ask leaders and teams to consider "How are you growing?" something changes. Their energy goes up and a whole new set of ideas emerges about how to tackle the challenges of the day. Simply asking "How are you growing?" in the face of a challenge unleashes ideas that weren't visible before. Giving difficult feedback turns into a practice of sharing a humble perspective with honesty, care, and detachment to outcomes; working toward a stretch goal becomes a team practice of giving our best, growing more closely together, and questioning limiting beliefs that made the goal seem impossible before; and stress management turns into an exercise of learning to say a firm "no" to what no longer serves us and a wholehearted "yes" to what does. Growth Leadership opens our eyes to hitherto hidden resources within ourselves and others. As we become more aware of who we truly are, we discover more of our inner wealth.

Have you ever been in a meeting where people were talking but no real conversation took place? Perhaps they were saying what was expected, not what was true. Who was talking, their wise owls or their defensive crocodiles? It probably was a crocodile exchange. When we are committed to getting to know ourselves, we learn to connect with others from that more authentic place—our owl. We put more of our true selves in the conversation. We don't "phone it in" but are completely here. When we are more present, it encourages others to do the same. In the workshops I lead, we usually ask leaders of the group to vulnerably share their true aspirations and fears for the meeting at the outset. Imagine being in a meeting where your managers would openly convey their true aspirations and fears. Wouldn't that inspire you to also be more transparent? In an atmosphere of openness, where people have dropped their borrowed crocodilian masks, conversations go much more smoothly. Instead of worrying about looking good, we focus on the truth about the issues at hand. Elephants in the room no longer create tension, as they are discussed and explored together and become opportunities for learning and bonding. A shared mind-set of inner curiosity about who we truly are, beyond our borrowed personas, connects us to each other and to the real things that need speaking about. Growth Leadership helps us relate to ourselves and each other more fully.

CHOOSING TRUE GROWTH OVER GETTING

There are at least two ways in which we can approach our journeys of growth: we can grow to get to some destination we have in mind, focusing on the outcome alone; or we can choose growth for its own sake, completely open to where it may lead us. When we choose growth with a predetermined destination in mind, we limit our expansion by defining the outcomes based on what we know—our borrowed ideas. When we choose growth without agenda as a compass for our lives, we may find that we unlock endless fascination, inspiration, creativity, and power with that decision.

When I look at myself and others, I see that instead of choosing growth detached from outcomes, many of us have learned to live from a mind-set of growth for the sake of getting. We keep telling ourselves that we want to get "there": get results, get approval, get to answers, get to our destination. We seem to have created a world that drives us to want to always get more, often at the expense of growing more deeply into who we really are. When I stop the car at a red light, I see people all around me checking their phones, and I feel an inner tug to do the same. I ask myself—how much fulfillment are we getting from the e-mails, texts, and apps? Are we becoming so focused on getting what we think we want—a text message from a friend, an e-mail from our boss, a score from a game, a "like" on Facebook, or a follower on Instagram—that we forget what really matters to us: lasting fulfillment?

Becoming absorbed in getting can lead to a disregard for our ecosystem, resulting in ecological disasters. It can lead to constantly deepening economic divides—"I get more and more and you get less"—and growing social tension as different groups point fingers at each other, trying to get validation for their respective borrowed worldviews and ways of living. Our "Getting Mind-set," one of the ideas we have collectively borrowed from the past, may have outlived its usefulness.

Many of us seem to sense we're at the end of an era. There is a concern about the lives our children and grandchildren will have in this world that we leave behind—this world full of political, social, economic, and environmental turmoil. Depression, anxiety, and other psychological afflictions are at an all-time high. Companies are spending exponential amounts of money in providing psychological treatment and support for their employees. Employee engagement in the United States hovers at a mere 30 percent, according to Gallup. Do we wish to continue in this direction? Or can we leave behind our crocodiles and foster an environment that encourages true growth and learning?

A GUIDE TO GROWTH

I wrote this book to help guide our journey of growing into who we really are, going beyond our borrowed ideas of self and the world to help us express our true essence while we inspire others do the same. It is a reflection of the learnings that I and others have had in our quest to uncover our essential selves *and* be leaders in the world that we love and care for. We call it being Growth Leaders. As Growth Leaders, we see every moment, every interaction, and every change as an opportunity—an opportunity to become fully present to who we are now, to grow more into who we truly are, and, from that authentic place, to selflessly help others and give our best.

We have deliberately structured this book. It's organized based on leadership journeys that we have guided over decades with organization leaders, teams, and families—large and small.

We start the journey by diving more into how we grow and how we keep ourselves from growing, and then ready ourselves for our first big step: selecting a purpose, a calling that we wish to grow into and serve from. Once we have defined our purpose (something that often evolves over time), we will move on to study the core of the matter more deeply: ourselves. How can we use everything (in our inner and external world) as fertilizer for growing into our full potential? And how and where do we wish to contribute? We will follow up by looking at what we can learn from our fears—our crocodiles—and how to tame them, how we can balance right- and left-brain-oriented leadership styles, and how to inquire into our most sticky limiting beliefs so we can unlock them to see greater truth—while learning from stories told by great leaders who have walked this path or are walking it now. In the process, we will learn how to cultivate unflinching fascination for our learnings, which will help us overcome old crocodilian conditioning that tells us to abandon this journey into our authentic selves altogether. Our crocodiles are formidable defenders of the status quo. They may already be telling you to stop reading now, as this journey into self will get them nowhere!

After exploring ourselves this way more deeply, we will look at helping others grow. We will explore how we can use every conversation as an opportunity for inner development, from which both parties can walk away feeling taller on the inside. And finally, we will learn how to actively coach and inspire others, one-on-one and one-to-many—so that we can lead those who surround us to adopt a Growth Leadership Mind-set, routinely transforming our crocodiles into owls, together.

How to use this book? It's up to you. You can read this book as a journey in the order it is presented, or you can start your journey in any chapter where you feel drawn. Each chapter provides its own stand-alone tools for growth and you will find Fieldwork questions at the end of each chapter that can help you practice the tools. This is not "homework." Do what floats your boat and leave the rest.

The book is also a companion manual. I use it in my leadership work with clients, including in the Columbia Business School Executive Education "Leader as Coach" courses. You can take the journey outlined in this book by yourself, or together with others, whatever makes sense for you. Doing some of the Fieldwork together with someone you trust is a great way to deepen your learning.

Many of us, including me, have taken this and other growth journeys multiple times, as they provide new insights every time. You can read this book once, then go back and do the Fieldwork practices; you can select a particular chapter you believe will help you grow through a situation you are facing; you can take a paragraph or sentence and write about it in your journal . . . you decide how you will use this material for your growth.

WELCOME

Reading all of this, you may think, *but I like my life the way it is.* But take a moment to listen deeply. What does your heart tell you? The heart is the compass that has guided many, if not all, of the great leaders before us. Ask yourself, "What if I were to die in a year, how would I want to live? What would I want to discover? How would I want to relate to others? How would I want to better the systems that I'm a part of (my family, my organizations, my business)? And on a scale from one to ten, how much would I want to really, fearlessly know myself?"

See how this sits with you. What if every moment became an opportunity for you to become more present to yourself, learning about who you truly are, and contributing your best from an ever more authentic place? What if you could stop reacting from your fears or based on borrowed values? What if you could be free from the crocodiles that may have been limiting you?

The next chapter of life always begins in this moment. This book may challenge you to step deeper into your own life and leadership. Keep asking "How am I growing?" and let yourself be present to whatever calls to you.

I am grateful for the chance to offer these writings to share a path for our growth. It's my deep intention that the pages ahead will touch your heart and guide you and the people around you to ever greater freedom, self-love, and love for our world. Let go of what you think you know about yourself and open to a new experience of you.

Enjoy the reading and the road ahead.

TAMING
YOUR
CROCODILES

CHAPTER 1

Cultivating an Attitude of Growth

"The human mind always makes progress, but it is a progress in spirals." —Madame de Stael

STAGES OF GROWTH

WE HAVE EACH been through multiple growth cycles in our lives, growing up from infant, to child, to teenager, to young adult and so on. With each of these stages come deep learning experiences—we can call them awakenings—that have the potential to bring us closer to our true selves. For as long as I can remember I have been fascinated by these awakenings, and as I have gone through them, I have noticed that this type of learning is what makes great leaders. When we learn, we become bigger on the inside and more capable on the outside. Learning, in particular self-discovery, is essential to becoming an effective leader and creating a fulfilling life.

How do we cultivate this life-giving quality we all share—our capacity to learn? One way is to become aware of how we learn and how we don't. In my own life, growth has sometimes come only after a long period where I failed to learn the lessons being offered to me. We may respond instantly to feedback we receive from friends or colleagues, or we may only learn after our sticking to an old script for too long leads us into trouble. Growth often comes from letting go of mistaken beliefs we inherit and are attached to; you can think of these as crocodiles that have dominated our reptilian brains for eons.

Here is part of my growth story. As you read it, see how it may be similar to yours. Also notice common learning patterns I was falling into.

I was born and raised on a farm in the north of the Netherlands. I remember always being interested in the beauty of the region: the fields, the church steeples on the horizon, and the ever-changing display of clouds, grass, animals, and light. What I wasn't interested in at all were the tractors, tending to the cows, and the farming itself—all of which interested many of my friends and family. My mantra early on became: *get me out of here as soon as possible.* I longed to see the wider world.

Driven by this yearning, I ended up in New York City in my early twenties. I still remember arriving there for the first time on a Greyhound bus and looking out of the window, just before entering the Lincoln Tunnel. I gasped at the beauty of the tall buildings standing in stark contrast to the dark-blue September sky. In that very moment, I fell in love with Manhattan, and decided that I was going to get to the top of one of these buildings as soon as possible—not as a tourist, but as a CEO, managing partner, or owner: I was aiming high.

I got part of the way there. I was elected one of the youngest partners in the consulting company I worked at, I got a corner office on Lexington Avenue, and I thought I had it made. Not so fast, it turns out. Life had some lessons in store for me.

I remember being at a holiday party right after my election to partner, where one of my colleagues came up to me and said, "Hylke, you seem to be really good at what you're doing, but do you really like it?" I thought it was a dumb question. I hadn't loved working the farm as a child—it felt like something I had to do. Work and joy were not connected in my mind.

And then something else happened. I was leading a large consulting team. The manager on the project was reporting to me, and he and I were quite close—or so I thought. About an hour before we were going to present our final recommendations to our client, the board of a German pharmaceutical company, he approached me and said, "Hylke, we need to talk. I have some bad news for you." The worst-case scenario flashed through my head—after five months of deep analysis, had our numbers come out wrong? I asked him what the problem was. My colleague said, "Hylke, you are the worst manager I have ever worked for. It's painful to work with you and I will never work with you again!"

Strangely enough, I felt relieved. *Phew . . . nothing's the matter with what really matters: the numbers for our client,* I thought. Since I had been to feedback training, I said, "I'm sorry to hear that, why don't you schedule some time with my assistant so we can talk about it when we're both back in New York." Needless to say, I heard his feedback and didn't change anything as a result. I didn't think that being the worst manager ever was a problem, because, growing up, I knew several very successful farmers in the Netherlands, and they became successful—or so I thought—by being feared by their farmhands. Employees rotated through their farms frequently, and I thought they often needed to be cajoled or criticized to do their work. I thought that was the way you managed a successful company.

A few months later it came time for the annual performance reviews. I loved performance reviews—I had gotten high marks all throughout my life thus far, first in school and now at work, where I was earning big bonuses, fast promotions, and good projects. This time, my boss said, "I have three pieces of news for you. One piece of good news and two pieces of bad news." I thought he was playing with me. I had yet again more than made my numbers that year and thought I was up for another promotion.

"The first thing is that I will fire you in six months unless you drastically change your behavior." That seemed like an odd comment to me. Did he want me to sell even more? I thought my numbers looked good. He continued: "The hardest thing for me to share with you is that no one in this firm really likes working with you anymore—they try to avoid it." That hurt. "Finally," he concluded, "I want you to take a week off, totally off. Don't check your voicemail—nothing—and think deeply about what I have said." That was supposed to have been the good news. Even though I didn't love my job, I derived a sense of security and identity from it, so being disconnected didn't seem like such a great offer.

That week out of the office, I talked to my friends about what had happened. Some told me that my boss was crazy, given all the hard work and great results I was giving him. One or two others cautioned me, and said I should look into the feedback and at least get a coach so I could keep my job. That seemed like a wise idea. And so I did. I got a coach and we worked together for a year and not much happened. Yes, I learned some valuable techniques, but at the root nothing shifted. I continued to believe that I was better than most people there, and that only a few people were better than me. This meant I had to be nice to the better-than-me group, and tolerable with the others—going through the motions of the be-kind-and-clear communications processes I had learned that year in coaching.

And then I hit a wall. I had developed severe asthma and my insomnia was intensifying. Sometimes I wasn't able to sleep for seven days in a row. In one of these sleepless weeks I was on vacation with some friends on Ameland, an island off the north coast of Holland. We were sharing rooms. While my friends were snoring the night away, I was lying there at 2:00 a.m., 3:00 a.m., 4:00 a.m., wide awake, with my body aching from not having slept. Suddenly it dawned on me: Something big had to change. I couldn't go on like this. What had happened to the sweet boy who loved the fields and the music and had lots of great friends growing up? All I could see now was a robot who achieved, achieved, achieved and not much else. And even the achievements were no longer coming the way they used to, as my body and social structures were crumbling.

Does any of this sound familiar? Your own growth journey will likely take a very different form, but it may include a similar pattern of stagnation or struggle. Growth is not a linear process. Life is messy and sometimes it seems like we're going backwards for a long time, before anything changes. I went through a decade or more of inner decline, where life got harder and harder as I became more and more brittle on the inside. Difficult as it was, that was what it took for me to evolve. Our path is sometimes smooth, sometimes not, just like a river.

Even though life and growth may sometimes seem difficult and unpredictable, we may also notice some patterns in how we learn. This awareness can help us become more skillful in navigating our learning journeys, as we become able to recognize and let go of our crocodiles.

In 1999, I trained for my first marathon. It was held in New York City. The first time I did a long-distance run to prepare for the big day, I was caught off guard by the pain and fatigue I experienced around mile twelve. When marathon day came, I knew what to expect and how to move through that dip in my energy—I had learned to rely on steady pacing, gentleness, and perseverance as my helpers. Similarly, we can learn to ride the waves in our learning journeys. These waves follow common patterns and we can train ourselves to move through them—equipped with specific mind-sets and behaviors.

Stage 1: Unconscious-Unskilled

Let's take a look at the first stage of growth, which we can call "Unconscious-Unskilled." Unconscious-Unskilled is a phase where you don't know what you don't know. For me, I had blind spots in huge areas of life and leadership. I had no idea that life (especially work life) and joy had anything in common. I hadn't a clue that seeing the greatness in colleagues and treating them with sincere respect is important, and that it makes work a lot more fun. I had no idea who I was. And I didn't know that my crocodiles were keeping me stuck.

Life is our greatest teacher. We hear this all the time and yet, how much are we listening to life? I certainly wasn't. I had completely closed off, thinking I had it all figured out: make lots of money, nurture a few friendships, and become part of the uber-elite that runs the world was my credo then. With this fixed mind-set, I didn't appreciate the wisdom in my colleague asking me whether or not I liked what I did. Nor did I hear the cry for transformation from my colleague who gave me the "bad manager" feedback. I even rationalized my boss's feedback, despite the fact that he had told me that he was going to fire me. He had fired people in the past and I knew he was serious about it with me. And yet it didn't sink in. Why not?

I had a very deeply entrenched belief system about what constitutes a good person and what I needed to do to be happy. I thought I had to perform to be happy, even if that meant alienating others and, most painfully, myself. I can see this now. Back then I was totally unconscious of this performance-over-all-else orientation. So I was powerless over it—it was running my life, without my knowing it.

"Listen to the whispers, so you don't have to hear the screams" is an old Cherokee saying. My own whispers told me time and time again that I needed to stop, take a step back, and introspect. But I didn't want to. I closed my ears to all the signals that had been coming my way, leading a life that, looking back now, seems in many ways to be a bit absurd. The Dutch priest Henri Nouwen wrote: "The noise of our lives makes us 'deaf,' unable to hear when we are called, or from which direction." According to him, our lives become "absurd" when we lose touch with reality as it is, or deaf to life's natural song. He points out that the word *absurd* has the Latin root *surdus*, which means "deaf." I would have benefited from opening my ears earlier to the natural rhythms that I was called to live by. The words *hearing* and *healing* have only one letter difference—we could call this a coincidence or consider it as pointing to the transformative healing power of tuning into the natural rhythms of our lives. Until we do so, we remain Unconscious-Unskilled, unaware of where we are stuck and where we must grow.

Stage 2: Conscious-Unskilled

Eventually I did start hearing the screams and became conscious of where I was unskilled. Paradoxically, my insomnia woke me up to the realization that I needed to transform. "What had happened to the sensitive boy, who loved the fields, the church steeples, and nature and who had many wonderful friendships?" I wondered. It dawned on me that I had become a robot, driven by my attachments to performance, prestige, and power. The person who I had become had very little to do with the boy I remembered I had been. And I saw that my life had become unmanageable—my health was failing, I couldn't sleep anymore, I had only some superficial friendships left, and my work was becoming rote. That sleepless night during my vacation on Ameland was the moment where I entered the next stage of growth: I became "Conscious-Unskilled," or in other words, I now knew that I didn't know. I saw that there were huge parts of my approach to life that needed changing so that I could start living from a much more authentic place.

I reached the Conscious-Unskilled stage by allowing myself to become more present, more aware of what was really happening—opening myself to the feedback I was receiving from life. One way in which we can accelerate our growth is to be present to what is and to fully let in what we notice. When we pause long enough, with concentrated attention on what is happening in our lives, we may create sufficient distance from our habits to see what is holding us back and where our biggest opportunities for growth are. Often, we resist doing this because being honest with ourselves feels too threatening for our crocodiles. But it's our only avenue for real learning.

Stage 3: Conscious-Skilled

The move from the Unconscious-Unskilled to Conscious-Unskilled phase is the beginning of growth. This transition is important, as we can only grow once we have gained awareness of what we have yet to learn. We are becoming aware that we don't know everything (often through realizing our own specific crocodilian shortcomings), but we haven't yet acquired the knowledge and skills we need to grow out of it. It's not until we come to a crossroads and make the deliberate choice to develop ourselves more fully that we start to move from Conscious-Unskilled to "Conscious-Skilled." We need to develop the *inner resolve* to fully address our area(s) of not knowing. During that night of insomnia, I sensed I *had* to change my life if I wanted to have a shot at being happy again. I became determined to find a new way to live, no matter what. I looked for books, teachers, and eventually meditation found me. Through it I started to find a path back to who I truly was. I discovered how to let go of old, borrowed beliefs that had kept me stuck, like "I should be recognized," "I am better than others," "I should be perfect," "I should have it together," and "I should know the answers." Dropping these beliefs led me to perceive and behave in new ways, and helped me develop my formerly lacking people skills. We become Conscious-Skilled when we start acquiring new capacities, mindsets, and behaviors and start applying these in our daily lives. My new skill of being gentle with myself, which I honed on the meditation cushion, led me to take time to investigate what I truly wanted to do with my life. This inquiry led me to almost becoming a monk, and then deciding to dedicate my career to helping others access and apply the peace and compassion I was finding on the meditation cushion to leadership, by becoming an executive coach and team facilitator.

The journey from each growth stage to the next is different for everyone. Generally, though, when we're first on our new way, it may feel disorienting. We may feel that we don't know who we are anymore. If we have lived a whole life based on being "the special one," it may feel off to "only" be one of many contributors on a team. If being "the nice one" has been our go-to borrowed persona, the first time we say "no" without apology to someone we care about may feel like jumping out of an airplane. If we are used to being "the rescuer," allowing someone who is struggling to find their own way without us jumping in to fix it for them may feel like blasphemy. At first this new way of being and doing felt very new and uncomfortable to me. I was still only Conscious-Skilled. I was tempted to go back to the rat-race way of living that I knew so well. Conscious-Skilled is like driving a car just after having obtained our license—it might not be second nature yet, but it is becoming a functional part of our lives. We are starting to live and are slowly getting used to our new way of being and doing—it's no longer just a whisper in the background.

Stage 4: Unconscious-Skilled

We move from Conscious-Skilled to Unconscious-Skilled when we begin to effortlessly integrate our newly found aptitudes into our daily lives—they become second nature. Then we drive the car, without having to think much about driving it. Our newly found awareness has been translated into skills we perform naturally—like breathing in and out.

To get to this point requires at least three things from us. First is repeated practice. The second is a sense of courage—a sense of being wholehearted, and not giving up, whatever obstacles we may encounter. The third is humility. The first two, practice and courage, are probably quite intuitive. The latter one, humility, might be less easy to understand, and yet it is a crucial ingredient throughout all stages of growth. Let's explore what we mean when we say *we need to be humble to learn.*

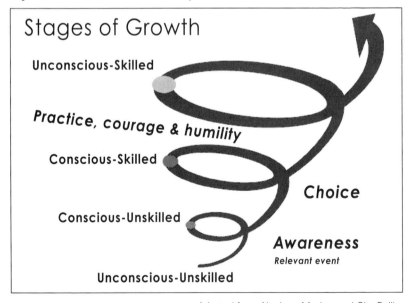

Adapted from Abraham Maslow and Gita Bellin.

CULTIVATING GROWTH THROUGH HUMILITY

The word *humility* has a very beautiful root—it comes from the word *humus*, which means "ground." Humility means being willing to accept that we don't know. It means being willing to question everything in our lives for truth. We need to be willing to say "I have lived my life based on beliefs that I don't know are true. I am willing to question and to let go of those beliefs, if I discover that they are not true. I am willing to let go of everything about me that is not true, to make space for what is."

To truly evolve we need to find the wherewithal to meticulously and continuously look at our unexamined beliefs and motivations. Humility enables us to keep growing out of who we are not, into who we truly are. For me to grow, I had to be willing to question my beliefs, for example about being special, being better than and all-knowing. According to Gandhi, "The instruments for the quest of truth are as simple as they are difficult. They may appear quite impossible to the arrogant person, yet most natural to an innocent child. The seeker after truth should be humbler than the dust. The world crushes the dust under its feet, but the seeker after truth should so humble himself that even the dust could crush him. Only then, and not until then, will he have a glimpse of truth."

Humility is not a one-time event. It's an ongoing practice. Do you dare be so humble that you admit you don't know everything yet? Dare you question your entrenched beliefs about yourselves and the world enough to take challenging moments as opportunities for self-reflection?

Stillness Practice

Reflecting on awakenings I have witnessed in myself and others brings out one other aspect of humility. This is *stillness*. We seem to grow by leaps when we allow ourselves to become still. When we let go of our activities and the chatter of everyday thinking, we become more open to seeing ourselves from a different angle. Sometimes life throws us into a stillness we can call the night of the soul, when we have no other option than to do nothing and reflect, like that night on Ameland when my insomnia woke me up to pause and take an honest look at my life. We can choose to go into this stillness anytime we want, pausing everything we are doing and allowing ourselves to become quiet on the inside. This can mean taking a moment to stop what we are doing, taking a walk, or looking at the sky. Then we can ask ourselves, without any expectation of the answer, *How am I growing? What are the whispers telling me? What beliefs that I have held onto as true are not? What is true about me now?* Or maybe we drop all questions and simply surrender to the moment and let be what is. Stillness will speak, when we have the humility to listen to it. Maybe do it now. Take a moment to be with yourself, dropping everything. Be still.

LEARN TO LOVE THE PROCESS— ADOPT A METAMIND-SET OF FASCINATION

Growth is not a linear process. The path of learning is something like being on a spiral—we get to see the same things over and over again, but from a higher altitude. It's a messy process and to stay in it, throughout all the stages of growth, requires ongoing commitment to learning. As Patrick Connor, one of my teachers, taught me, an unflinching metamind-set of fascination for learning can motivate us to keep going no matter what, even when life throws us "curveballs," such as loss, disappointment, and rejection. We can always rely on our fascination. It's simply a choice we repeat over and over. We know we can step back and reflect "How am I growing?" any time we like. Watch what happens when you commit to "How am I growing?" as a regular practice. You may discover a hidden strength, a grit, to face whatever comes your way today, ready to learn a bit more about who you truly are and who you are not from your current situation, *whatever* it is. Sometimes I kindle my fascination by choosing to be in awe with this present moment, asking myself "What could this present moment be teaching me?" As I adopt an attitude of AWE (Always Willing to Evolve), I feel more rooted in my journey of growth.

Growth Instant

When we face ourselves more fully, with concentrated attention, we come to see what is true and what isn't about us. Often there is a trigger, what we can call a *"relevant event,"* that provides the impetus for our new awareness. Yet before we accept an event as relevant to our growth, we tend to ignore many, frequently more subtle events that hold the same teaching. I had made my colleagues' and my boss's comments *"irrelevant events."* Eventually insomnia became my relevant event. Now looking back, I remember hundreds of little and big situations that I could have learned the same lessons from—and yet I had brushed all those aside. I thought I was too busy, too important, too old, and too invested in my ways to listen and consider a change.

Think of the whispers in your life you have made irrelevant—maybe because you thought it wasn't the right time to stop your momentum, or because you dismissed the person telling you, or because you were afraid of the changes that it would require. It's very human to want to dismiss the whispers and yet, for us to grow, we must find the courage to open our ears and listen.

To remind us of the power of relevant events to help us grow, we also call them "Growth Instants." When we are triggered, or when we feel a subtle whisper, we can stop and ask ourselves, *How am I growing?* We don't make any moment irrelevant. We see every moment as a potential Growth Instant. We don't want to take a second of this life away from our awakening into our fullest potential. Instead, we listen to all the feedback we receive and never dismiss any signs that we may be headed down a dead-end road. We don't ignore nudges to proceed a new way that will help us grow.

I-We-It Whisper Awareness

Whispers come from different directions. Fred Kofman, another one of my teachers, provides a way to organize them. Keeping this organization in mind helps to open ourselves also to areas of our lives where we don't typically look.

He describes perception of reality as a stool with three legs: "I, self," "We, relationships," and "It, task." The "It" part of our perception of reality is our focus on that which is tangible—what we do, how well that goes, how effective and efficient we are. The "We" part describes our attention to our connection to others—how much trust and empathy there is, how deep our bonds are, and how much we are enjoying being together. And the "I" dimension speaks about our inner lives—how aligned we are with our values, how we feel, and how fulfilled we are.

It's a three-legged stool, as our perspective on life is balanced only when we pay attention to all three areas. It's out of balance when we focus on one or two aspects of reality at the exclusion of the other(s). When we only focus on the task, we may be successful for a while, and yet if we ignore our relationships and our inner life, we may burn bridges with others and become strangers to ourselves. When we prioritize relationships over all else, we may lose focus on our tasks and lose touch with our authentic needs and aspirations. And when we focus only on our inner lives, we may become disconnected from others and unable to take care of our basic tasks.

Ask yourself, where does your attention habitually go to? I, self; We, relationships; or It, task? What is the impact of that on the other two dimensions in your life? And in which area do you hear the strongest whispers? How are you growing doing this reflection?

In my journey, I had become so focused on the It that I had completely lost touch with others and with my true self. When I lay awake that night on Ameland, I started to hear the screams from all three aspects of reality. I was deeply unhappy (I), I had become completely estranged from those I cared about (We), and even in my area of focus, the It, I was losing out, as I was becoming less and less effective on the outside, while becoming more brittle on the inside.

The Eyes of Love vs. the Stare of Judgment

Remaining courageous, humble, and fascinated makes us more open to seeing where we have opportunities to grow and learn. And there are other mind-sets we can adopt to keep on the learning path. One I especially like is looking at ourselves and others with what we can call "The Eyes of Love." It's about choosing to be gentle with ourselves, especially when life gets tough, rather than giving in to our crocodilian reflex of self-judgment.

We grow so much just by being gentle with ourselves. Think about how quickly children grow when they are in an atmosphere of love rather than judgment. Unfortunately, as adults, most of us have PhDs in judgment. Our inner critic is super strong. We judge and criticize ourselves for not knowing better and for not growing faster, or tell ourselves that growing is too hard, that we aren't worth it, and that we don't have time for it.

Looking at ourselves through judgmental eyes slows down our growth. We end up in a downward spiral. Let's examine how this self-limiting pattern works.

Afraid of judgment if we try and fail, we look the other way from our growth opportunities. As a result, we slowly become *unable* to see those opportunities—we become deaf to the whispers in our lives, since these ask us to make changes and take risks that our inner critic fears. This means we end up making the same, self-limiting choices over and over again. Then, because we can't easily overlook the consequences of our self-limiting choices, such as dysfunctional relationships, lack of fulfillment, and lack of effectiveness, we start judging ourselves for these self-created misfortunes, feeling even worse about ourselves. As we stay in our unconscious, self-punishing, downward spiral, the layers of self-judgment become so thick that they paralyze us over time. We feel bad about ourselves, and bad about feeling bad, becoming ever more resistant to letting go of old limiting ways. With every setback, we judge ourselves more, feeling worse and getting more entangled in this downward spiral, which then discourages us even further.

I have been stuck in this self-destructive pattern many times, like during the ten years before that night on Ameland. I sabotaged my learning by refusing to acknowledge the increasing pain in my body and mind. I didn't want to admit that I wasn't loving myself or what I was doing, and that the quality of my work was decreasing. I didn't want to accept that my colleagues were fed up with me.

To deal with my pain, I alternately chose self-punishment and blaming others—working harder and harder and becoming more and more aggressive with my colleagues. I was numbing myself with work. Job performance had become a poor substitute for the more difficult task of looking inside, re-evaluating my priorities, and changing course. I tried to make my restlessness go away by adopting more self-judgment strategies—working even harder and isolating myself more as a result, leading to greater pain, more frustration, and more self-judgment. I was caught in a downward spiral.

Thankfully there was a way out of this pattern. When I woke up after my insomnia, I made a conscious choice to learn myself out of my despair, whatever it was going to take. My decision and subsequent actions helped me to gradually transform my workaholic downward spiral into a growth journey—replacing despair with hope, stagnation with creativity, and loneliness with connection.

What has kept me going? Gentleness and radical self-honesty: I have been learning to see myself with the eyes of love, not through a judging lens.

Reflecting on some of the following questions with kindness can help us snap out of a negative judgment spiral:

- What can this station in life teach me?
- What old ways of thinking are limiting me?
- How have these ways of thinking helped me? How are they common and understandable strategies of the mind to help me live?
- What do I not want to see? What if I allowed myself to see these limiting thoughts?
- Who would I be without these ways of thinking? What new ways of thinking can I adopt that fuel fulfillment, connection, and effectiveness?
- How can I respond differently to my current situation?
- What am I grateful for? How can I bring more of the things that make me grateful into my life?

Or, in one question: "How am I growing?"

Sometimes, we may find the answer is "not at all" or "not in the ways I would like"; that's when we know we need to find the courage and humility to keep pursuing our own expansion, without self-judgment.

As I pondered some of these questions after that sleepless night on Ameland, with honesty and a newly found gentleness, I discovered underneath all my travails a deep longing to be myself, the real Hylke; to see how I was not the thoughts and actions that were driven by my past conditioning to be special, and that I could choose another path that offered more growth and authenticity—one where the little guy inside who loves nature, music, and the truth of life would get to take the driver's seat.

Take a moment and contemplate some of the questions above for a challenge you may be facing. Look at yourself with kind eyes—the eyes of love. Do you notice a space that opens when you give yourself a moment to reflect more compassionately on how you are growing and where you may still be stuck? Do you notice inner strength becoming available to you when you let go of some self-judgment?

When we start to see the new opportunities for growth that become available with gentle inquiry, we gain motivation to keep approaching every challenge with the eyes of love. When we see that gentleness works, we become even more motivated to use it.

CREATING A GROWTH CULTURE TOGETHER

We can adopt the practices of courage, humility, fascination, and gentleness on an individual basis, and they also work in collectives such as teams, entire companies, even families. When an organization's leaders instill an atmosphere of fascination with growth, work starts to become exciting, no matter what is happening. Like a child, we start to love learning more about ourselves, and what we are truly capable of. With this enthusiasm comes confidence. Then our offices and our homes become places to discover and share truth with each other. As a result, our families, teams, and organizations become "sadhu-like." *Sadhu*, among other things, means "an efficient one." In a sadhu culture, not a moment gets wasted on ego-serving goals that don't contribute to real learning. Everything is for our higher growth and service. Customer and coworker feedback becomes an opportunity to access and apply more of our creativity; a reduction in force turns into an opportunity to access greater firmness and compassion in ourselves; and the start of a new project invites us to become even clearer about what we really wish to contribute at work.

Imagine if we can reach a point when that will be the prevailing atmosphere in leadership worldwide. What will happen with our so-called problems? We may grow through them and solve them from our collective ever-expanding consciousness. The rewards may be tremendous—a healthier world, and maybe most importantly, deeply fulfilling lives.

MAKE IT YOURS

So how do you keep fueling your fire for growth? In the end, it's up to you. Maybe your deeper awareness of the stages of learning you go through will help you to stay the course of growth when things get tough. Maybe you will find that greater humility and allowing yourself to question more of your beliefs will open up new avenues for growth. Or it could be that steadfast courage to examine whatever is presenting itself to you for learning without flinching will help you. No matter what you choose, stay gentle with yourself. That's something we can always fall back on, no matter what happens.

You create your own path of learning. Take a moment and think about how you will design your journey in a way that appeals to you. Make it attractive to *you*. Maybe you add a bit more courage. Maybe a bit more gentleness. Possibly some regular moments of stillness or meditation. Maybe you intend to have at least one Growth Instant every day. Or, what about play? It can be a very powerful tool for learning as well. Whatever you do, make it yours. And then take the first next step, however little. See how it feels. Celebrate any progress, however small. It's like watering little saplings that have just been bold enough to sprout. Going from being blind to a part of ourselves to seeing it consciously can be a seismic shift. Allow it to happen. First there was just a seed and then there is this beautiful green thing popping up—a big miracle indeed!

Take a moment to pause and thank yourself for taking the time to pay concentrated attention to your own growth. And then, when you are ready, continue reading.

FIELDWORK

1. What are the whispers saying in your life? And what are the things being said to you right now that you may not want to be hearing? This could be direct feedback from your coworkers, supervisors, clients, or employees; it might be requests for more attention or respect from family members; or it could be a message from your own body.

2. Where is your own biggest growth opportunity? Is it on the "I"-dimension (self): awareness of your values, who you are, your fulfillment? Or the "We" (others): impact on others, relationships, trust? Or the "It" (system): how you contribute to the system you're a part of, long and short term? Or some combination of these three dimensions?

3. Given your reflection on questions 1 and 2, what is one thing you are becoming aware of that you are Conscious-Unskilled in? What would Conscious-Skilled look like? Write it in table format, such as below:

FROM: My Conscious-Unskilled State	TO: My Aspired Conscious-Skilled State
e.g., I am overworking myself	e.g., I work with ease and have balance in my life

4. What will you choose next in order to move from Conscious-Unskilled to Conscious-Skilled and then to Unconscious-Skilled? What will you practice?

5. In what ways do you judge yourself for being Conscious-Unskilled in this area of your life? What does your self-judgment crocodile say about you not mastering this yet? What is the impact of this crocodile on your learning? What happens to your learning when you relax these crocodiles?

6. How can you act on the whispers with more compassion for yourself? Keep asking yourself this question until you sense you have found an answer that resonates with you.

7. How are you growing?

CHAPTER 2

Finding Our Fearless Calling

"Select your purpose . . . and then use selfless means to attain your goal. Do not resort to violence even if it seems at first to promise success; it can only contradict your purpose. Use the means of love and respect even if the result seems far off or uncertain." —Mahatma Gandhi

CONNECTING TO YOUR TRUE PURPOSE

WHEN YOU WAKE UP in the morning, do you have a sense what you aspire your day to be about? Do you have a sense of purpose? Or are you reacting to what shows up in your inbox, or on the screen of your mind—the tasks, feelings, and ideas that are there when you wake up? Having a sense of purpose can help us focus. It's like going on a hike where we set out to reach the top of a mountain. That sense of direction will help us plan our trip and stretch us beyond what we may feel most comfortable doing in the moment. We may not stop for as long in the coffee shop along the way, and we may carry some extra water to stay hydrated, even though it adds weight to our pack. Our intention fuels our resolve.

Deep down, we all feel called to something great in this life. The more we have a clear idea of what this is, the more energy we may feel. Our calling is very personal—it's unique to us and not something that someone else can tell us. It's something deep inside of us that energizes us—it helps us to start our day, to focus our priorities, to address the challenges we encounter, and to motivate us to keep growing. The only person that can define that calling is the person reading this sentence. (In case you wondered, yes, that is you.)

Where does our calling come from? There isn't really one answer to that. What we do know is that we are influenced by other people's priorities—

often without realizing it. Let's reflect for a moment. What do we learn about our purpose from our families, schools, jobs, friends, and the wider world? We receive tons of messages from the tribes we live in. Here are a few: to survive you need to be busy, to belong you need to conform and not rock the boat, to be successful you need to be better than others and make lots of money, to learn you need to get to know the answers fast, and to be worthy you need to be special . . .

Because we want to survive, belong, be successful, grow, and be good, and because we prefer not to question the priorities of those closest to us, we conform our lives to our tribe's priorities, rather than our own—often without knowing it. Or we rebel and reject the tribe's priorities, and live the opposite of what they value. In both cases we are at risk of leading borrowed rather than authentic lives. We are unconsciously reacting to our environment.

Why do we live borrowed lives? Because we haven't yet found out who we truly are, what our true calling is, and committed to that. Rather than first finding out who we are and taking a stance for that, we are swayed by our tribe, and stand with them, or against them. For a while, I lived my tribe's focus on wealth, climbing the corporate ladder as fast as I could. Then I rebelled and almost became a monk, thinking I wanted to live without ever having to think about money again. Neither path was sustainable for me, as neither reflected who I truly am. Instead of my authentic self, these orientations had money at the center—getting lots of it, or having none of it. After ongoing reflection, I learned that my calling had to do with something inherent in me—my desire to grow and discover more and more of who I am and who we are together. To find our callings, we have to be willing to look inside and disentangle ourselves from the messaging and programming all around us.

The one thing we know for certain about life is this: We all will die. Contemplating our mortality can help us clarify our calling. One of my uncles, Gerrit Visbeek, died of cancer when he was sixty-two years old. We spoke often during the last few months of his life. He told me that his biggest regret was putting off getting to know who he really was until he was on his deathbed. He shared then that he was discovering that his essence had something to do with love that goes on, even after death. Rather than focusing on this love and extending that to others, he realized he had spent a big part of his life being devoted to other priorities—priorities he had borrowed from those around him, like being someone in the world, being successful, and accumulating wealth.

For all we know, we may not wake up again tomorrow. How do you want to live the next few hours? Who do you want to be? How do you want to live out your calling a bit more today? Even if you don't have a clear sense yet of what your calling is, reflecting on this can help you move toward it. These are essential questions for our growth. Gerrit learned from his father, Douwe Visbeek, that being successful and important was required to survive and live a good life. This is understandable, as my grandfather came from very humble beginnings and had to work hard all his life, first to gain financial stability and later to maintain his wealth and status as a prominent dairy farmer in the north of the Netherlands. My grandfather likely learned about his life's priorities from his father, and my great-grandfather from his father, and so on.

Many of us are operating off these borrowed "get rich" or "get important" compasses that were so important to my uncle and his father. As Gerrit's life shows, a borrowed life compass can take us very far in external terms—he ended up owning one of the largest greenhouses in the Netherlands—and yet, as he taught me at the end of his life, a borrowed compass can never lead to a truly fulfilling life. There is so much more inspiration in authenticity.

✔POINT

On a scale from one to ten, how much of your energy do you spend on priorities that are truly authentic for you (rather than borrowed ones from your tribe)? Circle one.

1   2   3   4   5   6   7   8   9   10

DISCOVERING OUR COMPASS

Discovering our life's purpose can be like walking up a mountain. Our initial intention may be to reach the peak, only to discover on our way up that the peak we had been able to see was not the actual highest part of the mountain, and so we refine our target. The same happens in life.

Over time, we get to know ourselves in deeper and deeper ways—many of us grow our vision of our life's purpose as we age. That has been my experience. When we're five we may identify our calling as: "To be an astronaut." By the time we're twelve we may reinvent our calling: "To be a teacher and help others." And by the time we're forty, our calling may be: "To give our best every day to parenting our children toward their own discoveries."

I always have sensed that my life's calling has something to do with helping others and about making the intangible tangible. I have always loved how music—in particular the music played on the great seventeenth-century church organ in the village where I grew up—could transport me to a space of aliveness, awe, and inspiration I knew only there. When I was a young boy, I started playing melodies on my French horn in the hopes that I could stir a similar experience in others. Yet I also had a strong drive, inherited from my family, to be someone in the world. This drive led me to prioritize being special and wealthy, climbing the corporate ladder in Manhattan as fast as I possibly could. And that got me part-way up my personal mountain. I learned how to think and interact with other people on the consulting teams that I was part of in exciting ways. I began to appreciate the wonders that can happen in a conference room when people put their whole hearts and minds into creatively solving a complex problem.

When this purpose ran out of steam for me, I stumbled across meditation while on a trip to Vietnam. I had heard about meditation and had even done short stints of it in yoga classes. When a friend of mine took me to a temple at a noisy street in Ho Chi Minh City to practice meditation, I thought I knew what I was in for—some gentle breathing and relaxation exercises, not much more than a quick mental workout. Instead my friend asked me to sit down on a cushion on a concrete floor, to hold my body still, breathe naturally, and place all my attention on the in- and outgoings of my breath, letting thoughts and sensations pass through me, without paying attention to them. He suggested we practice that way for one hour. I did it; liked some of it; found a lot of it painful, especially sitting cross-legged; and was relieved when it was over. Afterward I felt sore, and also relaxed and somewhat joyful. I didn't make much of the experience and we got on with our day—seeing the sights around town.

That night I managed to sleep a sound seven hours, which hadn't happened for me in years. And I achieved that while my internal clock was upside down, being eleven time zones away from my New York apartment. All of this, after just one hour of concentrating on my breath, with lots of distraction in the background by the loud noises of Ho Chi Minh City traffic! I felt deeply thankful for having been introduced to this practice of meditation. I was so moved by the experience that, in what was practically an overnight decision, I decided to dedicate myself to mindfulness. I started meditating every day and thinking about how I could bring mindfulness to everything I was doing. As I did more meditation, I reconnected to the peace, joy, and love that I had experienced as a young boy listening to the organ music in the village church. I was discovering a way out of my restlessness! It's hard to put this experience into words. Let me try anyway. I know I will fail the best way I know how.

I was starting to experience a stillness that is like the sky. It holds everything, it doesn't take any position, it is clear, embraces everything, and doesn't want to change anything. I found that I would access this inner spaciousness by becoming really present to this very moment, and by letting any thoughts about the past or the future just pass through me. I started to see that when I become mindful to what is, I experience peace, aliveness, and love that is available to me in every moment. It's not available some of the time, it's there all the time. It's just a matter of me connecting with it. Mindfulness meditation practice became one way for me to access this replenishing stillness.

Because I fell in love with this sense of peace, I decided to devote my life to it. My life's purpose had evolved from pursuing importance and wealth at all costs to cultivating this sense of inner peace and joy, day after day. Inspired by this new calling, I found myself rethinking my life completely, including considering becoming a monk. I spent a great deal of time in retreat centers and monasteries at that time.

Even though my purpose seemed pretty final to me then, I never made that final step of becoming a monastic. Something inside of me told me not to do it and I listened to that whisper. I discovered that going into the monastery wouldn't be a fit for me. I sensed a fire in my belly that

FINDING OUR FEARLESS CALLING   25

didn't want me to go. While I was committed to finding peace, a part of me wasn't fulfilled by it. I started to see that I would not be satisfied by inner growth and introspection, in a relatively secluded setting only. I also would have to honor a deep longing to express myself and be of service in the world in other ways.

This longing fueled the next stage of my journey. During that time, I stumbled into a way of life that seemed to merge the draw of monastic life and the intrinsic rewards of the business world. While still a partner in a consulting firm in New York City, I was being guided by Karen Aberle, a seasoned executive coach. Working with her to discover more about my true calling, I started to see that I could have it all—deepen my experience of peace through mindfulness *and* be in the world, helping people. People just like me working in corporations and looking for something that would give them more lasting fulfillment. I share some of the questions she asked me in the fieldwork at the end of this chapter.

What makes you come alive? What do you really wish to contribute to your world? were two of her questions I still think of often. With Karen's help, I saw that a big part of my calling was about helping others in the world grow. It was a way to share my experience of the meditation cushion with people where they spend most of their waking lives—at work. And so I became an executive coach and team facilitator, working with people to realize more of the peace and joy that is at the core of our being and apply that in their day-to-day work. I still remember Karen's e-mail when I messaged her I was considering signing up for a yearlong training program to become a coach. "Jump!" is the only word she wrote. I did. I remember how excited I was by my decision.

"Eureka!" I thought at the time. "Now I have gotten to what I am supposed to be doing here!" "Not so fast," said life. There was much more evolution to come and some of it sprang from meeting other inspiring people. They have helped me see life and my place in it with new eyes. One of these people is Gene White.

Meeting Our Purpose

Gene is the president of the Global Child Nutrition Foundation, which works to eradicate child hunger in the world. She is one of those people whose sense of purpose is immediately apparent and she inspired me to take another look at mine. She works twelve to fifteen hours a day, travels all around the world (mostly in coach), has more energy than most people I know, and is in her mid-nineties. I got to know Gene while interviewing her for an article that I was writing on great leaders. I showed up at her home on Whidbey Island, near Seattle, Washington, around 1:45 p.m. on a sunny day, fifteen minutes before my scheduled appointment with her. I didn't want to knock just yet (as I expected that a woman of her age might be just finishing up a nap), so I took a seat on the bench next to her front door to wait out the time. To my surprise, within moments of my sitting, the door flew open and Gene was standing right in front of me to welcome me into her home.

We spoke for two hours without stopping, after which she asked me what I'd like to do next. I told her that I was curious to get to know her neighborhood. Without hesitation, she accompanied me to the car and hopped in the seat next to me, from which she kept sharing her insights, now about Whidbey Island. When we made it back to her home and finally said goodbye, she was about to take a conference call. What was her secret?

Gene makes no fuss about herself or her level of energy—she feels she is just an ordinary person doing her part. In our interview, she shared wisdom from her nine decades of living and serving, and in doing so, helped me to create a picture in my mind of how we can "have what she's having." What is the secret behind her incredible level of energy?

In one word—purposefulness. I have come to see that being clear about and staying committed to her calling is one core driver behind Gene's magic. But how did Gene find her purpose? Or how did the purpose find Gene?

When I was first talking to Gene at her home, it became clear very quickly that she is laser-focused. After making sure that I was comfortable, she asked, "Shall we talk now?" ready to dive in. I decided to drop the big question first: "Gene, you are not eighteen anymore; where do you get your energy?"

"I am a very fortunate person in the sense that I believe in what I am doing," she responded. Reflecting a bit more, she gazed up at the ceiling and started telling me about an event that had changed her life while she was in her mid-thirties. I will share her recollection of the event in full, as it contains some clues on tapping into our intrinsic motivation:

"Life-changing experiences come in many different forms. For me, it occurred in Tunisia when I was on a volunteer work assignment for the US Agency for International Development. One of my assignments took me to the south of Tunisia in the Sahara Desert, and before leaving I visited the US Embassy canteen to purchase a few supplies that included a small box of animal crackers.

"A week later I arrived at a small oasis village where the longevity of adults was thirty-five years, meaning many children had no home or parents. They were both gone and children were foraging the countryside in little packs, desperately looking for food. When I got out of the car, I was surrounded by starving children with hands outreached for anything I might give them. Well, this was clearly an animal cracker day if there ever was one. There were so many children that I started breaking the crackers in half—giving the head to one little fellow, the tail to another—until I was out of crackers.

"I suddenly felt someone pulling on my dress and looked down to find this tiny girl, three or four years old, begging for her cracker, and I couldn't believe that I had no way to help her. Her malnutrition had progressed to the point that cell structure was breaking down; heavy discharge was running from her eyes, nose, and mouth and maggots were crawling in the filth on her face. Her hair had never been combed and looked like fur on her tiny head. I knew this child was dying and although I had training in child nutrition, I had nothing to give this starving child, not even an animal cracker.

"Although I don't know the name of the child or even the village, I do know that I decided then--that day, in that oasis village—to do all I possibly could to prevent tragedies like this from happening. This happened many years ago and I am still trying. A starving child in Tunisia set me on a path with new direction and I am so very grateful for this."

I could see tears in her eyes as Gene told me her story. Before her visit to this Tunisian village she had seen her work as "a nice thing to do"—something through which she would learn a lot. After meeting this starving girl without having anything to give her, Gene's life changed forever. She committed her life to eradicating child hunger. This purpose has been guiding her for more than sixty years now.

And there is another aspect to Gene's inner compass that fuels her vitality. "I read a lot, love music and especially classical music; am in book clubs, a writing group, on the board of a local food bank, and immersed in community activities. I live in an incredibly beautiful area in the Pacific Northwest and many evenings I visit the beaches to watch the sun set, reflect on the fullness of life, and consider ways to further enrich the future." People ask her why she doesn't quit all this learning. What is it for? "I can't imagine living in a rapidly changing world and not changing with it. I sometimes find people who, regardless of age, resist change and are 'old' in spirit. Conversely, many older people are forever 'young' in their will to learn and contribute." She explains what having the outlook of an old person looks like. "Regardless of our age, we should have no sacred cows. In other words, we should not be so committed to tradition, so committed to the past that we have to perpetuate it. To me there are no sacred cows, they are best used as hamburger."

Gene sees young people who seem old, having internalized their environment's sacred cows about what their place is and what they can and can't do: "Perhaps they are insecure, afraid to try something new and believe in themselves." She sees people getting stuck in their careers, in their jobs. Gene believes we have multiple careers in our lives. Looking me straight in the eyes, she says: "You do too." I hear the sacred cows inside of me mooing in protest.

One sacred cow Gene has ground up into hamburgers is the idea of retirement. "Some people believe it's a time to kick back and forget the world's problems. I see retirement differently, instead as an opportunity to reach out and do things not possible before. You're not so committed to schedule, to routine or the expectations of others. You find a whole new opportunity to be who you are and fulfill things that are important to you." Gene has been learning all her life and will continue till the end.

I ask her, "What would you do if you knew you had six more hours to live?" Gene muses: "Exactly what I am doing now. No. I don't think that's quite right. If I knew I was going to leave tonight, I wouldn't clean the house today, someone else can worry about that. Frankly not much different from what I am doing. I wouldn't be on the phone calling a bunch of people. I would simply kick back and say 'well, this is the start of something wonderful' and ease myself into what's out there. I'd feel at peace."

Not all of us are so lucky as to have a direct purpose-giving experience, as Gene did in Tunisia. Yet, even without it, we can find our calling—the thing that drives us deep, deep down. Learning from other leaders, such as Gene, can help us in our discovery process. Gene stayed curious and saw what was needed, applied her talents and skills, and committed herself to a cause bigger than her individual identity. Her choices have been life-giving for those she serves (as well as herself) ever since.

We know we have arrived at a sense of calling when it's something we can rely on to give us energy consistently, no matter what is happening in the external world, or in our lives. Our calling is very personal—no one can tell us what it is. In part inspired by Gene's fascination for life and dedication to ending child hunger, I evolved my purpose from pursuing my own inner peace to dedicating myself to self-discovery *and* service.

Gene and other great leaders like her—some of whom you'll meet later in this book—kindled my fascination with the apparent limitless potential that lies within each of us. I decided I had to find out their secrets, and excavate more and more of this internal wealth that lays dormant deep inside.

Traveling toward Who We Have Always Been

So what lies inside of us? In what follows I will share what I have discovered so far. It's not meant to be *the* answer. I am writing it only as signposts for your journey.

At our core, we are like the sky, which radiates awareness, unconditional love, limitless potential, and unopposed peace. Awareness, love, potential, and peace are big concepts. Let me try to describe what they point to. Some of it may seem esoteric to you. Please don't let that bother you. It's not meant to be an exact description. Read it more like you would look at a painting or listen to a piece of music. Take in whatever resonates and leave the rest.

When I become still and let myself become completely disinterested in the fleeting thoughts, feelings, and sensations of my body and mind, I notice a space in me. This space has no boundaries, which becomes clear to me the more I surrender to it. From this space, I am present to the moment. Being present, I am aware of what is happening around me and inside of me, and inside and outside—myself and the world—stop being different. This awareness, like the sky, has no boundaries: it doesn't change, it just notices. It's always there, although I sometimes forget that awareness is watching. And it's discerning. From skylike awareness, it's more clear what is true and what is not, what is wise and what is unwise, what is helpful and what is not. Awareness helps to put things in a true perspective.

Our essence is also unconditional love: caring for everything and everyone, without any need for reciprocity. It doesn't place conditions on others or circumstances. It has no agenda and doesn't want anything from others. Gene does what she does because she wants to help. She doesn't do it for the rewards. Her service *is* her reward. Like a flower, she freely shares her fragrance. That's her nature. As Gene says, "Kindness has no statute of limitations." That includes everyone and every situation. At our essence, we seem to be loving toward everyone and everything, even if our fearful crocodilian mind has other ideas.

Our core is about potential too. We can make ourselves into anything we choose. If we decide to be caring, we find ways to care for others. If we decide to be innovative, we find new ways to look at things. If we decide to be productive, we get things done. Conversely, if we decide to stay angry, we can hurt ourselves and others. Of course, we can also use our anger to set boundaries—another creative act. If we decide to give in to fear, we experience smallness. And if we give in to despair, we experience misery. It's really up to us how we use the potential that we are.

Try this out next time you're stuck in traffic. Decide to think about all that you are grateful for, instead of giving in to impatience or frustration. You may notice the comfort of your seat, the gentle breathing in your stomach, the beautiful child looking out of the window in the car next to you, the play of the clouds in the sky, the sound of a singer on the radio, and maybe a glow of radiance inside of you, that is becoming stronger as you contemplate what you are grateful for. Notice how you have unlimited potential to create your experience, no matter what happens on the outside. In one of my favorite movies, *La vita è bella*, we watch a Jewish father take care of his son in a Nazi concentration camp. Through song, kindness, laughter, stories, and endless other forms of care, he manages to provide his son a beautiful experience, in the midst of a concentration camp. I think of this often when frustration starts to block my inner vistas of what is possible. I remind myself then to shift my attention to something I am grateful for. Looking with the eyes of gratitude is a great way to access joy. When I notice how quickly my experience shifts, simply through a shift in mind-set, I am reminded of the limitless potential that I am.

I also sense we are unopposed peace, like the sky, as it includes such opposites as clouds but is not touched by them. When we become very quiet, we may experience this sense of peace that goes beyond our rational understanding. Then we may sense a stillness that doesn't want anything and yet underlies and envelops everything. It's even there when we are grieving. Last summer I lost a dear friend. I felt so much sadness that I was afraid of it at first. I thought it would destroy me, and so I suppressed it. Then a still voice inside of me nudged me to open up to my emotions and let them out. As I did and let myself cry, I felt this uncanny sense of relief—a peace that went way beyond the understanding of my rational mind. The peace that we are is here always, even when we're having a hard time. It's just that we may not always notice it.

What Is Your Calling?

Awareness, unconditional love, limitless potential, and unopposed peace—these are how I view the summit of the mountain of self-discovery now. And I realize that my perception inevitably will change as I keep walking on this path. Resting more and more in the realization of being skylike in essence, and experiencing the joy, strength, and compassion that come online with that, I feel more motivated to help others find out more about who they really are.

How do you see the summit? What do you sense lies at your core? Whatever words, images, and sensations come to you, let them be there. Including absolutely nothing. Take a moment and take note of what you are seeing. This reflection may help you discover more about your calling—what you wish to dedicate your life to.

It doesn't matter what your calling is. As long as it floats your boat, it will be helpful in your journey of growth. Once you have committed to it, you may notice increased energy that supports you. It may motivate you to keep learning and contributing, just like Gene's purpose—to end child hunger to create peace—has given her focus and drive for the last sixty years.

Once you commit wholeheartedly to your purpose, all kinds of opportunities come into view. "I've never doubted this," Gene reflected during our talk. "The paths opened up in quite amazing ways. After the

Tunisia experience I volunteered with several international organizations, worked in other countries, and later became involved in the newly established Global Child Nutrition Foundation (GCNF), where I continue to serve today. Our purpose is to expand opportunities for the world's children to have access to nutritious meals at school using foods supplied by local agricultural production. In GCNF we have the privilege of helping countries advance the health and education of children through school nutrition programs. It is hard to imagine anything more important for children and their countries."

Purposefulness Replaces Competition

Clarity of purpose unites us with each other, and, when deeply understood, transcends competition. According to Gene: "I often find that well-intended humanitarian organizations choose to work independently rather than in partnership to achieve essentially the same goals. Alleviating poverty and hunger are mega-issues that can't be solved alone; no one has all the answers; personal agendas need to be put aside; we must share information, skills, and the many other resources needed to create a more secure and peaceful world.

"This gets back to my basic point. We should not compete, we can't afford it—the issues are too big. We must learn and work together at this critical time in the global community."

We may think, *Well, but I still need to compete with others for market share, for promotions, for jobs, for a place to live, etc. How can it be true for me that we don't need to compete, that purpose transcends competition?* Gene teaches that when we are clear about our unique contribution and we are truly open to seeing what is needed, places to live and serve become available to us. When we make ourselves available to life, life becomes available to us.

Working with companies and teams for the past twenty years, I have noticed that the ones that last are those who are dedicated to making their unique contribution to the world, not those who are distracted by comparison to others. They have transformed their view of other organizations from competitors into partners who serve a common goal, and who they can learn from and with. This makes logical sense. The more we think about how to beat others, the less attention we place on cultivating our unique talents and discovering what those we serve really need. Seeing other companies as competitors rather than partners is an old borrowed belief, a sacred cow that we can grind into hamburger.

UNCONDITIONAL INTENTION

You may have a sense of your life's purpose or calling. To test it, to make it stronger, you can ask yourself: "Am I willing to live this calling every day, starting now?" Discovering one's calling is like bringing life into the world—the calling grows and develops within us, and once it is born it will always be ours to love, no matter what happens. I am inspired by mothers who day-in-day-out are there for their children, from the moment they gave birth to them. Life callings grow and mature as children do; we help our calling live and grow by our unflinching, continuous commitment to it.

For us to stay continuously committed, our purpose needs to be non-contingent on outside conditions. Compare these two callings:

Calling 1: I intend to help people be their best, no matter what.

Calling 2: I intend to give my best, no matter what.

What do you notice? Both can be seen as beautiful callings, and yet, one of them has more power to withstand the storms of life.

However subtle, the first calling speaks about how I will help people, which implies some conditionality, or dependence on the outside world. How will you feel on days when the world just doesn't seem to want your help? For example, your colleague may be in a bad mood, your spouse may be upset about something, or your friend may just choose to stay down. If you try to help others in these circumstances, that can backfire and drain your inspiration.

I notice this in growth workshops. Sometimes there are people who aren't interested in what we're doing. A part of me feels I should help everyone to be their best. However, when I focus my attention on those who don't want my help, they get frustrated; other workshop participants who are interested get less of what they came for; and I feel drained by the end of it. There is a sense then of my being in opposition to what is needed.

When I operate from calling 2, giving my best no matter what, I am operating from a place that is unopposed. I can *always* give my best. For me giving my best is being present, loving, learning, and contributing, no matter what.

And when we look a bit deeper, we can also discover some conditionality in calling 2. What about the moments there doesn't seem to be anything in me left to give? When I am tired or sick? When "my best" is tied up in words and actions, it's conditional on my being able to think, speak, and act. And on some occasions, that may not be possible. So even this intention of giving my best is not life-proof. What would be an intention that is 100 percent unconditional?

For me, that is "I am." I am here—present. That is something I can always rely on. I have found that being present is a powerful gift I can give to myself and others. And it's unopposed, not dependent on anything. Ask yourself, on a scale from one to ten, how present are you now? "10" is being totally here, as present as you would have been when you held your newborn for the first time, or when you asked your spouse to marry you, or when you asked that person you really were interested in out on a date. "1" is being completely distracted, maybe thinking about your to-do list, or obsessing over what didn't go well today, or fantasizing about what you want to have happen next. Notice what happens when you ask yourself this question several times: "How present am I now, on a scale from one to ten?" You become more present as you keep repeating the question. We become present by placing our attention on the here and now. Coming back to presence is a choice. And when we become present, what do we notice? A sense of stillness, aliveness, clarity, and vitality may come to the foreground. Also, some difficult emotions and sensations may become more noticeable. Presence doesn't mind what we notice. It's present to anything, no matter what. It is a reliable friend. Presence is always here.

When looking at these three callings again, what do you notice—which one is most robust, able to withstand whatever happens?

Calling 1: I intend to help people be their best, no matter what.

Calling 2: I intend to give my best, no matter what.

Calling 3: I am present.

Calling 3 is even more independent from circumstances than calling 2. It is not affected by outside events, nor by our inner moods—we simply observe all of it from presence. Presence is 100 percent unopposed by anything. It's simply here, like the sky.

Reflect on what may be an unconditional intention for your life. What is something you can always rely on? You may find it helpful to have a dual calling—one that is 100 percent unopposed and lasting, and one that involves the external world and is thus more conditional. Jesus is one incredible leader we learn from about holding a dual calling. He dedicated Himself to loving action for everyone, including prostitutes, tax collectors, and lepers—the outcasts of society at the time. When he was no longer able to act physically, he remained steadfast in His love, his unopposed calling. We get a glimpse of His unopposed love at the very end of His life, when He caringly encourages the criminals hanging on the crosses next to His not to despair but to have faith and know that all is well. He taught "Be in the world, but not of it." Have a worldly calling, which you know will be somewhat conditional, and at the same time stay firmly rooted in your unconditional calling. Your unconditional calling may have something to do with being love, presence, and peace.

My unconditional calling is being present. My worldly calling is to discover who I am, and help others do the same, to create a peaceful world. At work, my commitment to being present helps me to stay aware of myself, others, and what is needed, without getting entangled in any of it. And when I do get entangled, being present helps me to notice that I am entangled and let go of the thoughts and feelings that have me in their grip, like "I need to be liked," "I need to be special," and "I need to rescue."

My worldly calling of self-discovery and helping others with their journey helps me to stay focused on working with myself and others on inner growth and saying no to activities and projects that are not about this calling.

What is your calling in the world? And what is your unopposed calling?

CRYSTALLIZING OUR CALLING IN THE WORLD

We'll explore a few other lenses from which to explore these questions now. Over the years I have seen different leaders, like Gene, live their calling in the world. Almost all their callings have a sense of helping others in them. Here are a few better-known ones. Steve Jobs once said, "We're here to put a dent in the universe, otherwise why else even be here?" And Jeff Weiner, CEO of LinkedIn, writes that he is here to "expand the world's collective wisdom and compassion." We are all the CEOs of our own lives. In what ways do we wish to use our lives to contribute to the world?

Seven Motivations, Seven SUCCESS-Intentions

Our calling can be seen as a composite of what we deeply value and what is needed in the world. This is different for everyone and also can evolve over a lifetime. Richard Barrett, the British author and leadership development pioneer, re-conceived Maslow's hierarchy of needs, based on researching thousands of leaders and organizations, to help map organizations' states of consciousness. I have slightly modified his work, to create a map of seven levels of motivation we can use to orient our growth journeys. I found this map helpful to gain more clarity about our callings.

Take a look at these seven motivations below. Ask yourself: Where do I place most of my attention? Spend some time with this to let any patterns in your motivation become clear to you.

1. Survival—making a living, providing for my family

2. Relationship—having healthy, fulfilling relationships

3. Self-esteem—having a strong sense of self and accomplishment

4. Discovery—learning about who I really am and evolving

5. Making a contribution—leaving the world a better place than I found it

6. Cohesion—seeing and making connections between everything and everyone

7.   Wisdom and compassion, enlightenment—selfless service, realizing and living my essence, seeing myself as everyone and everything

You may notice that the first three motivations are about taking care of our smaller, personal worlds; the last three are ways of interacting with the world and life as a whole; and the fourth one, discovery, is a bridge between the personal and the larger world. We tend to start off in life being focused on surviving, and creating a network of belonging around us. And then as we grow, we become curious about who we really are and how we can care for others in the world around us.

Gene's calling reads as follows: "Eradicate hunger among children so they can focus on their education and become peaceful contributors to society." It's almost all about motivations 5 and 6—helping children (motivation 5) to create a peaceful society (motivation 6). My calling is primarily fueled by my interest in self-discovery (motivation 4) and living who I truly am (motivation 7) and I have added an element of contribution, creating a peaceful world (motivations 5 and 6). This doesn't mean I don't care about finances, relationships, or doing my best. It's just that those values don't drive my calling. This means I live simply and engage in money, relationships, and work as ways to grow in consciousness.

You may find it helpful to contemplate these seven motivations and include the ones that resonate with you into your calling. This is more of an art than a science. To help work with these seven motivations as we consider our calling, I think of these motivations also as seven intentions we can choose for our lives. I have summarized them into an acronym to remember them more easily: seven SUCCESS-intentions: Samurai, Uniting, Centered, Curious, Extending, Sensing, and Simple.

Take a look below and see which ones, if any, you would like to integrate more into your calling.

1.   *Samurai*—having the warriorlike courage and fortitude to take care of my basic needs, and face my challenges resourcefully without being overwhelmed by them

2. *Uniting*—creating authentic, empathetic relationships that welcome everyone and go beyond tribal us-vs.-them dynamics

3. *Centered in purpose*—being driven by my inner compass, pursuing my goals wholeheartedly and with focus, and seeing every "failure" as part of moving forward

4. *Curious*—opening my heart to life's teachings—the whispers—no matter what, and seeing every moment as an opportunity for discovery, bigger vision, and being innovative

5. *Extending*—expressing my gift to others unapologetically and caringly

6. *Sensing*—using intuition, looking for the connection between everything and everyone, integrating the seeming polarities in life, creating cohesion

7. *Simple*—seeing what is needed and doing it, letting go of all ego personas, simply being and contributing who I am

Play around with these seven SUCCESS-intentions. Which ones are you most attracted to? Which ones least? Why? What does that tell you about your calling? Don't worry about getting it right. Your calling is something that is yours and can evolve over time.

Consider this calling of a young woman named Selina Taylor Townes. Her calling is to help organizations learn how to resolve conflict and increase productivity by encouraging employees to communicate and operate authentically. She is currently applying for entry-level HR/employee relations positions to gain professional experience and then plans to pursue a PhD in Industrial Psychology and Conflict Resolution. Selina's calling includes intention #1, Samurai, choosing to make a living as a counselor working with employees; #5, Extending, helping others at work; and #7, Simple, not being absorbed by "little me" but serving a specific need in the workplace in a way that reflects her essence.

Or what about Thomas Neergaard Hansen, EVP of Carbon Black, the provider of next-generation endpoint security? His calling on LinkedIn reads: "I lead people and organizations to go further than they otherwise would." Which SUCCESS-intentions do you read here? I see #3, Centered in purpose—he is asserting his leadership role, which, given how I know

Thomas, is natural for him; #4, Curious, "going further than otherwise"; and #5, Extending, "helping people and organizations."

And here is Augusto Muench's calling for a specific role in his life—coaching. He wrote it during the Leader as Coach Columbia program where I met him. Augusto is a coach, and president of the South America Region for Boehringer Ingelheim, the life sciences company. His calling reads: "As a Coach I intend to be here for you, for me, for us, for love, for the love of learning: to be present and flow with your own energy to find your path together within the unconsciousness of our daily routine." I read #1, Samurai, "within the unconsciousness of our daily routine," #2, Uniting, "for us," #3, Centered in purpose, "I intend to be here," #4 Curious, "for the love of learning," #5, Extending, "for you," #6, Sensing, "flow with your energy," and #7, Simple, "to be present."

Lastly, here is Debbie Lynd's calling. Debbie is a close friend, an amazing coach, and so many other things. She also cofounded the Growth Leaders Network. Her calling is: "I will delight in every person I meet." I hear all seven SUCCESS-intentions in her short but oh-so-powerful declaration: Samurai, Uniting, Centered in purpose, Curious, Extending, Sensing, and Simple.

Take some time to let your calling come to you as you reflect on these seven SUCCESS-intentions. Maybe you find it helpful to think of someone you admire. Which of the seven SUCCESS-intentions do they live? Chances are you have similar aspirations to theirs. Take some time and let your calling come to you.

Take a Walk

To discover your life's calling, it may be helpful to spend some time by yourself in silence. Silence is the most reliable and loving teacher I know. Also, going into nature can be very helpful to discover your calling. Nature—in particular, nature that has not been touched by humans—is a powerful teacher. Have you ever come across untouched nature that didn't inspire some sense of beauty and majesty? Nature is always in harmony with itself, integrating all its unique components in a vibrantly alive whole that uplifts the human spirit because it is a reflection of it. Nature mirrors back to us who we really are. There is something very simple and very profound in each of us that is our essence; that wants to express itself without apology. Just like the flower blooming on the rock, giving its full colors and fragrance to the world, unburdened by the opinions of others. Dare you to live as the flower, knowing your essence and sharing it freely?

As you take a walk into nature, either literally or in your mind, be mindful and kind with yourself. Let your innermost self tell you about its dreams for your life. Undoubtedly your dreams will find you when you start listening deeply to them. It may take some walking before there is clarity, simply because many of us are so used to listening to others' opinions that we have forgotten how to listen to our inner voice. It is ready to speak to us from a place of deep, deep stillness, to guide us into who we are and how we may care for life now. If in doubt, keep walking, meditating, checking in with your dreams and know that your calling is waiting for you. When you find it, it may set you ablaze with strength, creativity, and warmth.

A DAILY CHOICE TO BE YOURSELF

Some days you may not feel like living your calling. Instead you may want to give in to parts of your mind that tell you to play small. *Don't be who you really are, other people may feel insecure around you*, you may think. Or, *you have never done this before, you won't be able to; you don't have the strength for this, you need to back down.* When you hear these voices, you can remind yourself that as a human being you have a unique capacity to choose how you respond, both to outer events and to your inner thoughts and feelings. On days that I have felt most vulnerable to smallness—days where I wanted to forget I had a choice—I have found it helpful to remind myself of people I admire for their ability to be who they really are in the most trying of situations. One of these people is Viktor Frankl.

Viktor Frankl was a Jewish psychiatrist with a flourishing practice in Vienna, Austria, during the 1930s. When he was given the option to immigrate to the United States, he chose not to, as his parents couldn't join him and he didn't want to leave them behind in the looming darkness of the uncertain times. Frankl ended up being incarcerated in four concentration camps. Not only did he survive, but he chose to stay present to what was happening, and be curious about it. Weeks after being liberated from a concentration camp, he wrote a book that has epitomized the power of choice for millions of people around the world since then—

"Man's Search for Meaning." As a human being and psychiatrist living in those concentration camps, he wanted to comprehend how people could survive the grueling reality of murder, starvation, torture, and disease. How did the few people who weren't put to death survive, living in unimaginable hardship, day-in, day-out, without an end in sight?

Frankl reflects in his book: "We who lived in concentration camps can remember the men who walked through the huts comforting others, giving away their last piece of bread. They may have been few in number, but they offer sufficient proof that everything can be taken from a man but one thing: the last of the human freedoms—to choose one's attitude in any given set of circumstances, to choose one's own way."

Frankl's example teaches us that we always have a choice how we respond. The act of realizing that brings inspiration to stay true to my calling now, no matter what is happening.

To stay true to your calling, the key is to choose it every day, no matter what is happening. If you find yourself wanting to give up—as you feel you can't, believing it's too hard and too uncomfortable—do it anyway. Surprise yourself. If Viktor Frankl could stay true to himself in a concentration camp, can you stay true to you in your life today?

Take a stance for who you truly are. And let yourself be surprised by the strength that comes with that.

FIELDWORK

1. Read the following excerpt from "Long Walk to Freedom" by Nelson Mandela:

   "I was not born with a hunger to be free. I was born free—free in every way that I could know. . . .

   "But I then slowly saw that not only was I not free, but my brothers and sisters were not free. I saw that it was not just my freedom that was curtailed, but the freedom of everyone who looked like I did. That is when I joined the African National Congress, and that is when the hunger for my own freedom became the great hunger for the freedom of my people. It was this desire for the freedom of my people to live their lives with dignity and self-respect that animated my life, that transformed a frightened young man into a bold one, that drove a law-abiding attorney to become a criminal, that turned a family-loving husband into a man without a home, that forced a life-loving man to live like a monk. I am no more virtuous or self-sacrificing than the next man, but I found that I could not even enjoy the poor and limited freedoms I was allowed when I knew my people were not free."

   Please reflect for a few minutes on the following:

   "It was this desire for the freedom of my people to live their lives with dignity and self-respect that animated my life . . ."

   What animates your life?

   What is the contribution you wish to make to the world?

2. Another way to look at your calling is as your "Growth Vision." Your Growth Vision is a statement of WHO you wish to become and WHAT you wish to contribute. Take some time to review and answer the following questions:

   A. What did I love doing as a kid? How did I like to play?

   B. What makes me come alive?

   C. What is my gift that my community cannot afford to lose?

   D. Which poem or quote captures the essence of who I am?

E. What fears do I have about being who I truly am?

F. When and from whom did I learn these fears?

G. Who would I be without these fears?

H. Which of the seven SUCCESS-intentions am I most attracted to now? Choose at least two. What would happen if I practiced this intention two times in my life?

   1. *Samurai*—having the warriorlike courage and fortitude to take care of my basic needs, and face my challenges resourcefully without being overwhelmed by them;

   2. *Uniting*—creating authentic, empathetic relationships that welcome everyone and go beyond tribal us-vs.-them dynamics;

   3. *Centered in purpose*—being driven by my inner compass, pursuing my goals wholeheartedly and with focus; and seeing every "failure" as part of moving forward;

   4. *Curious*—opening my heart to life's teachings—the whispers—no matter what, and seeing every moment as an opportunity for discovery, bigger vision, and being innovative;

   5. *Extending*—expressing my gift to others unapologetically and caringly;

   6. *Sensing*—using intuition, looking for the connection between everything and everyone, integrating the seeming polarities in life, creating cohesion;

   7. *Simple*—seeing what is needed and doing it, letting go of all ego personas, simply being and contributing who I am.

I. How do I wish to contribute to my world?

J. What does my world really need?

K. What vision do I commit to, no matter what?

L. In what forms will I manifest my vision initially?

   Using your answers to the questions above, create your Growth Vision, eventually refining it into one sentence.

CHAPTER 3

Growing through Challenge— Transforming Crocodiles into Owls

"Stop being afraid of what could go wrong, and think what could go right." —Author Unknown

MIND OVER MATTER

WHEN DO WE make our greatest leaps in learning? When things go well, or when we are challenged? Learning can happen any time, if we are open to it. We can transform any moment into a Growth Instant. Yet difficulties may be our most powerful learning opportunities—they are huge doorways for our growth. We can see them as moments of truth. Will we respond from smallness or from greatness to the obstacle on our path? And where do we find the wherewithal to keep learning and contributing, even when we are under stress?

I found some clues studying leaders I consider great. Some of them are well known, such as Mahatma Gandhi, Nelson Mandela, and Franklin D. Roosevelt, while others are lesser known, such as Chris Capossela (Chief Marketing Officer of Microsoft), Gene White (President of the Global Child Nutrition Foundation), Robert Tarkoff (CEO of Lithium Technologies), and Gerrit Visbeek, my uncle who was a greenhouse farmer. What makes these leaders great in times of challenge? *How do they respond to obstacles?* And what can we learn from them?

Eighty years ago, FDR faced one of the biggest and most pressing leadership challenges that the United States had ever known in its 150-year history: The Great Depression, which sent the country and the world tumbling into a downward spiral. Some people feared that the decline might never end. In the United States alone, nine million savings accounts had been wiped out, the unemployment rate was above 25 percent, and things were only getting worse. In February 1933, there was another run on the banks, further eroding the stability of the financial system. A visitor to the White House said to FDR, "You're either going to be our greatest President or you're going to be our worst President," to which FDR responded, "No, if I fail, I'll be our last President." John Maynard Keynes, the British economist, was asked if anything like this had ever happened before. He responded, "Yes, it was called the Dark Ages and it lasted four hundred years."

FDR responded decisively to the crisis. William Silber, an NYU economist, describes FDR's actions the day after he became President: "On Sunday, March 5, 1933, after a month-long run on American banks, the newly inaugurated President of the United States proclaimed a four-day suspension of all banking transactions, beginning the following day . . . On Thursday, March 9, FDR did not reopen the banks as planned; rather, he extended the closure for three days."

FDR made a courageous decision, instating a bank holiday that closed all the banks. He explained later that this was a "first step in the government's reconstruction of our financial and economic fabric." The bank holiday was a huge departure from the past—never before had there been a complete stoppage of the US payments system. And it was a huge gamble, as many feared that people would storm the banks when they reopened in even greater panic than they had before.

On Sunday, March 12, at 9:30 p.m. Eastern Standard Time, the evening before the banks' reopening and eight days after his inauguration, FDR went on the radio to give his first Fireside Chat. It lasted fourteen and a half minutes, and most Americans with access to a radio gathered to tune in. To this day, this speech is one of the most remarkable acts of great leadership that I know of:

"My friends, I want to talk for a few minutes with the people of the United States about banking—to talk with the comparatively few who understand the mechanics of banking, but more particularly with the overwhelming majority of you who use banks for the making of deposits and the drawing of checks. This bank holiday, while resulting in many cases in great inconvenience, is affording us the opportunity to supply the currency necessary to meet the situation.

"After all, there is an element in the readjustment of our financial system more important than currency, more important than gold, and that is the confidence of the people themselves. Confidence and courage are the essentials of success in carrying out our plan. You people must have faith; you must not be stampeded by rumors or guesses. Let us unite in banishing fear. We have provided the machinery to restore our financial system; and it is up to you to support and make it work . . . It is your problem, my friends, your problem no less than it is mine. Together we cannot fail."

The day after FDR's speech, people made another run on the banks. This time it was not to withdraw money, but to return the hoarded cash. According to the *New York Times*: "The public plainly showed that it recovered from the fear and hysteria which characterized the last few days before the banking holiday was proclaimed. It was obvious that people had full confidence in the banks which received licenses to reopen from the Federal Reserve Bank." At the end of that month, people returned two thirds of the cash that they had hoarded since the onset of the panic. With hindsight, we see that FDR's bank holiday and his first Fireside Chat ended the bank runs that had deepened the Great Depression.

What can we learn from FDR's handling of this challenging moment in history? FDR had a very clear strategy and process to stave off financial collapse. And yet that is not what people remember most about his leadership. FDR's first fireside chat is known as his "More Important Than Gold" talk. So, what was more important than gold? According to FDR, "that is the confidence of the people themselves. Confidence and courage are the essentials of success in carrying out our plan." FDR focused on mind-set more than matter to help address the financial crisis. In the span of less than fifteen minutes FDR transformed the mind-set of a nation paralyzed by fear and hysteria into one with courage and confidence in the system.

Peter Drucker, the management consultant who is described as the "founder of modern management," is said to have asserted that "culture eats strategy for breakfast." He points to something FDR understood very deeply—our mind-set, how we see ourselves and our world, shapes how effectively we can act. A mind-set paralyzed by hysteria will lead to hysterical actions that produce disastrous results. A mind-set of courage and confidence enables us to act boldly, to learn and move effectively, and to create new possibilities for excellence, prosperity, and connection.

To great leaders, mind-set is just as important as strategy and process. Some see mind-set as the *most* important asset we have in addressing challenges. I agree with them. Think of Gandhi leading India toward an attitude of nonviolence and self-reliance, or of Mikhail Gorbachev nourishing an atmosphere of openness in the former Soviet Union to create a path out of communism, and of Satya Nadella, CEO of Microsoft, transforming the company by emphasizing a Growth Mind-set.

A METAMIND-SET FOR GREATNESS

If cultivating a mind-set conducive to success is so important for a leader to be effective, is there a specific mind-set great leaders focus on when working through an obstacle? While studying the greats I have come across a plethora of mind-sets that help to address challenges. This includes the following mentalities:

- Taking a self-mastery instead of victim mind-set: focusing on the aspects of the situation that are under one's control, rather than blaming the situation and people involved;

- Adopting a learner's mind-set: having the humility to see the limitations of one's own perspective and the merits of other perspectives, being willing to question all assumptions to arrive at a more comprehensive understanding of reality;

- Taking a one-team mind-set: appreciating the benefits of deep collaboration over heroic independence.

All of these foci can be effective for a leader . . . until they are not. Any strength overplayed can become a weakness. It's the beauty of human development that things that worked well yesterday may not work so well today. This provides the impetus to reinvent ourselves constantly—to grow. Overly relying on self-mastery can lead to alienation from others, leaning on learning alone can lead to indecisiveness, and overemphasizing collaboration can lead to lack of accountability.

So what metamind-set, what overarching orientation, can leaders come back to no matter what challenge they are facing?

I think of my uncle, Gerrit Visbeek. He was a farmer who owned and ran one of the largest greenhouses in the Netherlands. In April 2009, he was diagnosed with cancer. At first, his priority was continuing his life as usual. A few months later the doctors told him there was nothing else they could do for him and he had to prepare to die. After hearing this news, my uncle and I began speaking over the phone, almost on a daily basis. In our last few conversations before his death in December 2009, Gerrit taught me something that gave me a clue about what my life may be about and therefore what an enduring orientation for life and leadership may be, even in the face of our greatest difficulties.

When we initially started talking during the summer of 2009, my uncle would often tell me about the pain he was feeling. There was the physical pain of his body turning into a skeleton as the cancer ate him up, the emotional pain of having to say goodbye to his wife and children, and also the mental pain of having to part with all of his possessions—his beautiful home, his company, his yacht, his car, his clothes—everything he had worked so hard to acquire in his life.

Then the tenor of our conversations started to shift. Gerrit's voice became deeper, more melodious, and softer—I sensed more gentleness in him. He told me how placing his attention on the love that he had for his family helped him not feel the pain; how, surrendering to that love, he was feeling content; and how he knew that his love would not die with his body. "One thing I wish is that I had found this love in myself earlier in life. And yet, I am very grateful to know it now," Gerrit shared. A few weeks before he died, Gerrit told me he was no longer afraid of his passing, saying instead: "If life has been this much of an adventure, how much greater of an adventure will death be?"

Gerrit inspires me to this very day. His memory teaches me to be loving, and to stay fascinated with life and who I really am, no matter what. His example tells me to greet the darkest of times as my great teachers to help me discover more of who I really am. I sense that Gerrit's teachings are timeless, and that they align with the following philosophy taught by one of the great Indian sages, Nisargadatta Maharaj:

> *"Once you realize that the road is the goal and that you*
> *are always on the road, not to reach the goal, but to enjoy*
> *its beauty and wisdom, life ceases to be a task and becomes*
> *natural and simple, in itself an ecstasy."*

FDR exemplifies the same energy. When I look at him in documentaries and photos, I see an unflinching warrior who smiles and remains resourceful, even in the face of tremendous challenges, like the polio that crippled him at age thirty-nine, and the Great Depression and World War II that almost destroyed the world as he knew it. It was as if he could see the promise of new possibilities, even in the darkest moments.

FDR, Nisargadatta Maharaj, and Gerrit Visbeek point to a metamindset we can come back to, no matter how big the challenge and who we're leading—whether it is ourselves, our friends and family, or our coworkers. We call this mind-set a Growth Leadership Mind-set.

A GROWTH LEADERSHIP MIND-SET

A Growth Leadership Mind-set is one where we see every moment, every interaction, and every change as an opportunity for presence, self-discovery, contribution, and excellence. When we adopt a Growth Leadership Mind-set we are continuously feeding the fire of fascination with ourselves, with others, and with our larger world. We start seeing the so-called "problems" in our world as opportunities for our evolution. We ask ourselves "How are you growing today?" as often as we ask one another "How are you doing?" We are equally committed to both our inner growth and growing our world.

A Growth Leadership Mind-set has four core ingredients: presence, self-discovery, contribution, and excellence. We can think of these ingredients as being part of a soup—presence is the broth and self-discovery, contribution, and excellence are the other ingredients we add to give it substance. Together they provide a nourishing orientation from which we can live fulfilling lives and help lead others do the same, even in the face of challenge.

Introducing Presence

Of the four core ingredients that make up a Growth Leadership Mind-set, presence is for many the most abstract, even though we may have heard about it in the context of mindfulness meditation practices that have been introduced to us by wisdom pioneers such as Jon Kabat-Zinn, Eckhardt Tolle, and Jack Kornfield.

What is presence and why is it foundational to being a Growth Leader? As human beings, most of us spend a substantial amount of time living in our heads. Whether we are worrying about what we'll make for dinner, remembering that summer five years ago, or wondering what our partners are thinking, our minds always seem to be somewhere else. Presence means letting go of the past, the future, our speculations, and any other distracting thoughts; to be here in our bodies right now, in the moment that is unwinding before our very eyes. *Presence is the effortless art of observing, appreciating, and being fully here now.* This is especially important when we are having difficulty. Our minds may be going crazy with regret, guilt, fear, and other forms of anxiety. Resting in presence, we simply observe our mind and disentangle ourselves from our mental noise.

Some of us are familiar with this idea we call "presence" in this book—others are now discovering it. If the concept of presence ever gets a little bit muddled or hard to grasp, try substituting the word *presence* for one of these other words:

1. *Mindfulness*

2. *Awareness*

Mindfulness is the practice of bringing our attention back to this present moment. When we practice mindfulness, we become present. Resting our attention on our breathing is one way of practicing mindfulness. The breath is always here now and when we focus on it, we become intimate with the part of us that is timeless, neutral—that which is always here now. You could say mindfulness is a tool to focus our attention on the present moment.

Awareness is the ground from which we have the wherewithal to notice our thoughts, feelings, and sensations. Being aware, we notice what is happening, without getting caught by what we observe. When we do get caught, we observe that too, dispassionately, and come back to being the neutral observer. And we can even train ourselves to become aware of awareness itself—we can observe the observer. Awareness is presence, and can give us a sense of contentment and confidence.

Like a superhero who must learn how to control their superpower, the more we practice being aware, the more quickly it will become second nature. Life will become clearer and feel less stressful. We will feel calmer and more cheerful. Since it's always there, awareness, presence, or whatever you want to call it can become your best friend and partner in life and leadership. It's a space you can always return to, no matter what challenge knocks on your door.

To become more present, you can do a mindfulness practice. You will find one example below. If you think you are too busy to do it now, you would probably benefit even more from doing it anyway. One caveat: there are thousands of mindfulness practices—this is just one of them that I propose to you because of its simplicity.

Twelve-Breath Presence Practice

Here we go.

Smile, and gently close your mouth. Allow yourself to become aware of the in- and outflow of the breath through your nose. Allow the breath to deepen and become aware of the breath moving your stomach in and out. Let any thoughts and feelings just be there and keep bringing your attention back to the in- and outflow of the breath. After you have felt the breath this way for a few seconds, close your eyes, and take twelve slow in- and out-breaths into your belly. Keep bringing you attention back to the breathing while you do this. Let any thoughts and feelings be there. Don't touch them. Keep coming back to the breath and rest your attention on it.

Now pause the practice and rest for a moment. Then ask yourself, How present am I now on a scale from one to ten? You may have become more present by doing this twelve-breath practice. You may be more in the now. You may be enjoying this moment more. You may feel calmer, maybe a bit more clear. Whatever your experience, it's all good. You can't do it wrong. Simply doing the practice will help you become more present over time.

I do this short practice often between meetings, on planes, waiting in line (with my eyes open to stay aware of what's happening around me), or after lunch to help re-energize myself. When might this practice be helpful to you? Start by picking a set time once a day and practice it at least seven days, if possible on consecutive days. That is how often we need to repeat a new practice before we start experiencing the benefits more than the discomfort, colleagues of mine have found (and I agree).

"Be here now."

That's one way to summarize presence. Gently reminding ourselves to "Be here now" is another way we can practice mindfulness, anytime, anywhere.

You will find an additional meditation practice in Appendix 1.

Introducing the Other Three Ingredients: Self-discovery, Contribution, and Excellence

Practicing presence in our daily activities and interactions, we open the door to the second ingredient of Growth Leadership: self-discovery. When we become more aware of what is going on in the moment, we can discern more easily what is true for us and about us. We notice our thoughts and feelings more vividly, we learn what we do and don't like, and through this learning mitigate the risk of falling back into self-limiting behavioral routines. By practicing self-discovery and applying it to every situation, we benefit from any challenge that life throws our way. When we see an obstacle as an opportunity for learning rather than as a defeat, we find excitement and inspiration to keep growing and evolving. From this perspective, we can be grateful for every challenge we receive as leaders, be it difficult feedback, a stretch goal, a hard conversation, or a cash flow challenge—these are all lessons from life to help us find out more about who we truly are and who we are not. Feedback can point us to a blind spot, a goal can help us access hidden strength, a conversation can remind us that we are not alone in our work, and a cash flow challenge can unleash latent creativity in us.

Like self-discovery, caring for and contributing to those around us, the third ingredient of Growth Leadership, provides us opportunities for our own growth as well, especially in the face of challenge. Parents experience this while raising children, employees while serving customers and working with one another, and managers while leading their teams. We are like trees, which as they grow taller provide shade, shelter, and nourishment to countless creatures. Managers who grow their capacity to lead are often entrusted with leading larger organizations, which gives them an opportunity to further grow their capacity to inspire and care for others. To lead more people, we need to access more resources within ourselves to care for them. When we become more experienced leading more people, we tend to be asked to lead even more people—and we're onto our next growth challenge. Growth, contribution, growth—it's an infinite cycle.

Growth Leadership is also about excellence. The word *excellence* comes from the Latin verb *excellere*, which means "to surpass." When we commit to excellence, we are called to go beyond what is currently here, to create something that we feel proud of. Like a flower blooming, we share our very best. From this perspective, difficulty becomes our next invitation to excel and surpass our limitations. Excellence requires focus and creation. Creation demands inner growth and inner growth fuels excellence— another infinite cycle.

The four ingredients of Growth Leadership are like a four-legged table—removal of any one of the four leads to imbalance. Self-discovery without contributing to others can lead to narcissism and isolation. Contribution without excellence can lead to stagnation and boredom. Excellence without presence can lead to perfectionism and restlessness. And presence without self-discovery, contribution, and excellence can turn into rigidity and isolation. All four together provide an inner foundation for endless inspiration, connection, and creativity.

Contemplate these four orientations: presence, self-discovery, contribution, and excellence . . . Are they not part of our innate humanness? Do we not all have a longing to be present (aware of what is going on inside and around us), to learn, to contribute (to ourselves and the people and systems we care for), and to excel?

If Growth Leadership is part of who we are, then why don't we practice it all the time? Let's dive into the land of neurons, habits, and history.

A CONTRACTION MIND-SET— PART 1: THE CRINGING CROCODILE

Think of how we typically react to something not going our way. We shut down. We get overwhelmed by a sense of dread. Our self-talk may be: "Oh, no!" Our upset feelings bring about uncomfortable contractions and tensions within our body. We may feel frantic or helpless. Why is this?

Modern neuroscience gives some clues. It claims that our nervous system is wired primarily for our survival. Each of our brains contain the amygdala, an almond-shaped group of nuclei, which is on 24–7 alert for danger to make sure we don't get hurt. If we are crossing the street, and are forced to jump out of the way of a careless driver, we can say to ourselves: "Thank you, amygdala, for saving my life once again." Just after receiving a signal of danger, the amygdala orchestrated the release of adrenaline and hormones that made our blood rush and our muscles contract, and gave us the quick reaction of dodging the oncoming vehicle. That is the good news about the reactive "reptilian" part of our nervous system.

The bad news is that the amygdala often gets it wrong. This is why we may mistake an innocent vine for a poisonous snake and flee from it. And because this part of our brain is a rough-and-ready alarm system, it doesn't distinguish between physical and emotional threats. From the perspective of the amygdala, someone disagreeing with us, or our boss disapproving our proposal, feels as threatening as a tiger jumping on us to eat us for lunch. Psychologist Daniel Goleman pioneered this concept in the 1960s, and in recent research he has found that our society is in a constant state of low-level amygdala hijack. It's called a "hijack" because when we're under the influence of the amygdala we tend to be controlled by it, unless we are very mindful of what's happening. It's constant because in today's world, we don't give ourselves enough real rest to calm down our amygdala. We tend to opt instead to browse the internet, play cellphone games, watch TV, and keep working—anything to keep us stimulated. We are forgetting how to rest and our amygdala stays on high alert.

The amygdala is part of the "crocodilian" or reptilian part of our brain. It is primitive and aggressive/defensive-reactive. When driven by the amygdala, we have limited capacity for self-discovery, contribution, and excellence. Instead we are driven by an immediate reaction to fight, flight, or freeze. Instead of operating in a way that leaves room for growth or care, this crocodilian "Contraction Mind-set" tends to operate on the level of victimhood, a "safe" state that is meant to foster self-preservation and, as a side effect, keep us small.

We know we're in the grip of this crocodile when we react based on a tension in our emotional or physical bodies. As a side note, we'll call this reactivity the "Cringing Crocodile" to distinguish it from its sibling we'll meet later in this chapter. Reacting, in this case, includes giving in to negative *thinking*, even if we don't respond verbally or physically to a situation. We may notice that we feel edgy, stressed, agitated, overwhelmed, arrogant, despondent, shocked, anxious, angry, or a combination of these. We resist reality, which makes the world feel very small and keeps our chances of growing slim-to-none.

Under the influence of the Cringing Crocodile we resort to fight, flight, and freeze reactive behaviors. We dominate, control, shout, judge, manipulate, argue, overwork, overtalk, and push others aside, caught up in a fight reaction. In flight, we may please, defer to others, play small not to rock the boat, avoid conflict, gossip, and appease. And in freeze? We get tongue-tied, get flustered, shut down, repress our thinking, and make ourselves invisible. The fight/flight/freeze repertoire of the Cringing Crocodile is vast. Think about the reactive behaviors you may fall into when under the influence of this crafty creature. It may be some of the behaviors listed before, and there are many others as well. They are fear-based and all of them block us from learning.

We have another clue that we are in the grip of these crocodiles, besides noticing tension in our bodies, and catching ourselves in fight, flight, or freeze behaviors. This is the language of our thoughts, our self-talk. As the crocodile works for our survival, it is not interested in nuance—that would take too much time. The crocodile doesn't want us to think, it wants to act now. A tiger is about to eat us! We can't wait. So the crocodilian part of our nervous system makes instantaneous judgments and doesn't check them. It immediately labels everything as black or white, right or wrong, good or bad, safe or dangerous. To keep it simple and actionable now, the crocodile takes no time to verify assumptions. That's why it states them as fact. Our crocodile will often say something like "X is Y." Here are a few common ones:

"I am never going to learn this."

"I am this way."

"I can't."

"There is nothing I can do . . ."

"We are the best."

"They should/shouldn't have . . ."

"This is how it is."

"There is no other option."

"They are this way."

To become aware of crocodilian language, take a moment and list the Crocodile Statements you notice in your self-talk, especially when you feel challenged. It's all about stating your assumptions as facts.

Crocodile talk can have big implications when we listen to it. Take note of the following:

"Everything that can be invented has already been invented."
—Charles Duell, Director of the US Patent Office, 1899

"Sensible and responsible women do not want to vote."
—Grover Cleveland, US President, 1905

"There is no reason for any individual to have a computer in his home."
—Ken Olsen, President, Digital Equipment, 1977

The crocodile makes up its mind about how things are, and states them as absolute truth. Great for physical survival—it's handy to have unambiguous information telling us to run now when a tiger appears—but not so great for the rest of our lives.

What is the cost of these Crocodile Statements? Let's go back to the three dimensions of perceiving reality: I, We, and It.

On the I-dimension Crocodile Statements cause stress, as we worry about being right. And when we know we are not, our crocodiles will create even more emotional turmoil by having us fabricate assumptions disguised as facts, to back up our judgments. Ever been in a meeting where you learned something new that contradicted a conclusion on your PowerPoint slide and you somehow found yourself making up reasons why you were right?

Crocodile Statements also corrode the We-dimension, our relationships, as there is no real dialogue possible when we are right and they are wrong.

And how about the It-dimension, our effectiveness? If Mr. Duell, Mr. Cleveland, and Mr. Olsen had been correct, we would have missed out on all the innovations from the last hundred-plus years. Nothing new would have been invented. Women would not be voting. And the computer on which I am writing wouldn't exist.

Crocodiles are invested in the status quo. Why? It's better for our survival, from their reactive, needing-the-answer-now-or-die! perspective. When they are in control of our nervous system, we don't learn. Instead we stay invested in unchecked assumptions and base our lives on this crocodilian pseudosense of certainty. That's the bad news.

There is some good news about our nervous system as well. Let's see what we can learn from FDR about another part of our nervous system that, as it turns out, can tame our crocodiles and help us learn from our obstacles as well. There were quite a few crocodiles to be tamed in 1933.

BRINGING THE CROCODILES UNDER THE AEGIS OF OWL WISDOM

Franklin D. Roosevelt didn't know about crocodiles, as studies of this topic were not public knowledge during his time in office. Yet, he did recognize fear as one of his country's greatest challenges, in particular in facing the banking crisis. As he famously said at the outset of his inaugural Presidential Address: "Let me assert my firm belief that the only thing we have to fear is fear itself." FDR went on to emphasize the importance of combating fear three times in his 14.5-minute Fireside Chat a week later, concluding, "Let us unite in banishing fear . . . together we cannot fail." He made people aware of the crocodilian traps that could undermine the nation's recovery. And he let people know he wouldn't support fear-based behavior, stating: "Let me make it clear to you that the banks will take care of all needs except of course the hysterical demands of hoarders—and it is my belief that hoarding during the past week has become an exceedingly unfashionable pastime in every part of our nation." Neither FDR nor the banks would feed the crocodiles.

FDR coached a whole nation to tame their crocodiles and grow in wisdom. We can refer to the opposite of the crocodile as "owl wisdom," pointing to the wise and compassionate part of our nervous system, which we now understand is related to our heart area and prefrontal cortices.

Imagine an office scenario in which we receive criticism for a task we just finished. How can we respond to that with more owl wisdom, rather than crocodilian hysteria? And how would our crocodile want us to react? Do you see how many more options we have when we respond from owl wisdom? We'd want to find out more about the feedback, learn the specifics to see where we did well and where we could improve, and we'd probably want to understand how we could more effectively address the task going forward. Conversely, the crocodile would just be defensive, making the other wrong, ignoring the feedback, or trying to fix the problem in a rush.

Historian David McCullough remarked: "FDR made speeches that wanted people to rise, to be better than they thought they could be." FDR helped people excel—to surpass their imagined crocodilian limitations. He helped shift the collective consciousness of a nation from a crocodilian fear-based Contraction to an owl, heart-based Growth Leadership Mind-set, helping them to see the Great Depression with fresh eyes. Instead of acting from "poor me," people grew to re-conceive their overwhelming problem as a shared growth challenge. *How can I contribute to the solution*? became their new perspective. And contribute they did. Remember, they voluntarily returned two thirds of the hoarded cash to the banks by the end of the month that FDR gave his "More Important than Gold" talk. FDR successfully coached people to transform their reactive crocodiles into constructive owl wisdom.

Crocodile-Taming Practice

Following in FDR's footsteps, we can coach ourselves from crocodile to owl when we are challenged. We can practice a Growth Leadership Mind-set—

choosing presence, self-discovery, contribution, and excellence over distraction, reactivity, getting, and giving up. Yet, in the heat of the moment, for instance when we are receiving tough feedback, this may seem like an impossible task.

To make crocodile taming more manageable, we can simply pause what we are thinking and doing, take a few deep breaths, and ask ourselves this question: *"Who's talking now, the owl or the crocodile?"*

When we're not sure, we can be pretty sure it's our reactive crocodile. If it is, we can simply *smile*, pause, and ask: *"How would my owl respond now?"*

See what comes up. Then acknowledge yourself for transforming this bit of your reactivity—taming the crocodile and finding a way to more wisdom by asking the core question of Growth Leadership: *"How am I growing?"*

It can be a big or small insight that comes. It doesn't matter. What matters is that you are learning, claiming a bit—or a lot—more of your owl wisdom.

Reflecting on these three simple questions tames our crocodilian patterns and brings them under the aegis of our owl wisdom. When we doubt it will work, we can think of great leaders like FDR, who tamed not only their own crocodiles but those of an entire nation.

I work with my crocodiles all the time. Here is one example out of many. A few months ago, I was on the phone with a client. He asked to postpone some of the culture development workshops we had planned. I felt anxious, as I wasn't sure I would have enough bandwidth that upcoming fall to accommodate the new schedule. My internal thoughts went: "Why could you not have thought about this earlier?!" "Now the whole thing will fail!" and "I did something wrong, that's why this is happening!" After the call, I paused, and asked myself the three crocodile-taming questions:

1. Who is talking now, the owl or the crocodile?
2. How would my owl respond?
3. How am I growing?

Doomsday and Pollyanna Crocodile Statements

Clearly, my Cringing Crocodile was talking. All my self-talk thoughts were filled with negativity and doomsday scenarios.

Anticipating the worst and presenting that as fact is another way our crafty crocodile tries to protect us. It spins a compelling nightmare hallucination so we will feel forced to go into a fight/flight/freeze panic. When we are stressed out, the Cringing Crocodile is happy. "At least I know we're on high alert," says our crocodile to himself, "I have done my job, we are preparing for the worst." This type of doomsday thinking can show up as overworking, fretting, perfecting, and other forms of obsessive behavior.

As a side note, crocodile talk does not only come in doomsday form. It also can be a Pollyanna. "We are the best," "That will never happen," and "I know the answer for sure" are ways in which the crocodile tries to make us feel safe by having us ignore what is really going on. We'll learn more about this type of Pollyanna-ish crocodile talk later in this chapter.

"How would my owl respond?" was the next question I asked myself after the call. I realized I could simply map out what this client needed and flag any conflicts in my schedule with other client engagements and discuss together with the client how we could address this. Yes, it was that simple.

Finally, I reflected "How am I growing?" I saw how much more joy there is in working with clients, being authentic with them, even about my constraints, unafraid of what might happen. If I let go of my crocodilian, worst-case projections, I get to experience flow, collaboration, and new possibilities to resolve issues.

When we bring the crocodiles under the aegis of the owl, our lives tend to become simpler, and more joyful. The key to crocodile taming? Noticing that we are under the influence of our crocodiles. Recognizing that we are caught is half the game.

Let's get to know another common crocodile that tends to keep us small and reactive. We'll call them the "Good Boys and Good Girls," or, in short, the "Clinging Crocodiles." Good Boys and Good Girls try to please others—similar to the flight and freeze behaviors of their Cringing sibling. Yet their inner workings are slightly different. The two crocodiles together keep us small, in a Contraction Mind-set.

A CONTRACTION MIND-SET— PART 2: THE CLINGING CROCODILE

How did your parents reinforce your behavior when you spoke your first words? And what did they say when you first learned how to spell your name? What about when you got a good grade on a test?

Chances are you heard, "Yes, good!" many times in your life and developed a craving for that kind of response along the way. What do you say to yourself when you finish your work on time? When someone agrees with you? When you arrive at your destination? You likely say, "Yes, good!" And you may feel good as a result.

The problem with "yes, good!" validation is that it becomes a blocker to realizing our potential when we start to need it. And many of us seek it constantly, whether we realize it or not. Neuroscience helps us understand why. Remember that our nervous system is wired primarily for survival. One of the many ways it helps us survive is by motivating us to do what is predictable. Think back to prehistoric times. When we first heard the sound of running water and discovered a nearby stream, we were happy, because we had discovered a new, reliable source of nourishment. A rush of dopamine was released by our brains, which made us feel good and incentivized us to go back to what we had just discovered, a nearby supply of potable water.

We get a release of dopamine when we feel validated. So every time someone tells us, "Yes, good!" we get this little chemical lift. This is not a problem in itself. However, validation becomes an issue when we put excessive mental energy into getting it. Then, instead of focusing on being aware of ourselves and learning, caring, and giving our best, we tend to keep running back to our familiar validation-seeking tactics. The tactics include playing small, not saying what we really mean, acting in a way that is untrue to ourselves to get approval, overworking to feel worthy, and giving up our life's dreams to stay safe and coddled in the bosom of people who validate us.

And our dopamine-seeking "Clinging Crocodile" behaviors are also more basic than that. Anytime we make a prediction and get the response we want, we will receive some dopamine candy. When we check our devices, anticipating a message, and then get one—e-mail, text, like, etc.—we get a little dopamine hit. This may explain why many of us, instead of smoking, are now addicted to checking our devices, even when driving our cars, waiting for the bus, or sitting at the dinner table. Dopamine candy beats the taste of real food, apparently!

All these Clinging Crocodile reactions started as patterns we learned as children—patterns that our primitive dopamine function rushes us into to help us survive. Take yourself back to when you were a kid. You had no means of providing for yourself. Instead you had to rely on your caretakers to survive. When you received validation, it meant that you were doing well—you were on track for survival. To be reprimanded meant that you weren't doing well, which meant the possibility of abandonment, and therefore death, or so your young crocodile figured. To avoid this, you learned certain defense routines to get validation that became engrained in your nervous system.

How do we get out from under the influence of these Clinging Crocodiles? Just as with the Cringing Crocodile, the first thing is to notice them. Again, our bodies provide helpful clues. How do you feel when you get approval or recognition? Maybe you feel a sense of euphoria, relief, or some other form of mini, momentary high. Likely, it's the dopamine release you're feeling. Also your self-talk may be dominated by a specific type of tranquilizing thinking, which we call Pollyanna-ish Crocodilian. Since our Clinging Crocodile looks for validation, it will create an internal dialogue of smoothness by wishing reality away, thinking and saying things like:

"It's okay," when it isn't;

"I agree," when you don't;

"I feel great," when you feel bad; and,

"Let's do it," when you don't want to.

Notice that our Clinging Crocodile doesn't want us to challenge these statements as Pollyanna-ish. It only wants things to be smooth, nice, and predictable. That's the bad news. The good news is that becoming aware of this Pollyanna-ish thinking is the beginning of taming this Clinging Crocodile.

Once we've noticed this crocodile acting up, we can choose being still and present, instead of giving into its need for validation. And we can listen to what our owl suggests and focus on giving our best, over pleasing those around us. To support our process, we ask ourselves the three crocodile-taming questions we discussed earlier:

1.   Who is talking now, the owl or the crocodile?

2.   How would my owl respond?

3.   How am I growing?

When we no longer try to be a good girl or good boy, we free ourselves up to listen to our heart, and grow more and more into who we really are.

Neuroplasticity: Our Past Becomes Our Future

The more often we think and act a certain way, the more often certain neural pathways in our brain get activated. These routines become engrained, as "neurons that fire together, wire together." And like a track we walk down in the snow, the more often we walk it, the deeper the track becomes. The more often we think defensive thoughts, the more likely it is we will repeat those in the future. The more often we bring the crocodile under the aegis of the owl, the more likely we will be able to do that in the future. Over time we can become unconsciously skilled in crocodile taming. Scientists call this process "neuroplasticity." Neurons that repeatedly work together prepare new tracks in the brain that become highways after repeated use. This is true for all repeated thinking, whether it's Cringing or Clinging reactivity, or Owl wisdom. It doesn't matter; our mind will repeat what it has been programmed to do, just like a computer.

Let me give you a personal example of one Clinging Crocodile pattern that has been deeply engrained in me. When I was a child, I interpreted that being myself was not acceptable, and therefore not safe. My parents were very skilled farmers, and I didn't really like farming. If I said, "I'd rather read," I would be told, "You should be a good farmer's son and work." So what did I do when I was seven or eight years old, living with caregivers who rewarded "good farmer son" behaviors, while my crocodile wanted to make sure I survived? I chameleon-ed myself into someone I was not—a "good farmer's son." I tried to make myself into someone others would validate. Why did my parents act this way? They were and are very loving people. I admire them. I love them deeply and they love me deeply as well. And at the time I was a child, they were not yet aware of these crocodiles. How could they have been? They had simply learned these ways of thinking from their parents and their parents had learned them from theirs, and so on. Crocodiles are not personal. They are tribal and they get passed on from one generation to another, until someone says: No more, *the buck stops here*. You can be that person.

In the grip of "Good Boy" programs that "being myself is unsafe," and that "I must comply, or else . . . ," I spent my energy trying to create an environment that validated who I was, even if I was not being myself. I overworked to get accolades, I had a hard time saying no, I didn't express my feelings clearly, and I was oversensitive and compensated for others' emotional turbulence.

I am no longer seven or eight years old. Yet I still have some "Good Boy" programs in my system. It was a neurological highway I traveled down often. As I didn't become aware of it until I was about forty years old, it's still somewhat part of me, even after the work I have done to heal it. Thankfully I have seen these Clinging Crocodiles lose their power to dominate my thoughts as I have been doing my practices to tame them.

PRACTICING A GROWTH LEADERSHIP MIND-SET

Had FDR given in to a clinging crocodilian desire to please, he surely wouldn't have been able to act as decisively as he did during that first week of his presidency in March 1933. FDR was an extraordinary leader. Maybe we can learn to be like him. Maybe it is time to decisively leave behind our Cringing and Clinging crocodiles and focus instead on our "confidence and courage" to transform ourselves and our world.

Will we have an immediate transformation once we decide to let go of our crocodiles? Probably not. The great leaders of our time didn't just become that overnight. FDR was struck down by polio eleven years before being elected President. He spent years learning to walk with braces and crutches to be a viable presidential candidate. Instead of giving in to despair, which he experienced at the onset of his disease, he stayed committed to his recovery. He joined, and shortly thereafter bought and led, a polio treatment center, Warm Springs, to heal himself and help others heal also. From an early age he had been taught he could succeed at anything he put his mind to, and he passed that teaching on to his fellow citizens. Eleanor Roosevelt once said: "I have never known a man who gave one a greater sense of security. I never heard him say that there was a problem that he thought it was impossible for humans to solve. I never knew him to face life or any problem that came up with fear." And even despite that, even FDR had his moments of crocodilian despair. I sense he overcame the external circumstances of his life with his trademark "confidence and courage"— much "more important than gold."

Look at your crocodiles with the eyes of FDR, with courage and confidence—what possibilities for *presence, self-discovery, contribution, and excellence* do you see?

Cringing Crocodiles	Clinging Crocodiles

Fight
    Perfectionism
    Needing to win at any cost
    Overpowering
    Being argumentative
	Getting Validation through People
	    Pleasing
	    Compromising
	    Flattering
	    Lying
	    Masking
	    Denying needs
	    Colluding

Flight
    Avoiding
    Not rocking the boat
    Deferring to others
    Pleasing
	Giving up on myself
	    Rescuing
	    Victimhood
	
	Getting Validation through Tasks
	    Perfectionism
	    Overworking
	    Fretting

Freeze
    Being flustered
    Hiding
    Denying difficulty
    Being apathetic
	Providing silver-bullet solutions
	    Double-checking
	    Overdetailing
	    Needing to win at all costs
	    Checking off the to-do list

Remember that neuroplasticity means we can unlearn our crocodilian thinking, simply by repeatedly choosing a different way that reflects more who we truly are. By repeatedly bringing the crocodiles under the aegis of the owl, we will outgrow them over time. All it requires is an FDR-like courage to name and tame our crocodiles and approach them with owl wisdom. We can start now by taking a few deep breaths and asking ourselves the three crocodile-taming questions:

1. Who is talking now, the owl or the crocodile?
2. How would my owl respond?
3. How am I growing?

And then let the owl insights come to you as you rest in presence.

FIELDWORK

1. Think of an upset that you currently have, or of an upset that you had in the past that still feels unresolved. Write it down. The more juice it has, the more anxiety it causes, the more you can learn.

2. What Cringing Crocodilian self-talk do you hear when you think of this upset? Examples are "I'm not good enough . . . ," "I can't . . . ," "I should have known better . . . ," "They shouldn't have . . . ," "I hate them . . . ," etc.

3. What are some of the Clinging Crocodile behaviors that you fall into most often? Which ones may be active as you face this challenge? Select two.

   A. Checking phone and e-mail reflexively

   B. Not saying no

   C. Not prioritizing

   D. Agreeing when disagreeing

   E. Short-term bias

   F. Not being bold, holding back

   G. Doing only what feels good

4. Think back to your childhood. What is a Clinging Crocodile defensive pattern that you learned as a child to get validation that helped you survive? Write it down. How may it play a role in how you face your current challenge?

5. Given what you have observed regarding your Cringing and Clinging crocodiles, how can you use your challenge as an opportunity to grow and be more true to yourself?

6. If you like, do this coaching exercise to experience the difference between Crocodilian Contraction and Owl Growth Leadership. Think of a challenge you are facing. First do exercise A. Write down your answers to the questions by yourself, or do it in conversation with a partner. Really allow yourself to get into it. Watch your feelings and thoughts and what you (your crocodile) are getting out of it. Take about five minutes.

Then do the same for exercise B. Watch how you feel. What crocodilian reactive feelings and thoughts are getting triggered? What happens when you pause long enough for owl wisdom to surface? How are you growing? Take about five minutes.

Now look at the difference between your experience between A and B. What are you learning about your crocodiles by bringing them under the aegis of the owl?

A. Crocodilian Contraction Coaching

   1. What is the problem you have?

   2. What is the reason for the problem?

   3. Whose fault is it?

   4. What should the team members do about it?

   5. How should they be punished for not doing anything about it?

   6. What is a quick fix?

B. Owl Growth Leadership Coaching

   1. What is your challenge?

   2. What assumptions have you made about it? Who is talking now, the owl or the crocodile?

   3. How have you responded thus far? What has been the impact?

   4. How would your owl respond?

   5. How will you respond?

   6. How are you growing?

7. How are you growing?

CHAPTER 4

Learning from Our Seven Fear Families—Befriending Seven Crocodiles

"Perfect love casts out fear." —The Bible

STEPPING INTO GROWTH does not come without its fears. Soon after we have experienced the satisfaction of connecting with our calling, we may find ourselves in the belly of the whale, frightened of what might lie ahead. Will our relationships survive this? Will we have enough money? Will we still be successful? Will we be able to keep our sense of identity, our sense of who we are? Even taming our crocodiles brings up fear. Can we really afford to let go of the fear of survival? Will we be okay if we no longer let the fear of not fitting in drive our bus? What if we no longer feared failure—would we still be successful?

I can't remember a day passing without feeling fear. Sometimes it runs subtly in the background of my thoughts; other times it's very vivid, occupying the forefront of my mind. But the good news is that in moving forward, I have found that most of my concerns turn out to be "False Evidence Appearing Real" (FEAR)—an acronym that we can use to reframe fear into what it really is: an illusion created by our crocodilian mind that is so bent on helping us survive, it tells us untruths that feel real.

OUR RELATIONSHIP WITH FEAR

Even if we believe that most of our fears will not come true, it is unlikely that we will never experience fear again. What's more likely is that we will encounter lots of fear as we step further and further out of our comfort zones and into our fullest selves. Like birthing, evolution is painful at times. The human system is designed for homeostasis—to keep stable—and will do all it can to protect itself from change. Gandhi once said, "We live within a circle, the circumference of which is bounded by our fears." We will need to become masters of working with our fears if we want to have a chance of stepping outside of our comfort zones.

How do we become masters of working with fear? To master anything, we first have to get to know it intimately. We have to befriend it, to get to know it inside and out, like the back of our hand. Most of us are not comfortable or even familiar with our fears because we have been taught that fear is something to be avoided—that it is something bad that we "shouldn't" have. Let's contemplate these three words and notice our reaction: "My deepest fear."

The dictionary defines fear as "an unpleasant emotion caused by the belief that someone or something is dangerous, likely to cause pain, or a threat." It's no wonder we keep such unpleasantness away from the forefront of our attention. The fact of the matter is that, like breathing, fear is a part of our lives. As long as we are in our human bodies, we are going to experience fear. Fear is natural. Yet fear also engenders a sense of "stuck-ness." Our habitual response to fear is paralysis, fight, or flight.

What if we had a more friendly relationship with fear? We have a chance to transform the way that we look at fear; we have a chance to become fascinated with it, like a child who has received a new toy to play with. We have the chance to ask ourselves, "How can I grow through my fear? What is there for me to learn?"

When we let go of the fear of fear and replace it with fascination, imagine what becomes possible for us and our world. Would we still be so overscheduled, if we were no longer driven by the fear of not being good enough? Would we still compete as much with each other, if we saw through the fear of scarcity? Would we still have enemies, if we let go of the fear of being hurt? Would we still have as many broken relationships, if we saw through the fear of being fully honest with each other? Would we still be addicted to our smartphones, if we transformed our fear of being alone?

Growth leaders aren't just fascinated with fear—they appreciate the tremendous creative potential underlying it. According to Pete Carroll, head coach of the Seattle Seahawks, "We need to get a platform in place that allows fear to be part of it, to be comfortable with it, even to have fun with it, and that allows us to master it. Then we get some tools, like breathing or self-talk. That's how to thrive in situations we're not proficient in. Fear is really central to what we do."

Tackling our fears may not seem useful for the business world, but it is. It may be one of the most useful things we can do to improve our business. Think about how much energy we spend avoiding our fears, suppressing them by trying to overcompensate, please, and perform. We need to realize that isn't how life is; it's how we've learned life to be.

Fear is at the core of Growth Leadership just as fear is at the core of what limits us as human beings. Fear is the food our crocodiles live on—both the Cringing and the Clinging ones we met in the last chapter. Without fear, they would die. Without the fear of survival and abandonment, these crocodiles would no longer need to work so hard to keep us worried, on guard, validated—always anticipating that next threat.

Growth Leaders unblock their fear-based limitations and help others do the same. Fear is the primary blocker to realizing our potential and is thus also the primary fuel for growth. The CEO of one of the largest Australian financial services companies understood this. He shared his top fears in front of thousands of his employees. By making his fears discussable, he gave his employees permission to do the same, creating a culture of honesty, acceptance, and deep collaboration (of course employees didn't need his permission, and yet, in a corporate culture, when the leader makes something okay, it becomes a heck of a lot easier for others to do so as well). Fear became as common of a discussion topic within the company as revenues, employee engagement, and the bottom line.

This CEO's fears included *not being recognized, being wrong, being ridiculed, losing control of the situation or of his emotions, being let down or letting others down, hurting others or damaging relationships, not being accepted or belonging, being alone, and being treated unfairly.*

Read this list again. Think of which of these fears is strongest in you, if any. Imagine what becomes possible when you befriend that fear so that you can learn from it; so that you can find the possibilities that this fear is keeping from you, and use them to propel yourself to your next level of freedom and greatness.

BEFRIENDING OUR FEARS

One of the beauties of the human mind is its ability to see patterns. Patterning helps us to see the forest from the trees, and distill the wisdom from the chaos. When we study our fears closely, we can also glean some patterns in them. One thing we can notice is that they are universal—we share similar fears. We may also notice that when we experience a powerful fear, it feels like something we have experienced before and comes from somewhere inside of us. Our fears tend to flare up when we are faced with a triggering event—a crisis, a setback, a new opportunity, or any other type of change. We discussed in Chapter 1 that we can see triggering events as Growth Instants—opportunities to grow our consciousness, in this case learning to befriend and release our fears.

When we look closely at our fears we may notice that there is an inverse relationship between our capacity to be loving and present, and our fearfulness. The less fearful we are, the more present we can be. The more fearful we are, the less we're able to be present. I remember this as the following equation:

My Actualized Presence = My Full Potential Presence – My Fearfulness.

The Fear Paradox

The more we are in the grip of our fears—the more we are driven by fight, flight, or freeze reflexes—the less we will be able to be totally in the moment and be aware of what is really happening. Paradoxically, the more we are driven by our fears, the more likely our fears are to be realized. We call this the Fear Paradox.

Picture this scenario: I am in the grip of the fear of abandonment. I am so focused on earning your approval, so bent on being a perfect good boy, so as not to lose you, that the real me is nowhere to be found. I begin to judge myself and compare myself to other people. I become jealous and possessive. I try to control the way that you see me, and become disingenuous with you. After months of my acting as a good boy in response to my fear of being abandoned, you leave me, as your inner being misses connecting authentically with me. My fear of being abandoned led to my being abandoned.

Picture a similar scenario at work. I am paralyzed by my fear of not being liked by my colleagues. To make sure I am not rejected by them, I say what they want to hear, not what I really think, making promises I can't keep, and I hold back negative customer feedback about our product I think they don't want to hear. After months of this, I feel drained, and my teammates dislike working with me. My fear of not being liked has led to my not being liked.

And we can see the same pattern with our other fears. For example, my fear of scarcity can lead me to becoming so obsessed with keeping my job that I no longer contribute to my team, but rather I begin acting as a hero who outdoes others. I take credit for things I didn't do, take on responsibilities that belong to others, and go into long monologues in team discussions to let people know that I am important, more so than they are. Over time the team may get out of balance due to my behaviors and if I am not able to adjust, they may ask me to leave and I lose my job. Thus, my giving in to my fear of scarcity leads to scarcity.

When we notice a fear coming up, we can simply pause and ask ourselves the three crocodile-taming questions we learned in the last chapter, and add two new ones:

1. Who's talking? The owl or the crocodile?

After that add:

2. What fear may be active here?

3. Who would I be without this fear?

Followed by the questions we discussed earlier:

4. How can I respond from my wise and compassionate owl?

5. How am I growing?

As we do this practice, we calm our reptilian nervous system that is hell-bent on our survival, and give our wise and compassionate heart and neocortex areas a chance to catch up and help us see the situation from a bigger, wiser perspective.

ORGANIZING OUR FEARS

One way we can make sense of our fears is to see them as related to our motivations. If we didn't have any motivation, we likely wouldn't have any fear either. If we didn't have the motivation to live, we wouldn't fear dying. If we didn't have the motivation to be in a relationship, we wouldn't fear abandonment or exclusion. If we didn't feel the need to be someone in the world, we wouldn't fear failure.

We mapped our motivations into seven categories in Chapter 2. We can use these categories to organize our fears also. We will call each fear category a "fear family," indicating that these represent a set of different yet related fear energies. Let the word *family* also remind us that our fears are inherited—they are part of our familial and cultural history. We tend to carry the fears that our ancestors hadn't yet mastered or seen through.

Motivation	Fear Family
7. Wisdom, compassion, enlightenment	Losing identity
6. Cohesion	Complexity
5. Making a contribution	Hurt
4. Discovery	Uncertainty
3. Self-esteem	Failure
2. Relationship	Abandonment
1. Survival	Scarcity

Before we dive into exploring each of these seven fear families, think about which fear family you see in yourself most often. And how do you react when you are in the grip of these fears?

1. Growing through the Fear of Scarcity

Let's start with the fear of scarcity. Where does it come from? It is directly related to our motivation to survive. But do we need our fear of scarcity to survive, or will our motivation by itself be sufficient for our survival? Let's do an experiment. Imagine yourself dirt poor, with no job and no money. Will you manage? Chances are your motivation to survive will lead you to find shelter and something to eat.

How does the fear of scarcity influence your capacity to find shelter and food? The more energy you spend worrying that you will not eat tonight and wondering where you will sleep, the less energy you have to be resourceful and find a solution. The motivation to survive will keep us alert and therefore out of trouble. We don't need fear for that. Fear leads to dysfunctional thinking. By contrast, presence and motivation lead to clarity of mind, care, and resourcefulness.

Notice how the fear of scarcity shows up at work and in life. Because we are afraid that we won't have enough, we don't share. Instead we compete for everything, causing disconnection and fragmentation. In teams, people are so concerned with their own survival that they make everything into an act to prove that they are worthy—chewing up precious time and resources with endless PowerPoint presentations, overworking, not being truthful for fear of losing pole position, and taking shortcuts—prioritizing short-term wins over long-term sustainability.

The more we are driven by the fear of scarcity, the less effective we become and, paradoxically, the more scarcity we tend to experience. In a simple equation:

My Actual Resourcefulness =
My Full Potential Resourcefulness – (My Fear of Scarcity + My Other Fears)

Still, knowing that fear is not helpful will likely not have the effect of you losing it overnight. That is why it's helpful to massage the crocodilian mind with an antidote practice of kindness and understanding, which over time helps it relax.

When we notice the fear of scarcity within ourselves, we can think back to the words that FDR used to coach an entire nation caught in this fear: "Confidence and courage are the essentials of success in carrying out our plan. You people must have faith; you must not be stampeded by rumors or guesses . . . Together we cannot fail." When you're caught in this fear, take the opportunity to grow your courage and confidence muscle. *Courage* comes from the Latin word *cor*, which means heart. When we look deeply into the heart, we find limitless resources within ourselves to respond to any situation with dignity, wisdom, and effectiveness. We may then ask ourselves: "How can I respond with courage now? How can I grow?"

Notice where in your body you feel the fear of scarcity most strongly. For many of us we experience a contraction in our belly and sacrum area, or in other words the root of our torso. Once this fear is activated, its energy starts to travel up into our nervous system, driving all sorts of stress and dysfunctional thinking. When we are driven by a fear of scarcity, we may react by panicking, seeing scarcity instead of abundance, running back to the familiar, blaming others, overworking, hoarding, and not attending to our social and familial relationships.

Imagine we could tame our fear of scarcity today. Would the world still have as much poverty? There are plenty of resources on this planet for everyone to be supplied for. Without the fear of not having enough, we may grow into a state of consciousness where sharing with each other and not waiting for others to rescue us become the new norm. How would having less fear of scarcity change your life?

2.   Growing through the Fear of Abandonment

Besides the fear of scarcity (of not having enough), the fear of abandonment is active within us from the moment we are born. As a two-year-old, if your mother rejects you and you have no one else taking care of you, that means certain death, as you are not yet ready to take care of yourself. This is why, according to our crocodilian nervous system, someone leaving us, disagreeing with us, or simply frowning at us equals death. It is this reptilian perspective that we operate from as toddlers. The problem is that the crocodile never grows up and we don't either, as long as we believe the horror stories it keeps telling us. *Under the influence of the crocodile, we act like a two-year-old.*

Some of the things that this crocodile tells us may not sound like horror stories at all—they may sound normal and believable. It may tell us that we need to wear certain brands of clothing to be important, or that we need to talk about certain subjects to be interesting to others. These are very subtle ways that this crocodile tries to cajole us into not losing touch with the tribe—to fit in. Every time we give in to our abandonment crocodile, we deny who we really are, thinking we have to abandon ourselves to not be abandoned by others. I have noticed in myself and others that there is an inverse relationship between being authentic and believing my abandonment fears. Or simply put:

My Actual Authenticity =
My Full Potential Authenticity – (My Fear of Abandonment + My Other Fears)

The crocodile tells us things like: *If I truly show who I am, they won't like me . . . ; if they really got to know me, they would realize I am a fraud . . . ; if I say what is true for me, I'll lose the relationship I so deeply cherish . . .* In other words, "If I am authentic, I will be alone." When we are acting from this fear of abandonment, we fall into behaviors such as clinging, trying to please others, creating silos and cliques, not being true to ourselves, hiding who we are, judging others for not complying with the tribal norms, withdrawing, trying to change others, overrelying on others, and operating from "needing" somebody or something (our partners, our children, our jobs).

Chris Capossela is Chief Marketing Officer of the Microsoft Corporation. He is one of the most admired leaders in the company and it's easy to see why. He is friendly, super positive, supportive of others, and very smart, among other qualities. People I spoke to love working with him. Throughout his career he has learned a lot about the inverse relationship between wanting to fit in and being authentic. Sharing his true self is something Chris has been learning over time.

"We did one of these crazy leadership trainings called 'Doing Leadership,' you know, you go outside and you have people running around, and doing all kinds of crazy exercises. After spending some time with us, they put a bunch of us against the wall and they had a few of us rearrange us physically in order of who you would follow and who you wouldn't. About twenty-nine people put me at the front of the line as the person they would follow and one woman put me at the very end of the line as the least likely person she would follow. After we had talked for a while they asked the woman: 'Tell us, why did you put Chris at number twenty-nine? Did you get the order wrong?' She said that she hadn't. It was one of these things where people had to be incredibly blunt and honest, which was helpful for me. The woman said, 'I don't trust him, I don't believe the things I am seeing from him. I don't believe that's what he actually believes.' That was just an eye opener."

His coworker's words made Chris reflect on himself. "What have I done? I was behaving what felt like normal to me. Then I started working on it—being very clear about how I felt about something and giving as clear feedback as I could. That's when trust started to build.

"The key thing I had to learn was to be more direct about what I wanted and what I was thinking because the way I show up physically doesn't always match what I might be thinking or feeling," said Chris.

Any strength overused becomes a weakness. Peers would tell him, "You've got this optimism and that sometimes leads you to being unclear. If I do something bad you have to tell me if that wasn't good, not that it was good." People had learned to recalibrate Chris's scale, which started at good and went to awesome. As one colleague put it, "I had to learn when you said something was good, it actually sucked, and when you said something was awesome it actually was awesome."

"I had to learn to be more articulate about what I was thinking and feeling—what my opinions were—as opposed to sort of trying to be part of the team. I had to learn to say 'hey, I'm actually not with you on that.'"

It was a learning opportunity for Chris, as he had been trained from very early on to please and perform to fit into the workplace. Chris grew up in an Italian restaurant in Boston that his family owned. They lived on the second floor and worked the restaurant on the first. Chris started serving as a waiter from age seven, and it was all hands on deck all the time. "It took me a long time to learn how to be trusted by my coworkers, because they kind of thought, 'well that's him performing, that's not really him. He is doing the fancy specials—he is doing this fancy presentation and he's really good at it. But is that the real guy? I don't know who the real guy is. That is the guy waiting the table for two hours.'"

Chris may have learned that to belong (or in other words, to not be abandoned) we have to please and perform. And in the restaurant business that means giving guests the best time they can possibly have, regardless of how we waiters feel about it.

Being authentic continues to be an area of learning for Chris. When we spoke about Microsoft, he told me: "It's a very high-paced, crazy culture, and the speed at which things get discussed in meetings is extraordinary. So when I am with my peers I have to really push myself—to tell myself hey, don't hide, be active, get in the game, don't vacillate. Instead, lead and anticipate. When I am with my directs, it is much easier. You're the top dog. Also when I am with my boss [Satya Nadella] one-on-one it's super easy. But with my ten peers at our senior leadership team meetings, I really have to 'Come on! Get in the game!' It's still big work for me."

Each year, Chris practices a number of leadership learnings he sees as important for his growth to the next level. "Be kind. For everyone you meet is fighting a hard battle," is Chris's sixth learning from the past year, quoting the Scottish theologian Ian Maclaren. According to one of his directs: "It's certainly a statement that's consistent with how Chris operates."

While Chris no longer sugarcoats his feedback, even when it is tough, he is committed to being compassionate, no matter what, even with himself. That helps him and others learn fast, and may be why people look forward to one-on-ones with him. It's safe to bring out your best with him, even if Chris doesn't agree with what you're saying. Chris builds teams that match him in authenticity, kindness, and deep enthusiasm for others' greatness.

When we truly wish to relate to others, we share who we really are and encourage others to do the same. Chris's learning suggests we "get in the game" and serve authentically with kindness. We can choose this as a Growth Practice whenever the fear of not belonging is acting up in our system.

How do we notice the fear of abandonment is acting up, besides the usual amygdala reactions like heart racing, blood rushing, and sweat? Many of us feel a contraction in our lower belly—the area of our body that is associated with relating to others (it's also where we feel the butterflies). When we feel this sensation, we can take a few deep breaths into our lower belly to rebalance ourselves, and then ask: "How can I be a bit more honest and kind now? How can I serve them a bit more? What is great about them?" These questions can help us move from defensive dishonesty to authentic expression and service.

3.   Growing through the Fear of Failure

Besides not having enough and the fear of abandonment, the fear of failure is another deeply engrained conditioning in our collective consciousness. Think about it—how many of us got a good grade in school for asking a great question or for saying "I don't know?" Most of us got ahead in life by giving the right answer. This starts very early when we're rewarded by our caregivers for calling things by the correct name; doing things correctly, like eating our food; and doing what we're told.

Over time, the pursuit of doing things right can turn into a paralyzing fear of doing things wrong. And, as with our other fears, the more we believe it, the more likely our fear will actually manifest. When I am so obsessed with doing it right, I stop paying attention to what is needed now and lose my connection with reality. Thus, my effectiveness plummets. In other words:

My Performance = My Full Potential – (My Fear of Failure + My Other Fears)

The more I am focused on the fear of failure—the more I am replaying my past memories of what can go wrong—the less I am here to take care of what is needed. In the grip of the fear of failure, I may procrastinate or not take risks as a way of staying beyond reproach, or not give my all so I can say I didn't mean it. Or I may lose myself in trying to make something perfect—winning my little battle but losing the war.

When we are living in fear of failure, we may fall into some or all of the following habits: distracting ourselves (such as with social media, television, or the internet), putting excessive pressure on ourselves, irritation, telling ourselves "I can't," and giving up. Also, we may judge and try to control others, micro-managing or manipulating them to make sure our plan doesn't fail.

Gene White, the president of the Global Child Nutrition Foundation, has failed often in her more than nine decades of living. In pursuing her ambitious goal of eradicating child hunger to create world peace, she has faced many obstacles. Some she navigated successfully the first time around, others after a few tries—and some she is still working on.

Gene sees any and all challenges as opportunities for learning to realize her purpose. "I can't accept failure as closure but believe instead that it becomes valuable learning for new beginnings," she told me when I visited her the first time. "I say to my colleagues, 'Don't tell me you can't do it, simply tell me why.' Many times we build barriers by saying 'no' before trying. 'No' is a seldom-used word in our organization."

Challenges energize Gene, and fuel her love of learning. Learning from challenges helps her grow as a person and discover new ways to achieve her mission.

An ongoing challenge for Gene is her husband's passing, now three years ago. She applies the same learning attitude here. "I find we don't stop living or growing because of loss. It is an incredibly difficult time but learning slowly continues as we grow in understanding and compassion. Is not sadness a way of adjusting to what happened?"

When everything is seen to be a source of learning to realize more of our calling, rather than a "success" or a "failure," everything becomes energizing, whatever it is. Part of Gene's astounding vitality may come from living life as an ongoing adventure and growing every moment, from whatever situation presents itself—failure or success, happiness or sadness, living or dying.

Gene helps us to reframe the word *failure*. Looking at so-called failure without fear and stigma, failure becomes simply something that happened that is different from our expectations. Our expectations are mind-made. We can adjust our expectations at any time, and see them for what they are—sometimes useful guideposts that help us move forward. They become barriers when we mistake the guideposts for reality itself. When we experience so-called failure, we can reframe it as a "different-than-expected reality." Then it automatically becomes part of moving forward; part of the ever-exciting adventure of growth which is life itself.

Failure = Different-Than-Expected Reality.

Notice the tendency to make failure the end of the world. How do you feel when you see your so-called failures as different-than-expected realities instead? Do you notice any heaviness lifting from your system? How will you lead differently when you see failure for what it is—possibly only as a different-than-expected reality?

Notice also that if we take on the "doing everything right" conditioning as our borrowed purpose, we set ourselves up for continuous struggle. Conversely, when we are grounded in our authentic purpose, our deepest calling, like Gene is, we see so-called failure as part of moving forward, not as the end of the road. My dad once called making a mistake "accumulating insight." I like that mind-set. It helps us to move beyond the stuck-ness we may experience when our crocodile fixates on failure. Now, when we encounter a different-than-expected reality, we may ask:

"*How is this part of moving forward*? What is the opportunity for self-discovery and contribution now?" Those questions can become part of our Growth Practice to transform our fear of failure into greater purposefulness.

In our bodies, we may notice a contraction in our belly button area when we're afraid of failing. When we do, we can kindle our purposefulness by deeply breathing into our navel area and thinking to ourselves: *I will. I will. I will.* Take a moment and try it out now. Repeat to yourself, "I will, I will, I will," and see how it changes your fear of failure.

4.   Growing through the Fear of Uncertainty

When we fear failure less, we tend to take more risks, leaving our comfort zone and going into areas of life and leadership hitherto unknown to us. And the further we move out of our comfort zones, the more we will likely encounter yet another fear—the fear of uncertainty. It's a natural byproduct of our motivation to want to learn, to want to expand and grow more fully into who we are.

Uncertainty is another one of these words that our collective conditioning has created negativity around. Understandably so. One day, I was hiking up a snow-covered mountain in Iceland. I had been out there for a while, and I was about to give up my attempt for the summit, as I had lost the trail. Earlier in the hike, a dog had joined me. While I paused and looked around for the next part of the trail, this dog started running in another direction—and yes, that's where the trail continued. I felt relieved and resumed my journey upwards, where I was rewarded with beautiful vistas of a snow-covered glacier valley. Pausing to rediscover the trail helped me gain a wider perspective. My fear of uncertainty would have taken me back down the mountain, and I would have missed out on that Icelandic panorama.

In the grip of fear of uncertainty we may believe thoughts that tell us that we're forever lost, that it's never going to work, and that it's better to just give up. That makes sense, as our crocodile is operating to help us survive now, in this moment. It needs to have certainty now. Continuing on the known path now or running back to the valley are its only viable options.

When we allow ourselves to become really still, totally present to this moment, we may see uncertainty with different eyes. Then we can see uncertainty is simply a moment of not knowing, of being in the question—what now?—without the need to go forward *or* backward. To remedy this fear, simply be here now, trusting that the next step will unveil itself. Notice that this involves a quality of openness and surrender.

As a society we have created a world of pseudocertainty. We are scheduled back-to-back, our GPS will tell us by the minute when we will arrive somewhere and the route we will take to get there, our devices tell us at all times where our loved ones are, and we are in total control of the climate in our offices and homes. We have worked hard together to control our reality and weed out uncertainty. What is the impact? We become less innovative, we relate to each other as predictable robots rather than as dynamic and evolving humans, and we feel overwhelmed by all the things we need to do to keep it all together, increasing our urge to control even more.

What if we trusted ourselves more in these moments of not-knowing—even cherished them as some of our greatest doorways to growth? The poet Rainer Maria Rilke wrote: "Whoever you are, some day, take a step outside of your house that you know so well. Enormous space is near." We can evolve our relationship with uncertainty, appreciating that our world beyond presence is uncertain; that change is the only constant in the external world beyond presence. Then we can watch the constant external change with inner confidence and see it as continuous possibility.

Consider this: When we are driven by our fear of uncertainty, we close ourselves off from reality as it is, and thus from the endless possibilities that are offered to us every moment. In short:

The Possibilities I Notice =
All Possibilities Available to Me – (My Fear of Uncertainty + My Other Fears)

Great leaders recognize this. When Adobe published its quarterly results in March 2014, it showed net income down by 28 percent from a year earlier. It was the fifth quarter in a row that the software maker posted a sharp drop in earnings. For most NASDAQ-listed firms this would have meant fast erosion in market value. Yet Adobe's share price had soared over the preceding twelve months.

What caused Adobe's earnings to plunge? According to Shantanu Narayen, CEO of Adobe, "We were the first company to say we are not going to issue packaged software, we were going to [only] deliver software on the cloud."

Innovation leaders, like Shantanu, courageously address three types of challenges in leading through uncertainty, with equal strength, as innovation expert Vijay Govindarajan points out. As they do, they help their organizations continuously evolve into their next level of greatness:

Box 1: Manage the Present, being mindful of what is needed now;

Box 2: Selectively Forget the Past, letting go of what no longer serves;

Box 3: Create the Future, applying nonlinear innovation.

Shantanu and his leadership team decided to selectively forget the past, discontinuing packaged software, Adobe's cash cow, and create a new future of delivering software in the cloud. These were audacious Box 2 and 3 decisions. And, as it turned out, that was the easy part. Enlisting others in these decisions was more challenging. Interestingly, Adobe employees were the toughest to enroll. "The hardest part of it has been getting people internal to the company to see the vision," said Shantanu. What he calls system "antibodies" were always about to derail Adobe's transformation.

"If there was something that I underestimated, it was how important communicating this is—over and over and over again. As a management team you can get used to it and you're like, okay, we've decided: we're going to burn the boats with regards to desktop software. You just assume everyone is going to follow." People's crocodilian fears of uncertainty—of letting go of their proven ways of surviving and making money, to make space for the unproven new venture—can delay or derail the Box 2 and Box 3 actions, such as Adobe's move to the cloud. Employees needed to let go of their attachment to known sources of revenue and free up their attention to focus completely on the uncertain, new cloud business.

Shantanu is described by his colleague John Donahoe, CEO of eBay, as having a deliberate style and a "steeliness" once a decision is made. "He's a quiet person, he leads with his actions rather than his words. He's not a guy with a huge ego, but he has a lot of pride." When Steve Jobs criticized Adobe's Flash technology, Shantanu stayed in his owl. "He doesn't get distracted or intimidated," Donahoe remarked.

In addition to role modeling confidence, Adobe leaders used other symbols and processes to help people tame their fear of uncertainty. For example, a spoof video of a support group for "revenue addicts" was shown at a sales conference as a light way to let people know that it was time to let go of their habit of selling packed software and start selling cloud subscriptions.

What would happen if we all burned the boats that no longer serve us? What is your first reaction to this? Do you notice any resistance to considering what beliefs and habits you could let go of? Letting go of the past, our mind-created pseudocertainty, is an essential part of learning and letting a new future emerge.

We know that fear of uncertainty undermines our resolve to learn and let go. Where do we find the strength to burn our boats?

"The lens that you use to look at your opportunities will determine how aspirational you'll be or how ambitious you are," Shantanu said. "My job is to set goals where people say they can't quite connect the dots yet, because if you do it's probably not aspirational enough." Shantanu helps Adobe grow through their fear of uncertainty by confidently asserting his bigger vision. How can we center ourselves in a bigger vision when we notice the fear of uncertainty in ourselves?

One place that we turn to for answers is our head—our brain will give us a never-ending stream of pros and cons, leading to paralysis. Many of us notice the fear of uncertainty as a contraction in our chest—our heart area. This area can also serve as a space where we place our attention to open up to a bigger vision when we face uncertainty. Our heart knows and, if we give it time, will show us the way.

When we notice our fear of uncertainty, we can pause and place our hand on our heart, and say to ourselves gently: "What is my bigger vision here? What if I let myself be audaciously creative?" Let the flow of ideas come easily. Stay open, and don't overwork. We know that reality is full of possibilities. With the eyes of our heart we are able to see and act on them.

Standing on that mountain by the glacier, not knowing which way to go, my uncertainty crocodile was limiting my perspective, urging: "Turn around, or you will get lost!" Had I given in to this crocodilian perception, I would have returned home and missed out on the joy of discovering the way up the mountain with my new dog-friend. That's often how we approach uncertainty—we wish it away, by ignoring or controlling it, and miss out on beautiful new opportunities for growth.

In any situation where our fear of uncertainty comes up, we can remind ourselves that, as presence, we're always safe. Our task is to grow in freedom by letting go of this fear, false evidence appearing real. Then we start seeing and acting more from our heart and we open up to a bigger reality, full of possibility.

5.   Growing through the Fear of Hurt

We play a dual game of growth: an internal game transmuting our fears into freedom and wise action, and an external game working with the fears of others. There is a saying in Dutch that translates roughly to "Tall trees catch much wind." The more centered we are in our vision and the more we lead from it (in other words, from our inner strength), the more reactions we will trigger in the outside world, both pleasant and unpleasant. As our confidence grows, we will become strong champions for our vision, and possibly attract more attention, with the increased criticism and vulnerability that often entails.

I noticed in my own journey of wanting peace above all else first that I would hold back out of the fear of hurting others. Upon further reflection, I realized that this fear of hurting others was really my fear of *being* hurt, of being retaliated against. As a kirtan singer I remember an experience with this fear vividly. I lead kirtans, the ancient, East Indian mantra singing and contemplation practice, in addition to doing leadership development work with corporations. I remember singing at a retreat where I wasn't the leader. As the atmosphere seemed to me very introspective, I sang very softly and solemnly. Afterwards, one of the participants who knew that I had been trained in opera vocals said to me: "That didn't count, you must sing again and this time for real. Bring the house down!" I followed her advice and sang a few days later. Again, the atmosphere I sang into was very calm and contemplative. However, this time I followed my heart and sang wholeheartedly, without apology. I felt guided and fulfilled doing it and people were visibly moved this time. The singing touched their hearts as I let mine freely express itself.

And yes, expressing ourselves fully requires us to be vulnerable. Let's see what the dictionary says about vulnerability. The first definition reads: "Capable of being physically or emotionally wounded"; the second: "Open to attack or damage." *Vulnerability* is another word equated with being open to negative consequences, just like "uncertainty." Brenee Brown has done years of research on vulnerability. Her findings show that we are so afraid of being vulnerable that we close ourselves off; we numb ourselves against reality, and as a result of evading the pain we also miss out on the joy.

Our collective conditioning that we will expose ourselves to ridicule if we express ourselves freely runs deep. We learned to "behave," and in the process forgot to express our hearts. Have you ever felt you wanted to start dancing in the middle of a meeting, as you believed it would help the interaction? Or say something controversial? And then you didn't because you didn't want to "upset the apple cart"? We need to be willing to throw out the rule book and, as loving presence (seeing what is needed), act unapologetically from our heart.

There is an inverse relationship between our fear of hurt and our capacity to really help others. When we are holding back, we are not really here and cannot give the other person our authentic self, our unconditional care. In summary:

My Actual Care for Others =
My Possible Care for Others – (My Fear of Hurt [Others and Self] + My Other Fears)

Nelson Mandela experienced this firsthand as he worked to rebuild South Africa after Apartheid. In the 2009 movie *Invictus*, we watch him express his love for the country by making a very controversial decision about the national rugby team, the Springboks, up until that time the symbol of white domination over the blacks. He hears that his sports deputy has just decided, together with a large gathering of people, to abolish the Springboks, getting rid of one of many of the hated symbols of Apartheid. He decides to go to the meeting and convince the people to vote to reinstate the team.

Instead of giving in to any fear of his popularity being hurt, he went for what he saw was needed to rebuild South Africa in that moment. Mandela commenting on his decision to confront the gathering that had just voted to get rid of the Springboks: "In this instance, the people are wrong. And as their elected leader, it is my job to show them that." As Growth Leaders, we are not led by our fears of being misinterpreted or offending others by disagreeing with them, but instead are guided by presence and our purpose to move above those worries and act for the greater good, despite any immediate headwinds or challenges.

Mandela challenged the gathering deciding on the fate of the Springboks to evolve their consciousness when dealing with the white Afrikaners: "We have to surprise them, with compassion, with restraint and generosity. I know all of the things they denied us. But this is no time to celebrate petty revenge. This is the time to build our nation using every single brick available to us." He challenged people to grow through their crocodilian anger to a place of owl compassion and wisdom.

As it turns out, his risky move paid off. By a narrow margin, the meeting voted to reverse their earlier vote and keep the Springboks. The team—up until that time the underdog of international rugby—not only went on to win the World Rugby Championship of 1995, but also did so with full support from both blacks and whites, who ended up dancing in the streets together to celebrate their joint victory. Mandela saw what was needed and did it, without apology, without fear of hurting people's feelings, and helped his nation evolve to a more sustainable place.

When we notice the fear of hurt in ourselves, we can remind ourselves of Mandela. Had he given in to his fear of hurt—of being unpopular and misunderstood—and his colleagues' desire for petty revenge, the nation would have missed out on a tremendous opportunity for unity and reconciliation. The South-Afrikaners I met a few years ago still remember the day the Springboks won as if it were yesterday. Said one: "I still get goosebumps thinking of what happened then. It was the first time I saw a glimmer of how we could live together peacefully as one nation."

The fear of hurt tends to show up as a contraction in our throat area—we literally feel choked and aren't able to say what we really want. In those moments we can choose to breathe deeply and remember what we are there to really contribute—and speak from that, however much our crocodiles are protesting.

6.   Growing through the Fear of Complexity

One teacher shared this with me: "True learning is seeing the connection between everyone and everything. *See the universe as a university*." While this sounds wonderful and speaks to one of our deepest human yearnings— to understand, to make sense of, to make meaning—it also can feel overwhelming. How can we possibly be open to everything, to all of life? How can we stay curious about the connection between it all and not lose our bearings, our focus on what we're here to do?

The mind looks for certainty and for relevance—it filters out information that it has little use for. First it looks for what's relevant to our survival, then it scans for pleasure, a proxy for survival. By itself that doesn't leave much energy for higher growth. That's why *growth requires intention and attention*. We choose presence, self-discovery, contribution, and excellence—and that by itself becomes a new filter through which we train our minds to interpret our experience. By asking the simple question "How am I growing?" our attention shifts from survival to higher growth. When we allow ourselves some quiet reflection on this question, we may notice insights from our intuition. Intuition helps us navigate life.

That's the good news. The bad news is that the wider we spread our wings, the more inputs we get to process.

Whether we're a leader of many or of just ourselves, our mind is exposed to about one billion bits of information in any given moment and automatically filters out the bits that are relevant for our survival, then comfort, then learning, respectively, according to neuroscientists. Mental space is precious, so what we give our attention to matters.

If we are driven by a need to understand everything, we will feel paralyzed often, as our mind can make the case for infinite numbers of interpretations for what is happening and, therefore, of reasons to do or not do something. The more complex our world becomes, the less reliable a guide pure reason becomes. Reason can bog us down. This is why we rely more on something beyond reason—we call it intuition, or inner guidance, or the heart's compass—to guide us through complexity.

As most of us rely on our rational minds for many of our decisions, we fear letting go of it and letting intuitive knowing guide us. We fear complexity that goes beyond our rational understanding. And the more we worry about the complexity, the busier our minds get in trying to figure things out, and therefore the less space there will be to open to our intuition. In short:

Intuition that I Am Accessing =
My Full Potential Intuition – (My Fear of Complexity + My Other Fears)

The more we let go of the fear of "not getting it," the more we open ourselves to what is, the more insights arise naturally within us, like how the river knows which way to turn around a rock in a river bed. When we let go, and stay present, opening up to the wisdom of this moment, we just know what to do. How do we connect to our intuitive knowing, especially when the going gets tough?

Yvonne Higgins Leach, a former communications lead at the Boeing Company who is now a full-time poet, got to address increasingly complex challenges for the corporation. In 2003, Yvonne was asked to lead the communications for the Boeing 787 airplane program worldwide. She shared some of her insights about the experience with me. "It was an opportunity of a lifetime because the company only develops a new airplane every fifteen years or so. We did a lot of PR and marketing at first, going around the world telling everybody about the airplane . . . It was wonderful. It was awesome to be able to talk about what would become the best airplane yet—it was like the honeymoon stage, right?

"Then we realized that the program had some issues . . . Within two years, 2007 to 2009, we had seven program delays and I'm telling you, that was very, very difficult. We were committed to 'Okay, we are going to fly the airplane in December,' and then December came and we didn't fly the airplane. And you know about the media around the world . . . you put a date out there and they are just all over it." Yvonne was the global public relations lead for Boeing's 787 program during these seven launch delays.

It was clear that these events had made a deep impact on Yvonne, as she repeated the "seven delays in two years" theme a few more times. "Two years, and I'm telling you, I've never had to be more resilient in my career because it got pretty tough. I was the one that was taking the calls. We would have an executive explain the story but PR then does all the follow-up, so I was the one answering the media calls from around the world. It got rough. I mean they were accusing me of lying, that we knew more, that it was impossible that we couldn't know what the problems were." A complex job, explaining launch delays of a major airplane to stakeholders, became more complex with every additional delay. How did Yvonne work with this complexity?

Yvonne paused, then continued. "So I really had to believe that I was there for a reason and I had to be resilient and I had to believe in the long-term view, that we were bringing into the world this fabulous product that will make the world a better place. And so I just had to breathe in and out . . . lots of deep breaths before the phone started ringing, and I would say to myself: 'Okay, this is why I'm here, this is my station, I'm the one.'"

Trusting her inner guidance in the face of complexity wasn't new for Yvonne. "I connect with my higher power every day," she shared. When Yvonne was at Boeing, she woke up every morning no later than five o'clock. The first thing she would do in the morning was center herself. "I think how you start your day is important. No matter how busy life is, you have to start by pausing and praying, meditating—whatever you call it." Yvonne has a particular way that she does this. "I have this little book that I get every year and it's called *Daily Word* and it has prayers from the Bible and that always grounds me. I say my prayers and then I start my day. And part of that is saying to myself: 'Okay, this is my station now—You put me here, I am an instrument of Your peace. Please tell me what to do and I will do it.'"

The 787-experience helped Yvonne conceive of herself and her role in bigger ways. She intuited that her job was about both communication *and* compassion. "I was thinking how hard it is to gain perspective for a human being who doesn't live the experience that is being judged," said Yvonne. "The media didn't walk inside of the walls of Boeing—they didn't see all the hard work and the difficult decisions that were being made. I think the media shouldn't have believed we were lying, but I understood how hard it must be for them to communicate what was actually happening—which is the media's job. So my job was to try to give them more understanding and that's where I had to dig deep, and take deep breaths, asking my higher power, 'Please, help me tell these stories so there is more understanding.'"

And Yvonne learned a lot about herself in the process. "I learned that you need to keep your head held high. If you believe in something, you need to stay with that in a good way. And I just thought, I'm not going to let it get to me. I am not going to believe that we did something wrong or that the media shouldn't react this way. It's all part of the process. Airplanes are hard and require a lot of risk and that's what it takes to be innovative. . . . So I truly believed that and it helped to keep my head up high as we were delivering the message."

Anchored in her inner guidance, Yvonne helped herself and her team give their best every day, and grow from the experience. She did not give in to the fear that there would be no way through this complex challenge, bridging the inner world of Boeing engineering with the outer world of the media. Instead of giving in to the fear of complexity and choosing the easy way out—making Boeing wrong, or making the media wrong—she managed to stay on the razor's edge of being truthful about what was happening and staying respectful to the interests of all parties involved. Her daily commitment to serve from her station, letting her higher power guide her, helped her through this challenge and helped her grow from it.

The next time we feel overwhelmed by the fear of the complexity of the challenges facing us, we can remember Yvonne's guidance and ask ourselves: "What is the deepest truth for me? What does my intuition say? How can I serve best from my station now?"

Centered in presence, complexity becomes an invitation to let our intuition speak.

7.   Growing through the Fear of Loss of Identity

Here's a piece of advice that Rob Tarkoff, CEO of Lithium Technologies, said he would give to CEOs who have just gotten the top job for the first time: "First, make sure you are ready for something you're totally unprepared for. Second, enjoy the journey. And the third thing is, realize that the only mistake that you really can't afford to pay is being close-minded to what is possible. Thinking you know the answer before you go in. If you think you know where things will end up, you are wrong."

With this advice, Rob points to three core identities we need to let go of to become a great leader. First, we need to let go of the idea that we are someone who is prepared for what is to come. Second, we must leave the one behind who thinks he has the hard job and can't enjoy it. Third, and maybe most importantly, we need to let go of any idea that we're the expert. Besides these three, there are countless other identities that get in the way of effective leadership, such as: I am a nice person, I am a competent person, I am a person worthy of respect, I am a risk taker, I am an analytical person, I am a people person, etc. The more we lead, the more we find that any identity eventually will get in the way of our effectiveness. Why? All these identities are about us, not about the organization and its purpose in the world.

Rob shared some insight about learning to be a CEO and shedding obsolete identities: "Managing a board as a CEO is very interesting and different from what I was used to. Before this, I was a general manager for a huge business but I always reported to a CEO. And when you are a CEO, you have a board, and CEOs make the mistake believing they *report* to the board. They do not report to the board in the sense that a general manager of a large company does. CEOs are responsible for setting a direction, strategy, and execution and getting the board aligned on what to do, as opposed to asking the board what to do or reporting to the board what you think they want you to do." One identity Rob got to leave behind was that of being dependent on someone else's direction. The buck always stops with him.

We don't need to become CEO to shed our "dependence" identity. Many of us unconsciously put others on a pedestal and wait for their approval, as opposed to staying centered in our own truth and leading from that. For many, this is an important growth opportunity.

The downside to being independent is that it can lead to separateness—the lone wolf, another identity. According to Rob, "There are too many CEOs who think because they are responsible for setting direction they don't need a board. Most boards are there to help! Why else are these people spending time and going to work as board members? Most people on boards are very successful people, who generally aren't there for their own impact; they want to help. So, we as CEOs need to be open to asking for help, and that comes with confidence in the role. We need to be able to say: 'I think we should go this way, but what do you guys think?'"

Asking for help goes right in the face of the expert identity that many CEOs have when they get the job. "People who progress in their careers to a level where they get to a position of leadership in a company are typically people who have a lot of great answers and insights," Rob continued. "They are typically not the people that we see needing a lot of help or asking for help a lot. You are supposed to have less issues than normal people. And that perspective limits your propensity to ask questions and thus your effectiveness as CEO."

Letting go of who we think we should be requires vulnerability. And paradoxically vulnerability gives strength. "I am not afraid to be open with my employees about my own life," said Rob. "So as an example, one summer my family dealt with some health issues and we have been working through that. And I have actually been pretty open with my employee base. I have been really, really surprised at not only how responsible people have been with the information and not sharing it, but also the degree of trust that people are now giving to me because of the fact that I shared something with them. So I've started getting back from people—nobody has a problem coming up to me now with, 'Hey, I've got a personal issue, and I've got to leave early today to take care of that—are you good with that?' I say: 'Of course.' And then when they are not doing that, they are staying later. So I had some travel plans I couldn't do because of this situation, and I said to somebody: 'I can't do that because I can't leave right now,' and they said: 'Great, no problem, cancel.' I think being more open helps a lot—we're looking out for each other and they know I am sharing with them and they're sharing with me.

"You need to find a way to ask for help when you need help, and not only will your company get better, but you will be a better leader also," Rob summarized.

Great leadership requires great wisdom and compassion. Great wisdom and compassion require letting go of any personal agendas to build and protect our identities. Notice what identities may be standing in your way to grow as a leader. Become fascinated with them and imagine what's possible without them.

When I asked Rob what he'd title his life story, he responded: "Something like *Keep Imagining*.'" As Growth Leaders we constantly reimagine our role, as we are completely present to what is needed now and serve that, not reenacting an old role that is now obsolete. And as we rest in presence, no longer striving to be some identity, we see any identities we may have had as temporary clothes we wore when they were needed. We can thank them for serving us and then discard them to become what's needed in the current moment.

Take a moment to do an inventory—what is it that you'd really like people to say about you? Maybe that you are a compassionate leader, or that you are bold, or nice, or resourceful, or wise, or effective. How have you made those into identities that you have become attached to? How are they getting in the way of you being effective in this moment?

And who do you put on a pedestal—seeing them as more, better, richer, wiser, nicer, or stronger than you? In which ways have you identified yourself as less than or dependent on them? Conversely, where do you put yourself on a pedestal? How are these pedestal identities getting in your and others' ways? Who would you be without them?

STANDING ON THE SHOULDERS OF OUR FEAR FAMILIES

Our crocodiles, the reactive patterns that keep us small, have a lot of fear-food to feast on. We have explored seven kinds of crocodilian food, seven fear families—fear of scarcity, abandonment, failure, uncertainty, hurt, complexity, and losing identity. What do you feed your crocodiles with most often? Take a moment to note which fear families are most active in you. You may notice your fears being those fear families or combinations thereof.

As with any part of the crocodilian system, noticing it is the beginning of dismantling it. We name it to tame it.

Once we see which fear family is active, we can transform it into a Growth Practice, inspired by the example of other leaders. In this chapter we learned from FDR about using courage to face the fear of scarcity; from Chris about practicing kindness and authenticity to transform the fear of abandonment; from Gene about practicing enthusiasm for learning to lessen the fear of failure; from Shantanu about staying true to our bigger vision to overcome the fear of uncertainty; from Mandela about being an unapologetic contributor to heal the fear of hurt; from Yvonne about staying connected to our inner guidance to work with the fear of complexity; and from Rob about letting go and reimagining ourselves to address the fear of losing identity.

Imagine what will become possible for you and those you lead when you have seen more fully through your fears. Don't forget to enjoy the journey through them. When you see a fear show up, look at it with the eyes of a child who just received a new toy to play with. Be gentle with it, curious, maybe have fun with it. Fear is part of life. And remember you can work with and see through any and all of your fears. It just requires intention and attention.

SPOT THE SEVEN FEAR FAMILIES IN DISGUISE—THE SEVEN CROCODILIAN SUCCESS PERSONAS

To make the Fear Families easier to work with, I have translated them into seven "Crocodilian Personas" we adopt to cope with these fears. Personas may be easier to spot than fears, as they are a visible composite of the needs and behaviors we fall into under the influence of fear. Fear tends to show up in a confusing and overwhelming confluence of feelings and thoughts.

"Persona" comes from Greek and means "Mask." When we are under the influence of a fear family we tend to wear a mask as a strategy to make sure we avoid the worst-case scenario projected by that fear. You'll notice the acronym "SUCCESS" again, like in Chapter 2. This time we use it to label the fear-compensating personas. They are: Safe, Us vs. Them, Controlling, Certain, Essential, Sapient, and Special. Here is a summary:

SEVEN CROCODILIAN SUCCESS PERSONAS

Fear Family	Fear-Based Need: To Be . . .	Coping Behavior
1. Scarcity	1. Safe	Overworking, victim, short-term biased
2. Abandonment	2. Us vs. Them	Judging, complying, silo-oriented
3. Failure	3. Controlling	Perfectionism, manipulating, micro-managing

4. Uncertainty	**4.** Certain	Rigid, dramatic, close-minded
5. Hurt	**5.** Essential	Dominating, rescuing, hiding
6. Complexity	**6.** Sapient	Knower, paranoid, advice-giving
7. Losing Identity	**7.** Special	Pedestal, martyr, ivory tower-oriented

Let's get to know each of them:

1. *Safe.* When we are driven by the fear of scarcity, we look for ways to be safe, financially and otherwise. To make that happen we overwork, . . . and/or give up, blaming others and taking a victim stance. Also we focus on the short term only to stay (emotionally) safe.

2. *Us vs. Them.* Afraid to be abandoned, we create a clique around us. We make sure that people don't and can't leave us. We keep our tribe intact by judging anyone who thinks and acts differently and by making sure we are fitting in, complying with the tribal norms. At work, we create silos that ensure a pseudosense of belonging.

3. *Controlling.* If we are afraid of failure, we will want to control the outcomes of everything, so failure is no longer an option. We have to be perfect. We control ourselves and others by fixing things, even when it's better to let the learning process play out. We resort to quick fixes. We manipulate others to do exactly what we want, as another way to control outcomes. And we create bureaucracies around us to micro-manage the greatest number of people as easily as possible. We believe we are more likely to get what we want and avoid failure when everyone, including ourselves, plays by our often intricate web of rules.

4. *Certain.* If uncertainty is our core fear, we will pursue certainty at all costs, being rigid in our behaviors and thinking. We hold on to our opinions and feelings as facts. Our heart is closed to

uncertainty, and therefore the richness of this moment. We also keep ourselves and others tied up in emotional drama as a sure way to maintain the certain status quo.

5. *Essential.* If we are afraid of hurt, making sure we are indispensable—essential—may be a good strategy, thinks the crocodile. Then we're sure we won't have to face the ultimate hurt—which, from this perspective, is rejection. We also try to avoid this hurt by making ourselves invisible while telling ourselves we are really important to the team. *Rescuing others can be another great way to secure our place in the tribe forever,* advises the crocodile, or *just dominate and become the boss, that way you'll really be indispensable!* Or we do everything by ourselves. That way we never have to face the unpredictability of relationships.

6. *Sapient.* If we worry about complexity, we may find it comforting to believe that—in the end—*we* always have the answer. We are all-knowing, sapient. A great way to impress people with our knowledge is to paint doomsday scenarios, as people's crocodiles love to feed on this kind of drama—it keeps them on high alert, the crocodiles' favorite way to ensure survival. Since we know best, we also give people advice, often unasked.

7. *Special.* And lastly, if we are concerned about our losing our identity, securing "special" status can be a great insurance policy. What is the premium we need to pay for this? Placing ourselves or others we are associated with on a pedestal does the job, and being a martyr who takes one for the team is a great strategy also. We may find ourselves in an ivory tower, seemingly protected from the riffraff below us.

Our fearful crocodiles are cunning. To tame them it helps to get to know them in all their disguises. Take a look at the list above. See which personas you are most likely to resort to, especially under stress. Don't be disheartened. There is nothing unique about these masks. They are universal and ancient. They are innocent strategies from our young crocodiles to ensure our survival. Our opportunity is to unmask them and start living more into who we really are.

TRANSFORMING CROC SUCCESS PERSONAS INTO OWL SUCCESS INTENTIONS

To unlearn these Personas, we can apply the Growth Practices we discussed in this chapter. They correspond with the Owl SUCCESS Intentions we got to know in Chapter 2.

We transform our Crocodilian SUCCESS personas simply by putting our attention on the intention instead of the persona. Then each persona becomes a stepping stone for our growth.

FROM: CROCODILIAN SUCCESS PERSONA	TO: OWL SUCCESS INTENTION
1. Safe	1. **Samurai**—having the warriorlike courage and fortitude to take care of my basic needs, and face my challenges resourcefully without being overwhelmed by them;
2. Us vs. Them	2. **Uniting**—creating authentic, empathic relationships, that welcome everyone and go beyond tribal, us-vs.-them dynamics;
3. Controlling	3. **Centered in purpose**—being driven by my inner compass, pursuing my goals wholeheartedly and with focus; and seeing every "failure" as part of moving forward;
4. Certain	4. **Curious**—opening my heart to life's teachings—the whispers—no matter what, and seeing every moment as an opportunity for discovery, bigger vision, and being innovative;
5. Essential	5. **Extending**—expressing my gift to others unapologetically and caringly;

6. Sapient	6. **Sensing**—using intuition, looking for truth and the connection between everything and everyone, integrating the seeming polarities in life, creating cohesion;
7. Special	7. **Simple**—seeing what is needed and doing it, letting go of ego personas, simply being and contributing who I am.

Time for some more practice. Take a look at the summary above and pick one of the pairs that you are interested in. If you like, think about a challenge you are facing. How would your SUCCESS Persona approach it? How could you approach it differently from your SUCCESS Intention? If you think you're stuck in your old ways, ask yourself, *Who is talking, the owl or the crocodile?*

RELEASING FEAR ALTOGETHER

There are so many ways to work with fear. To complete our visit with our fears in this chapter, we will learn another practice to work with them: releasing them from our energetic body. What does it mean to release a fear? First, let's think about what it means to hold on to a fear. When we are holding on to a fear, we believe whatever the fear is telling us, allowing it to stay a part of us. In the grip of that fear, we feel physical and emotional discomfort. We feel contractions, a sense of uptightness, and may experience feelings of isolation, anxiety, sadness, lack of control, and resentment of self and of others. Conversely, to release a fear is to choose to no longer hold on to it.

Fear Release Practice

Let's practice releasing fear, working with the fear of abandonment. In which relationships does the fear of abandonment come up most strongly in you? Think about your children, your partner, your parents, your colleagues, your work, your friends, and so on. Picture the relationship that triggers the strongest feelings of being left—of not being needed—of being abandoned. Now picture a situation where your fear of being abandoned by this person (or your job) was triggered. Really notice the fear, and feel the way it builds up inside of you, the way it sits and moves in you. Don't worry about doing this process "right" or being "good"—just feel, that's all. Feeling the fear in your body, think of it as a cloud moving through—it can be a puffy one, a dark one, a thundercloud, a stormy one, or whatever. Don't worry about its intensity, noticing it is the beginning of its release. And like the sky, as you practice presence, you hold all the clouds and are not affected by any of them. Allow yourself to feel the fear, maybe in a way you have never allowed yourself to feel it before.

The gut reaction is to stop this process, to suppress the fear by pushing it out of our minds or distracting ourselves with other thoughts. Don't let that reaction win this time—instead become disinterested in those feelings and keep bringing your attention back to this fear, in this case the fear of abandonment. This is a concentration game. It's okay to feel fear. This is just a practice, and you are perfectly safe. Remember you are skylike presence. Keep picturing your chosen situation, and allow the fear to become so strong that you feel a constriction building inside of you.

Now, begin to imagine that the space in your body is not as constricted as your mind is making it out to be. Take a deep breath and picture the space expanding around and inside this fear. Now give the fear cloud room to flow out of you as you breathe slowly and surely. This fear is just energy. It has no power over you. It is passing through you like clouds in the sky.

Take some time do this practice. You will know when it's time to stop. You likely will have found some relief from this fear.

By facing fear this way, we begin to see fear as normal, and that it is workable. Notice the ways that fear might be resisting this practice. It is normal to experience thoughts like *I don't want to do this*, or *this is only making things worse*, or *this is irritating me*. Be kind to these thoughts and, like the fear, allow them to become light, to begin to dissipate and pass through you. Allow any thoughts that keep you from being present to go. See them as your crocodilian mind trying to hold on to the fear. The crocodile is afraid you are taking away its food. You are! Say yes, and choose to be ready to face your fear, and explore it kindly.

In a way, the mind feels comfortable with fear, and so it holds on to it. We believe that without the fear of abandonment, without feeling like we "need" another person, we won't truly love them. We believe that without the fear of failure, we wouldn't have as much drive to succeed. We fear that without the fear of hurt, we won't be as compassionate, and that without the fear of uncertainty, we'll get lost.

Upon further inspecting these beliefs and challenging them, we can see that in reality, by not living in the fear of losing someone, we are free to love them more fully, unconditionally, and authentically, without suffocating them or trying to change them or ourselves. Without the fear of failure, we allow ourselves to be driven by the joy and excitement that we can find in working toward our true calling. Without the fear of hurt, we become free to let our lights shine and live an example that will ultimately liberate others and encourage them to do the same. When you see yourself reacting out of fear, whether at work or at home, ask yourself, "Who would I be without this fear?" and open yourself to the possibilities.

Notice that fears are with us, dormant or active, all the time: in every moment, in every conversation. You can practice releasing fear anytime it becomes active—not only when you are alone, in nature, or when you are in a secluded place. Whenever fear appears, no matter what fear it is, you can do the fear-releasing practice. Instead of suppressing the fear or trying to get rid of it, allow it to sit and move inside of you, and observe it changing as you breathe slowly. Remember that fear is just energy, and imagine that you are the sky, and that the fear, like clouds, will go as it came. Yes, it's that simple.

Enjoy this part of the journey of growing, *through* fear, more into your authentic self. Real growth is unlearning fear.

FIELDWORK

1. Of the seven fear families, which two are most active in you?

2. What is a challenge you are currently facing?

3. Which of these seven fear families may be active in you when you think about your challenge?

4. What reactive behaviors do you fall into when you are driven by your fear family?

5. What feelings and actions become possible when you apply a Growth Leadership Mind-set, using any of the Growth Practices suggested in this chapter?

6. What fear-based SUCCESS Persona are you most likely to fall into with this challenge? Which SUCCESS Intention can you practice? How?

7. How are you growing?

CHAPTER 5

Balancing All of Ourselves

"Wisdom without compassion is ruthlessness and compassion without wisdom is folly." —Fred Kofman

A S WE GROW out of our fears, we feel more freedom. We may become bolder, more focused, more creative, more compassionate, calmer, and more buoyant. Fear no longer holds us back as much as we grow more into who we really are. The more we grow by letting go of fear, the more another aspect of leadership becomes important—staying balanced in how we apply the greater powers available to us now. If we become only bolder, and not more compassionate, we may become disconnected from others. If we only focus on contributing and not take a step back, we lose perspective. If we only step back, we may not contribute. If we spend all our energy empathizing with others, we risk losing focus on our priorities, and if we don't empathize, we risk alienating others. Balance is an important ingredient of leadership.

Examples of balance are everywhere in nature. We see it in lightness and darkness; in sound and silence; in summer and winter; in hot and cold; in life and death. *Balance* comes from the Latin word *bilanx*, which means two scale pans. As one pan becomes heavier than the other, the scale goes out of balance; the same is true for human beings. We can see this within our body and our mind—we have a left and right side, a front and back. When one side is out of balance with the other, we feel out of kilter; off center. When both sides are in balance, we tend to feel in flow, in harmony with ourselves and others.

Sun and rain enable a beautiful harvest; silence and sound make beautiful music together; complementary colors create a vibrant picture; two different people can create beautiful friendship and partnership; rest and effort enable sustainability; left brain (logic) and right brain (intuition) together yield wisdom and compassion.

Think about what balance means to you. What does it look like? What happens when you get off balance? When you can't balance your work life and home life? Your friendships and your romantic relationship? Your hobbies and your chores? For me, I've noticed that I get off balance when I prioritize relationships over purposefulness, or conversely, I let myself get so absorbed in a task that I lose touch with those I care for. Notice for yourself what might be the behaviors that you fall into when you get off balance, or the ones that might cause you to get off-kilter in the first place.

As we mature as human beings and leaders, we learn to balance more and more seemingly opposite strengths. How can we be honest *and* respectful, with equal measure? How can we be decisive *and* inclusive? How can we be flexible *and* firm? How can we hold others accountable *and* coach them to be who they really are? We are constantly rebalancing ourselves.

And as we mature, our internal balance, or lack thereof, starts to affect others more. When we grow up, more people may be entrusted to our care. The greater the span of our responsibility, the more our internal equilibrium affects others. For example, if we manage a team, whether of a few people or of hundreds, and we only know how to be assertive without being able to listen, we risk creating a culture of competition where people work in their own silos without learning from each other. Conversely, if as managers we only know how to listen and not to be assertive, the culture around us may become one of indecisiveness—where nothing gets done as relationships may get prioritized over effectiveness.

GROWTH LEADERSHIP BALANCE: YIN AND YANG

What does internal balance look like for a leader? Let's start by looking at our nervous system. To simplify a complex mechanism, each of our brains has a left lobe and a right lobe—the left is in charge of the right side of your body and has more of a role in logic, assertiveness, and planning. The right lobe guides the left side of your body and informs intuitive, creative, and empathetic capacities.

In the East, they came up with a beautiful distinction to talk about these two sides of the same coin: Yin and Yang. Yin is the energy associated with the right side of our brain and the left side of our body, also called the feminine side. Yin is a feminine energy, and includes qualities like connecting, empathy, intuiting, and care. Yang is the energy associated with the left side of our brain and the right side of our body, which is considered the masculine energy. Yang qualities include assertiveness, purposefulness, will, and warrior energy.

You will find a summary of these energies in the table below. You'll notice that I have organized the energies across each of the seven SUCCESS Intentions we discussed in Chapter 2. As it turns out, SUCCESS Intentions 1, 3, 5, and 7—Samurai, Centered, Extending, and Simple— are Yang qualities, while Intentions 2, 4, and 6—Uniting, Curious, and Sensing—are Yin.

Pause for a moment and think about these two energies, Yin and Yang. Which one is strongest in you? This has nothing to do with your gender—these are just energies that point to your default leadership style. In our culture the words *masculine* and *feminine* come loaded with so much baggage—shame, guilt, pride, resentment; all sorts of things. From when we were young, we were conditioned to associate masculine energies with being stronger and more desirable when it comes to leadership, and feminine energies for being best suited in the home life. Before we continue, let's be aware of any such borrowed beliefs in ourselves and let them go. Neither energy is better or more suitable than the other. We will need to reach an effective balance of both if we want to realize our true potential as leaders.

Higher Yang: Purposeful	Higher Yin: Creative Connected
1. Samurai • Warriorlike (willing to stretch self) • Able to stay still in the storm **3.** Centered • Definite in purpose • With strong will, focused **5.** Extending • Assertive—internal strength and clarity, detached from outcome • Authentically contributing **7.** Simple • With enlightened intellect (for higher purpose) • With power through humility (learner)	**2.** Uniting • Caring • Compassionate, empathic • Kind, gentle, soft **4.** Curious • Creative, learning • Open • Comfortable with uncertainty • Inspiring innovation **6.** Sensing • Intuitive • Listening, collaborative, integrating • Patient • Creating cohesion

Adapted from Patrick Connor, Sharmadā Foundation, and Patricio Campiani.

My default energy leans toward Yin. I could hang out in intuition and empathy forever—this is why I am very comfortable coaching others. Now that I am coleading an organization again, I am challenged to grow my assertive and purposeful Yang side.

Guess how we look at any imbalance as Growth Leaders? Not as a problem but as another doorway for our growth. We are fascinated by it—this becomes another opportunity for discovering who we really are and leading from that place.

Remember Rob Tarkoff, CEO of Lithium Technologies? Any guesses what his rebalancing opportunity was when he became CEO?

"My father came from a very difficult background," Rob told me. "Both of his parents were Jewish immigrants in the United States. He was raised as an only child. His father died when he was thirteen years old, and his mother always worked to provide for him My dad worked every day of his life from age thirteen to about eight years ago when he faced some health issues. He is now over eighty years old. He didn't have the opportunities I had. Despite all of this, he became a successful physician and put himself through everything in life." Because of his father's difficult history, Robert learned from an early age about self-reliance—a Yang leadership trait.

And he became very good at it. Yet every time he got promoted he also experienced the limitation of self-reliance. "My entire career has been me thinking that I'm totally underqualified and underprepared for every role I have been given and that if I didn't come in every day, to prove my value to the people who chose me for that role, at some point this lack of qualification was going to be discovered. It's a kind of paranoia. I used to say to my wife: 'Is there ever going to be a time when I stop feeling like, you know, when are they going to find out that this was a mistake?' I think part of that comes from having a role model, watching my dad never take anything for granted. He always felt he had to earn the trust of his patients every day making really good diagnoses and using the learning to care for them. And so that's been the philosophy I've had . . . never take anything for granted."

Interviewing Rob, it became clear that he is a Yang-comfortable person, and yet, his learning is all about Yin. "You need to find a way to ask for help when you need help, and not only will your company get better, but you will be a better leader also," Rob shared with us in the previous chapter. As a relatively new CEO, Rob had to learn to ask for help—a Yin leadership trait: "the only mistake that you really can't afford to pay is being close-minded to what is possible. Thinking you know the answer before you go in. If you think you know where things will end up, you are wrong." His advice to other new CEOs points to more Yin traits: to connect with others and stay open to ambiguity—the possibilities that come from working with others.

Working on strengthening their Yin or Yang is common practice for leaders. Let's go back in time and take a look at another leader who learned to balance Yin and Yang within himself. See if you can guess who this is:

He has been president for two-and-a-half years and is reviled by most. A war has been dividing his country, and his army has just lost two major battles. People from his own party attack him for his compromising, indecisive attitude, and one of his generals reports there is open talk "of [his] weakness and the necessity of replacing him by some stronger man." After visiting him in January of that year, former Supreme Court Justice Benjamin R. Curtis reported on "the utter incompetence of the President . . . he is shattered, dazed and utterly foolish. It would not surprise me if he were to destroy himself."

It's June 1863 and Abraham Lincoln is President of the United States. Richmond's *Daily Dispatch* quotes Lincoln, stating: "The President said that it may be a misfortune for the nation that he was elected President; but having been elected by the people, he meant to be President, and to perform his duty according to his best understanding, if he had to die for it."

Now let's read a line from the *New York Times* of September of that same year: "We are grateful that the nation is led by a ruler who is so peculiarly adapted to the needs of the time as clear-headed, dispassionate, discreet, steadfast, honest Abraham Lincoln." And the *Chicago Tribune* takes up a similar tone, writing, "God bless Old Abe!"

What shifted in the summer of 1863? For sure, victories of the Union Army at Vicksburg and Gettysburg helped improve public opinion. Yet, even with those victories, the Civil War would not end until 1865, before which there would be many more heavy losses on both the Union and Confederate sides. In spite of the ongoing challenge posed by the war, Lincoln kept significant public support during the remainder of his presidency—from 1863 until his assassination in 1865. How come? And what can we learn from him about balancing our Yin and Yang?

Lincoln realized in the early summer of 1863 that he had two big challenges: reestablishing control over the Army of the Potomac and giving a new, much more aspirational direction to public opinion.

Lincoln, as a self-made man, relied heavily on tradition and convention. And he was very inclusive—a Yin trait. He would receive throngs of people from all parts of society at the White House every week, to hear about their lives and learn about the issues on their minds. But after he had been president for a while, his strengths of being inclusive and mastering the rules of any game he entered became weaknesses. As a civil leader, he believed he should leave the running of the army to his generals—that's how the game had always been played before. Instead of giving his generals firm orders, a Yang quality, Lincoln gave them only timid suggestions, which they, in turn, mostly ignored—a

Yin weakness. Lincoln's secretary, John G. Nicolay, despondently noted that the President habitually gave in to his top general McClellan's "whims and complaints and shortcomings as a mother would indulge her baby."

After many frustrating exchanges with a succession of ineffective generals, Lincoln recognized that his submissive (Yin) style wasn't working. And once he was convinced something had to change, Lincoln acted resolutely, without looking back. In the summer of 1863, he issued a series of direct instructions to his generals, leaving zero doubt about who was in charge. Lincoln wrote to General Hooker, a general who had repeatedly defied his suggestions: "To remove all misunderstanding, I now place you in the strict military relation to Gen. Halleck, of a commander of one of the armies, to the General-in-Chief of all the armies. I have not intended differently; but as it seems to be differently understood, I shall direct him to give you orders, and you to obey them."

Soon after Lincoln's augmentation of his Yang leadership, the Union Army booked a series of victories, notably at Vicksburg and Gettysburg. Instead of delaying and waiting for the perfect time, as they had before, the Union Army was now moving proactively, following Lincoln's firm orders.

The President had assertively left behind the conventions of the past—a Yang trait—and created a new relationship with the military. He had replaced indecisiveness with assertiveness.

Indecisiveness is a Yin weakness that typically comes from fear—think back to the fear of hurting others and the fear of uncertainty that we spoke of in the last chapter. Often when we get off balance, we compensate for it by falling back into a crocodilian fear-driven style first, before we manage to find new owl balance. We'll call owl-oriented Yin and Yang "Higher Yang" and "Higher Yin," and crocodile-reactive styles "Lower Yang" and "Lower Yin."

CROCODILIAN FIXES TO REGAIN BALANCE

At first when Lincoln wasn't able to get the army to work effectively toward his purpose—reunification of the nation—he defaulted to submissiveness. Submissiveness is often a fear-driven, crocodilian Lower Yin strategy. When we fall into submissive behavior, we are not standing in the strength of our purpose (a Higher Yang trait). Instead, the crocodile is pushing us into a quick fix: submit and hope for the best.

The crocodilian nervous system is there to help our immediate physical and emotional survival. Patience, fortitude, compassion, and wisdom are not part of its repertoire, as they don't lead to instant fixes, gratification, and validation. Our crocodiles want answers now. Instead of being firm and holding true to our purpose, our crocodile wants us to be safe now. We give in to others to get their approval—a Lower Yin strategy; or we overwork, preferably by ourselves, to create a quick solution—a Lower Yang strategy. Or, when a colleague is in distress, instead of being compassionate with them, and clear about our boundaries, our crocodile wants all the messiness gone now, so we ignore them and forge ahead carelessly—a Lower Yang strategy; or we go to the other extreme, and join them in their distress, try to rescue them, and give up on our priorities—a Lower Yin strategy.

Which crocodilian Yin and Yang strategies are we most prone to fall into? When we have a stronger Yin side (like I do), we tend to compensate for the weaker Yang side by applying Lower Yin strategies. Part of Yang strength is purposefulness—following through on our priorities. An overly Yin person will be great at connecting with others and weaker in taking a stand for their priorities. Deeply steeped in relationships, a fear-driven Yin person will try to get what they want by applying their Yin expertise—which can turn into manipulating or seducing others, submissiveness, or going into self-pity mode if they can't get the world to cooperate with them. Yes, I have tried all of these Lower Yin tactics in times of difficulty. They work for a short while and then they backfire, as I am not relating authentically to myself and others.

Conversely, if our Yang is our dominant side, we tend to go into Lower Yang when under stress, being arrogant and trying to outdo or control others. When there is disagreement, an overly Yang person may overuse their rationality. Driven by the fear of losing the argument, they may get so absorbed by their own reasoning that they forget to listen deeply and find common ground—a Yin strength.

Consider the strategies below. Which Yin and Yang crocodiles live in your system? In what situations do they get triggered, or in other words, when are you letting fear guide you to get what you want? To make these tactics easier to remember, I have organized them by the Crocodilian SUCCESS Personas we discussed in the previous chapter. Each fear-based persona has both a Lower Yang and Lower Yin side. Yes, our crocodiles are creative!

Lower Yang: Overdoing	Lower Yin: Pleasing

1. Safe
  • Overworking
  • Defaults to quick fixes
2. Us vs. them
  • Seeks to win, come out on top, be better
  • Judges others, right/wrong
3. Controlling
  • Perfectionistic, commanding, and pushy
  • Controls through doing and problem solving
4. Certain
  • Represses emotions, rigid
  • Uses logic and intellect at the expense of love
5. Essential
  • Heroic, is the answer
  • Dominates, or is self-sufficient and shuts off
6. Sapient
  • Needs to be right (Knower)
  • Has the answers
7. Special
  • Seeks respect and status
  • Proves self through achievement
	1. Safe
	  • Dependent on others, needs to be rescued, helpless, victim, weak
	  • Obsessed with security and safety
	2. Us vs. them
	  • Values relationship over purpose
	  • Gossips and blames to belong
	3. Control
	  • Manipulates through approval, pleasing, seduction, and vagueness
	  • Defers to others by default
	4. Certain
	  • Overwhelmed by emotions, volatile
	  • Seeks drama to protect status quo
	5. Essential
	  • Rescues others
	  • Worries a lot
	6. Sapient
	  • Knows what's best, advice-giver
	  • Predicts negative outcomes, paranoia
	7. Special
	  • Needs to be admired, vanity
	  • Becomes martyr, star, retreats to ivory tower

Adapted from Patrick Connor, Sharmadā Foundation, and Patricio Campiani.

There is nothing wrong with having these crocodiles—it's a natural part of our common, human evolution. We inherited them from our families and our culture. My father, like many hard-working dads of his generation, was somewhat absent from my childhood, and my mother was always there for me. She really nourished my Yin, for example, the creative qualities in me. She loved me making music. And she has always been a very empathetic person. The flip side, however, is that I also learned Lower Yin strategies in this relationship. As a child I interpreted that my mother had a fear of doing things wrong in my father's eyes—something she probably learned from her mom and other women of that generation. When I had a conflict with my dad, she would tell me that I shouldn't disagree, and that disagreeing was inappropriate. I didn't know how to talk with her beyond that. So I would start crying. I found that crying was an effective way to get what I wanted. So, when I got older, these mother-son interactions continued to inform my behavior, causing me to believe that being weak and timid would get me what I want.

Rob Tarkoff's family suggests the opposite pattern: relying on independent action to succeed (a Lower Yang strategy if overused), sometimes at the expense of staying connected with others.

Two very typical crocodilian compensation strategies are shown below. If we lack Yang purposefulness, we tend to please others to get what we want. If we lack the Yin ability to care and be cared for, we tend to compensate through overworking to earn love and don't develop the social connections that could provide that.

YANG LEADERSHIP	YIN LEADERSHIP
Purposeful	Caring
CROCODILIAN YANG FiX	CROCODILIAN YIN FiX
Overdoing (for relationship / compensate for Yin weakness)	Pleasing (for achievement / compensate for Yang weakness)

Adapted from Patrick Connor, Sharmadā Foundation, and Patricio Campiani..

Our crocodilian compensation strategies offer an important key to rebalancing ourselves. Instead of giving in to the crocodilian tendency that we most strongly relate to, which is often one-sided—either Yin or

Yang—we cultivate the higher qualities from the opposite side and grow through them. We rebalance our Yin fix of pleasing by becoming more purposeful (Yang) and our Yang fix of overperforming by becoming more caring (Yin).

When I am faced with a challenge and I see that I am not achieving what is needed, I practice assertiveness and purposefulness, with humility—an owl Yang strength—as opposed to giving into my Lower Yin traits of pleasing and self-pity.

Conversely, if your Yang quality is stronger, you may tend to overwork and try to control others to get what you want when you are under stress. In that case, cultivate your caring Yin side and ask yourself: "How can we do this together? What does the other person need to perform well?"

We may notice that our crocodilian fixes vary by situation. For example, with our boss, we may fall into blame (Lower Yang) or pleasing (Lower Yin), while with our peers we may try to outperform (Lower Yang) or manipulate them (Lower Yin), and with our direct reports and subordinates we may try to control (Lower Yang) or coddle them (Lower Yin). Awareness is the key. Once we identify a crocodilian pattern, we can never un-see it, and our awareness brings about the next chapter of greater growth.

We can also practice developing Higher Yin and Yang by implementing one or all of the following practices:

1. Taking a moment to pause when we find ourselves caught in Lower Yin or Yang;

2. Visualizing and channeling a person who has strong Higher Yin or Yang qualities;

3. Going somewhere we feel safe and practice (e.g., role play) our Higher Yin and Yang there;

4. Breathing deeply to calm the crocodile;

5. Intentionally focusing on those Higher Yin or Yang qualities when we are in a tough situation.

Will we ever be done rebalancing ourselves? It is unlikely. There are always going to be new situations, like levels in a computer game, where the stakes are higher and our Lower Yin or Yang sides will be triggered. So where do we find continuous balance?

FINDING CONTINUOUS BALANCE— ABIDING IN PRESENCE

Whatever we water in the garden grows. The same goes for our consciousness. Whatever we place our attention on grows in strength, whether it's a weed or a flower, a crocodile or an owl.

Neuroscience supports this. As we discussed in a previous chapter, neurons that fire together, wire together. The more often we use certain neural pathways—the more we repeat certain thoughts and feelings—the deeper the neural groove becomes, and the more likely it is that we will have similar experiences again later. This is called neuroplasticity. As we work to balance our Yin and Yang leadership styles, we create new neural pathways in our nervous system that come online when we need them next.

Against a changing environment, where can we *reliably* place our attention to keep from losing our balance? We can think of human attention as being given to three realities:

1. The *physical* reality: what we can see, our bodies, the outside world;

2. The *mental* reality: our inner landscape consisting of our thoughts, feelings, and memories;

3. The *transcendental* reality: what lies beyond the mental reality, the stillness that underlies everything, the peace beyond understanding. We have called this "presence" earlier in this book. It's the space of awareness in which everything is happening. It's skylike—it contains everything, doesn't oppose anything, and it is timeless and limitless.

Check for yourself. Where do you place most of your attention?

Chances are you are spending most of your attention on the first two realities: the physical and the mental. That makes sense, as these are the most readily identifiable. We know that when we are experiencing a stressful emotion or physical sensation, we tend to get absorbed by that.

On the path of growth we can get lost in either reality. In the physical reality, we may become so consumed by our drive to acquire more, to have a stronger body, or to be someone in the world that we lose touch with who we really are. On the path inward, we may get lost in obsessively monitoring our feelings, and end up solipsistic and isolated. We may get so focused on feeling good, or so discouraged by feeling bad, that we lose sight of the bigger picture of our lives.

For true growth, we need to look beyond our immediate, self-absorbing experiences, whether they are centered on exteriorities or interiorities. As we do, we may develop understanding of another reality beyond the habitual focus on our friends and family, our things, our results, our bodies, our feelings, and our thoughts. This is the third reality, or transcendental reality. In this book we have called it presence, but it is also known as unconditional love, awareness, and the peace beyond understanding. What would happen if we rested our attention there more often? What would happen with our capacity for growth, wisdom, and compassion?

Neuroscience gives some clues. When we connect our nervous system to an EEG, we can notice different brain wave patterns depending on where we place our attention. Our brain waves are measured in frequency (hertz or cycles per second) and amplitude. Depending on their range, neuroscientists have given them different names: beta, alpha, theta, and delta. The fastest brain wave frequencies, 14-38 cps, are associated with beta; the slowest, 0-4 cps, with delta. Each brain wave frequency is suited for different functions: beta for multitasking and logic, alpha for single-pointed focus, theta for aha insights, and delta for intuition and empathy. When we place our attention mostly on the first reality—the physical—we tend to be mostly in beta. When we are in the alpha and theta rhythms, we tend to be more aware of our inner landscape. And when we reach delta, we go beyond our inner world into the transcendental—the watcher, presence, awareness. This slowest frequency is also associated with deep sleep. Notice that in deep sleep we have no problems—that is the presence-like state.

BRAIN WAVE	PRIMARY FUNCTION	PRIMARY REALITY
Beta 14–38 cps	Planning	Physical & Mental
Alpha 8–14 cps	Single-pointed focus	Mental
Theta 4–8 cps	Aha	Mental
Delta 0–4 cps	Intuition	Transcendental

When our brain wave frequency is slow, our metabolic rate (the rate at which we transform food and oxygen into energy) is also slow—we tend to breathe more deeply and more slowly when we get to theta and delta. Many of us most easily experience a state of peacefulness that is not affected by outside stimuli when we rest our attention on the transcendental and are deep in delta. In delta, we tend to experience transcendental awareness—a state that cannot be captured in words. Problems are seen as luminous projections on a screen, not as a big deal, more like a play in which we participate as actors. We experience deep peace and connection with everyone and everything, and a state of bliss and harmony and spaciousness. Wisdom and compassion arise naturally and we lose the sense of being a separate doer; rather, we experience ourselves as an instrument of awareness. We become creative, inspired, and loving as we realize that to be so is our nature—not controlling, colluding, competing, or other ways of operating from fear.

We can begin accessing this state at will, as we can access any brain wave frequencies at will, by focusing our attention on presence—the stillness that underlies everything, like the sky that holds all clouds. We can learn to rest our attention there through conscious breathing, repeating a mantra, doing a visualization, and other meditation techniques. By training our brain to move out of hyperactivity, where our focus is on immediate wants and distractions, we can reach a more balanced state of mind.

"I have nothing to do," Irfan Khan, my tax accountant, reported to me on March 7, 2016, in the middle of the busiest time of the year for him. This is his mantra and he repeats it often. He reports that it helps him empty his mind and regain his energy, even when he still has twenty-five more urgent requests for help to address that evening. I have found this mantra, "I have nothing to do," very helpful to access the transcendental reality. It's like saying to the mind, *it's okay, you may rest now; it's safe.*

Try this out for yourself: "I have nothing to do." Let go of any feelings of resistance, of any internal arguing with this statement. The truth is that in this moment you have nothing else to do besides reminding yourself of that. Focus your attention on your breathing, on softly inhaling and exhaling as you repeat to yourself: "I have nothing to do . . . I have nothing to do . . . I have nothing to do . . ." This is the experience of presence: being with every breath, feeling the subtle warmth of the sun against your face, the subtle softness of your chair, the small rustles and hints of life around you. You can practice this before bed, in the shower, over a quiet breakfast, in the office, on your way home from work—anytime, anywhere. Even a few minutes per day with this mantra has incredible benefits. It's a way to reboot the inner nervous system, and to begin to explore the delta frequency. Besides giving you real rest, it can help you stay in balance, no matter what. No longer thrown off balance by the demands of the physical and mental realities—to have your outer and inner world in perfect shape, you can rest in presence. You no longer need to feel good, have people like you, have your problems solved and everything else under control in your life, before you can feel balanced. You can rest in presence through all of it, regardless of what is happening on the movie screen of your inner and outer life.

A few years ago, I would not have included this section in this book, as it might have been misunderstood by most as too spiritual and esoteric—strange and irrelevant to leadership. Today I come across many leaders who have had a glimpse of the love and serenity that you can access in delta, and I meet some who are permanently abiding in it and leading from it. It's even poked fun at on shows like *Silicon Valley*, whose CEO, Gavin Belson, has a guru among his staff. My personal experiences have shown me the dividends of being open to meditative practices in a business setting, but I'm far from the only one. The general mindfulness movement pioneered by Jack Kornfield, the Dalai Lama, Jon Kabat-Zinn, and Eckhardt Tolle, among many others, now regularly gets discussed in the corporate world, from the *Harvard Business Review* to the *Wall Street Journal*.

If you like, use the guided meditation below, the Stillness Practice from Chapter 1, or the Twelve-Breath Presence Practice from Chapter 3 to practice presence, unconditional balance. You'll find a few more meditation practices in Appendices 1 and 2.

Abiding in Presence Meditation

Begin by slowly reading the following text to yourself. When you come to the end of this text, close your eyes and rest for about three to four minutes.

Find a place where you can sit comfortably and undisturbed for the next few minutes. Allow yourself some time to relax. There is nothing to do—this is some time to be with yourself.

Relax your toes—they may feel like they soften. Relax your heels—they may feel like they are melting; relax your calves, your knees—they may feel like they are opening. Relax your hips and your sitz bones—they may feel like they are sinking into your chair or cushion. Relax your belly—it may feel like it softens; relax your solar plexus— it may feel like it becomes lighter; relax your chest—it may feel like it opens; now relax your throat—it may become soft like jelly. Relax your jaw—it may feel like it unhinges. Relax your tongue—it may feel like it shortens. Relax your eyes—it may feel like they descend; relax your forehead—it may feel like it's gently caressed; and relax the top of your head—it may feel like it melts.

Take three conscious, deep breaths into your belly.

Now become aware of any sensations in your body—aches, pain, tingling, fatigue, buoyancy, heart rate, breathing, perspiration—just allow yourself to be aware of all these sensations now. Take three conscious, deep breaths into your belly as you become aware of any sensations in the body.

Now become supremely disinterested in these sensations. Start to shift your attention away from these sensations to . . .

. . . your feelings. Notice any feelings you have now—joy, sadness, fear, anxiety, excitement, distractedness, awe, love, enthusiasm, guilt, resentment, resignation—

no need to change any of these feelings—just notice them. Take three conscious, deep breaths into your belly as you become aware of any feelings you have now.

Now become supremely disinterested in these feelings and shift your attention away from these feelings to . . .

. . . your thoughts. Notice any thoughts you have now—it doesn't matter what they are. Just notice them as you would notice clouds in the sky. Don't pay any particular attention to any of these thoughts more than other thoughts. Just see them as clouds in the sky. Take three conscious, deep breaths into your belly as you become aware of any thoughts you have now.

Now allow yourself to become supremely disinterested in these thoughts, feelings, and body sensations, and shift your attention to . . .

. . . attention itself, that what remains that is beyond thoughts, feelings, and body sensations. Rest as the awareness that is aware of all the thoughts, feelings, and body sensations. Allow yourself to rest as this presence—awareness—for the next few minutes.

If you get distracted, bring your attention back to the movement of the in- and outflow of your breath in your belly. Once you are resting your attention on your breathing, become supremely disinterested in that, again, and bring your attention to attention itself, presence, awareness, stillness—the sky that holds the clouds of sensations, feelings, and thoughts.

Now close your eyes and rest as presence for a few minutes. Nothing to do, only rest. You can't do it right or wrong, just do the practice and allow your experience to be as it is.

For a moment reflect on the possibilities of resting more often in the transcendental reality—in presence. We may think, *but how will I get my work done then?* We are so used to being absorbed by our thoughts, feelings, and sensations that we forget there's a more peaceful approach to life. We can learn to rest as presence twenty-four hours a day, while working, driving, taking care of the kids, being with our partner, or even sleeping. We do this by letting go of our attachment to thoughts, feelings, and sensations, and resting in the biggest picture of them all—presence. What would happen if all of us were to grow our consciousness to be more consistently in presence?

The more we stay in the moment, as presence, the more at peace we are. The more at peace we are, the less we ask from the world. The less we ask from the world, the more we can give it. The more we give, the more true leadership we provide.

Rather than asking the physical and mental realms for what they cannot give us, we learn to look to a higher source for motivation and inspiration. When we are guided by that vast transcendental perspective, we become our best bosses, mentors, team members, and contributors.

FIELDWORK

1. Where in your life, work, and leadership do you feel in balance? Where do you feel off balance?

2. What do you see as your strongest quality? Select one.

   A. Definitiveness of purpose, will (Yang)

   B. Assertive internal strength and clarity (Yang)

   C. Warrior energy, willing to stretch self (Yang)

   D. Ability to stay still in the storm (Yang)

   E. Power through humility (learner) (Yang)

   F. Inspirational (Yin)

   G. Creative, intuitive (Yin)

   H. Compassionate, empathetic, kind, caring (Yin)

   I. Listening, collaborative (Yin)

   J. Comfortable with uncertainty and ambiguity (Yin)

3. What do you see as your weakest quality, or growth opportunity?

   A. Definitiveness of purpose, will (Yang)

   B. Assertive internal strength and clarity (Yang)

   C. Warrior energy, willing to stretch self (Yang)

   D. Ability to stay still in the storm (Yang)

   E. Power through humility (learner) (Yang)

   F. Inspirational (Yin)

   G. Creative, intuitive (Yin)

   H. Compassionate, empathetic, kind, caring (Yin)

   I. Listening, collaborative (Yin)

   J. Comfortable with uncertainty and ambiguity (Yin)

4. What is the impact of this being a weaker quality for you? What is the impact on your relationships? What is the impact on yourself, on your sense of fulfillment and self-esteem, and what is the impact on your effectiveness in the world?

5. What do you see as your primary Crocodilian fix?

    A. Seeking power over others, pushy (authority, respect, status) (Lower Yang)

    B. Seeking to win, come out on top, be better (power through achievement) (Lower Yang)

    C. Repressing emotions, egotistical independence (self-sufficient, shutting off) (Lower Yang)

    D. Controlling through doing and problem solving (like being busy) (Lower Yang)

    E. Using logic, intellect, and reason at expense of love (Lower Yang)

    F. Seeking power through approval, pleasing, seduction (Lower Yin)

    G. Dependent, helpless, weak, timid, needing to be saved, victim (poor me) (Lower Yin)

    H. Obsessing about security and safety (Lower Yin)

    I. Needing to be admired (Lower Yin)

    J. Valuing relationships over purpose (Lower Yin)

6. How can you practice developing the Higher Yin/Yang side that is weaker in you? How can you mitigate the risk of you falling into Lower Yang and Lower Yin fixes?

7. What growth opportunities (Yin/Yang balance opportunities) are you discovering in yourself?

8. How will you commit to capturing those opportunities?

9. What difficulties do you have with resting as presence? Who would you be without these thoughts about it being difficult? What would be the impact on your ability to stay balanced if you learned how to rest as presence?

10. How are you growing?

CHAPTER 6

Truth Inquiry into Our Crocodilian Roots

"Truth resides in every human heart, and one has to search for it there, and be guided by truth as one sees it. But no one has a right to coerce others to act according to his own view of truth."
—Mahatma Gandhi

A S GROWTH LEADERS, we are committed to our vision for ourselves and for the world—our authentic purpose, growing every day more into who we are and expressing that in the world. Mahatma Gandhi devoted his life to truth and nonviolent protest, which led to India's independence. Gene White has dedicated her life to the end of child hunger to create world peace as president of the Global Child Nutrition Foundation. Rob Tarkoff, the CEO of Lithium Technologies, told me at the end of our interview that he is working to create a sustainable future for our children. And Andrew Blum, CEO of the Trium Group, a consulting boutique, whom we'll meet in this chapter, says the following about his motivation: "When I help people get clear, get connected, get honest with themselves about their business, I help myself get clear, connected, and honest with me."

As we continue to grow more into who we are, we are inevitably going to run into some crocodilian patterns and imbalances that seem to be almost intractable. You may think, *Hey I am this way and I will always be this way (a perfectionist, a pleaser, a conformer, a competitive person, an insecure person, a frantic person, a go-getter, etc.).* There is a tool that I have found a great measure of last resort to tackle these recalcitrant crocodilian obstacles to our growth. It's particularly adept at cutting through stickiness, getting us unhooked from seemingly unbreakable yet limiting habits. And of course, we can use it to tame any crocodile, not only the most stubborn ones. It's called "The Work" and was developed by wisdom teacher Byron Katie. Her method guides us to get clear on what is true, and what is not. Katie is far from the only one to make getting to truth the centerpiece of her teachings, though her approach is a particularly clear example of its power.

In addition to The Work, we'll learn another tool in this chapter, called "The Tree." It helps us get clear on the underlying belief systems that keep our sticky thoughts and behaviors in place. When we apply "The Work" of truth onto the roots of our limiting behaviors, we open ourselves to rapid and transformative learning.

Truth has the ability to transform any obstacle. Gandhi understood the power of truth and made it the central principle of his movement, which he called *satyagraha*, meaning "holding on to truth." He helped people see the fundamental truth that we're all connected. From that place of seeing the connection between all beings, Gandhi inspired his followers to practice *ahimsa*, or "nonviolence." This starts with nonviolence in the mind—not believing any thought that contradicts the fundamental truth of human oneness, e.g., the blame, judgment, and self-pity crocodiles—and then translating oneness into our actions toward others. Gandhi said: "The essence of holding on to truth is to withdraw support of what is wrong. If enough people do this, even if one person does it from a great enough depth—evil has to collapse from lack of support."

When we withdraw support of what is not true, or, in other words, become supremely disinterested in the untruthful content of our minds, our internal negativities collapse. Then our essence—unconditional love, peace, joy—can come to the foreground. I have experienced this time and again. When I stop believing a negative thought, I feel a sense of freedom, lightness, and buoyancy—like I am returning to my real self. "I am never going to make it," I may think, and feel bad. Then I ask: "Is that true?" When I really think about it, I realize that, of course, my negative thought is not absolutely true. It's only a thought. As I stay in this inquiry I feel the grip of thinking loosening its grip on me. It's like having the humidity in the atmosphere washed away by a big thunderstorm—afterward, the air feels incredibly clear.

In our journey through this book we have already learned some tools that can help us live our truth more:

1. *I-We-It Whisper Awareness*: Listen to the whispers in our lives before they become screams.

2. *Stillness Practice*

3. *Defining Our Authentic Unconditional Calling*

4. *Choosing a Growth Leadership Mind-set* where we see every moment as an opportunity for presence, self-discovery, contribution, and excellence.

5. *Twelve-Breath Presence Practice*

6. *Spotting our Cringing and Clinging Crocodiles*

7. *Releasing Crocodilian Fears through the Five Questions:*

   • Who's talking? The owl or the crocodile?

   • What fear may be active here?

   • Who would I be without this fear?

   • How can I respond from my wise and compassionate owl?

   • How am I growing?

8. *Growing through Our Seven Fear Families*

9. *Transforming Our Seven Croc SUCCESS Personas into Seven Owl SUCCESS Intentions*

10. *Balancing Yin and Yang*

11. *Abiding in Presence Meditation*—spending more time in delta

In this chapter, we're going to dive into the skill of being *radically honest* with ourselves, so that we can live and lead from that place. This is where our purpose will thrive, and where our leadership will take wing. The word *radical* actually comes from the Latin word *radic*, meaning "root." In our internal world, we have many layers—veils that keep us from living our truth. And to thin those layers out, we can either work with the tops of these layers, the weeds, or we can go for the roots. Applying Katie's deep inquiry for truth practice to the origins of our thoughts will set us free.

RECOGNIZING TRUTH

Truth sounds great in the abstract. But how do we know what is true for us and what isn't? According to Andrew Blum, "The truth always has a very clear feeling associated with it. It feels more neutral, more mature, and it has less emotional energy associated with it. It has clarity, and when you start to be familiar with what truth feels like, it's very clear when things are true or not." He followed up with an experiment to illustrate.

"How old are you?" he asked me.

"I am forty-three," I responded.

"Now," he said, "I am going to ask you a question and I want you to tell me a lie. How old are you?"

"I'm forty-five," I answered this time.

"You notice you feel a difference," Andrew explained. "There is always a slight charge . . . that is how lie detectors work. There is an electrical charge associated with lying that's different from the electrical charge associated with truth. How do you know what the truth is? Because you know it. The truth is the truth, and it always feels the same. Lies, equivocations, and intellectualizations often feel a lot like lies. They feel a little uneasy, unsteady, and delicate, because it requires a lot of mental energy to hold them."

Let's apply this truth litmus test to some of the beliefs and behaviors that underlie the conventional, borrowed focus of many leaders. Ask yourself these questions and see what you notice inside of you.

1. Is it true that you should be busy?

2. Is it true that you should be perfect?

3. Is it true that you should outdo your competitors?

4. Is it true that you should know the answer?

5. Is it true that you should not have conflict?

6. Is it true that you should defer to your boss?

7. Is it true that you don't have a choice?

8. Is it true that you should please others?

9. Is it true that you should always be reachable?

Do you notice any contraction inside of yourself while contemplating these questions?

We feel contraction when we believe false beliefs, as it is our nervous system's way of telling us that what we're telling ourselves is self-limiting lies, meaning there are other, more expansive ways to view reality. There are opportunities for greater truth, for growth of our consciousness into a bigger perspective than our limited belief. Our owl is saying *you know that is not true, think again.* That can feel very uncomfortable to our status quo-protecting crocodile.

Our crocodiles have been working very hard to build a belief structure that is designed to help us survive. One crocodile may have taught us to be perfect to gain approval, initially from our parents, which later it translated as our main orientation for life. Challenging such a deeply entrenched belief, like *I should be perfect,* after, in my case, having lived it for forty-plus years, feels uncomfortable, to say the least. It brings up confusion, disbelief, disorientation, maybe even embarrassment—*why did I let myself be fooled by this crocodile for so long? How will I survive when I am not perfect? How will others react?*

INQUIRY INTO OUR ROOTS

What lies at the root of all our mental chatter? Let's examine that now. Once we have clarity about the foundation upon which our crocodiles have built our inner house of cards—of false beliefs and limiting behaviors—it becomes much easier to dismantle the entire crocodilian system.

Human beings are like trees. Part of us is visible above ground—the other, deeper, more defining part, is hidden beneath the soil. At the surface, we can see our behaviors. Underneath those behaviors are our thoughts and feelings, which are another, less visible layer of our being. If we're looking closely, we can see thoughts and feelings manifest themselves in a person's expression, in their tone of voice, and in their body language.

Just as acorns fall from the tree and then grow again, actions, thoughts, and feelings come and go. The core of our individual inner landscape consists of beliefs, needs (met and unmet), and fears underneath these more fleeting states. When unconscious, these beliefs, needs, and fears form deeply engrained patterns that we reflexively hold on to, and without our realizing it, they inform our feelings, thoughts, and behaviors.

Therefore, if we want to transform any feelings, thoughts, and behaviors, we need to first look at the beliefs, needs, and fears informing them. But how do we address our beliefs, needs, and fears if they are buried deep within our inner soil?

We do this by looking at our visible patterns first: our behaviors and recurring thoughts—the leaves and branches of our being. But there are so many to look at, you may think. Where do we start? Life is a great teacher. It will show us where to look first, by having us experience results we are unhappy with. Those unsatisfactory results can be apparent or very subtle. Remember the I-We-It Whisper practice? We can scan our current situation for unsatisfying outcomes at the level of personal fulfillment (I), relationships (We), and effectiveness (It). This is the first stage of practicing radical self-honesty. Remember, the crocodiles like the status quo and do not want to touch anything that threatens it. Be honest with yourself, in spite of what your crocodiles may be saying (or screaming!).

Next we'll identify our behaviors and thoughts that may have contributed to the less-than-optimal outcomes. Once we have done both these inventories, we can slowly move down to the roots of our inner landscape. We call this inquiry "The Tree."

The Tree

The Tree consists of six questions. Let's work through them now, with radical self-honesty. As I go through these Tree questions with my personal example, apply the Tree to a challenge you are facing. Remember your status quo–protecting crocodile will not enjoy this. Be resolute and do it anyway.

We'll start by identifying the outcome that we want to shift by taking a look at the "I" (personal fulfillment), the "We" (relationships), and the "It" (effectiveness) in our lives:

1.   *What is a recurring result in my relationships, in my effectiveness, and in my fulfillment that I don't like?*

I see that I often feel a lot of worry and mental pressure when it comes to not being able to get everything done on time. For example, I stress about having all the materials ready on time for the next version of the online "Leader as Coach" program I will be leading for Columbia Business

School in the spring. The result I would like less of is that feeling of stress, which erodes my sense of joy and peace.

2. *What actions or behaviors are contributing to this unwanted result? Be deeply honest with yourself.*

When I look carefully at my life, I notice that I block whole days, sometimes a whole week, for work on my calendar and I don't take care of other areas of my life on those days. I ignore things like my partner, my family, my friends, my broader community, my hobbies, and my health. As a result, I feel like I am on a forced march, as opposed to enjoying the process of creation and being an instrument of presence.

3. *What thoughts and feelings are associated with this action, and may be driving it?*

Taking a step back, I notice ongoing mental chatter that says, if you don't stay focused, you'll never get it done. You mustn't have any distractions. It's the same inner monologue that guided who I was as a university student, which led me to sequester myself and study till I dropped. I feel stressed out when I am in this thought pattern. I feel a contraction in my heart area. Often while working, my right foot is tapping nervously, as if it wants me to keep running to get it done.

There is marked contrast when this nervous thinking is not driving the boat. When I am not thinking about getting it done, I am in the flow and am enjoying the creation process. This sense of flow is getting more common now, and yet the thoughts that rope me back into my familiar sense of nervousness are always there: *If you don't give it your all, you will fail.* I even use the greats, like Gandhi, who seemed to have such dedication to their cause that they chose to forego a lot of pleasures in their lives, as role models to justify my anxious running to get things done, no matter what!

4. *What history of beliefs may be driving these thoughts, feelings, and actions?*

When I look at my childhood, the first thing I remember is that my dad was always working, and the expectation for the family was that we would join him in that. As a child when I wanted to do nothing, or something I loved doing, like reading a book or playing music, I felt I wasn't a good farmer's son. Being productive meant being loved. Doodling or enjoying the moment (I don't think that thought even occurred to me growing up) meant feeling judged. I learned a belief system from my family that to be loved I have to produce. By the way, it wasn't my parents who came up with this idea. They learned it from their family, friends, and circumstances. My grandparents learned it from their family and friends, and so on.

I produce to be loved. Reflecting more deeply, I can see where my family and friends were coming from. They grew up in poverty and had to work hard to make ends meet. Production for them equaled survival and a way to love one another was to help the other survive. It's completely understandable they believed that. However, I got to experience the limitations of that belief system—namely that I can never produce enough to feel loved. As long as the belief "I should produce to be loved" is active, there will always be a sense of lack of love, which can never be filled by any action, as *no action can transform a thought pattern so long as the thought pattern stays unconscious.*

Knowing this, will I now easily discard the old belief system that I need to produce to be loved? Probably not—replaying this tape over the years has caused me to become attached to it, as if my life depends on it.

Asking another question can help create further perspective and, therefore, space around this engrained belief system. This question goes to the root of all of our thoughts and feelings. It's about our core fears and needs:

5. *What is the primary need at stake here? What is the underlying fear?*

I notice that my primary need is to be loved—to be in a loving relationship. And my fear is that I will not be loved unless I stay productive and have results to show for it. Being Hylke is not enough, I have to prove I am lovable by what I produce. Otherwise, the people I want to be loved by will abandon me. "The day I show up empty handed, without tangible successes, they will withdraw their love from me," so this crocodilian fear claims.

6. *How does the fear paradoxically create the result it fears the most?*

The more I give in to my fear of not being loved, the more I go into frantic production-mode, and the less connected I am to myself. Paradoxically, my fear of not being loved creates the experience of not being loved, as I stop being present to myself and others. I get so caught up in action that I am no longer present to this moment. I don't stop and notice the beautiful blossoms of the azalea on our porch, I don't notice my partner smiling at me, I don't smell the delicious food that is being prepared, I don't feel the soothing balm of the in- and outbreath, I don't feel my feelings, I don't notice the space that is aware of the feelings, I don't notice the sense of peace that comes with that, I don't notice what is here now. I am missing out on the love that life is giving me from all directions now. Why? Because I am so busy getting love, getting things done, that I don't notice that I am loved already now. The more I fear not being loved, the harder I run to prove myself, the more I disconnect from this present moment, and the more I have the experience of not being loved. *My fear of not being loved creates my experience of not being loved.*

And over time, the people around me will indeed stop being interested in hanging out with me and withdraw. Life is a great teacher that way. Who wants to be with someone who isn't present to them? My fear of not being loved creates the experience of not being loved, in more and more overt forms—like people leaving me. That's another reason the Cherokees advised to listen to the whispers before they become screams (see Chapter 1). When we notice we're driven by a fear, as we sense inner restlessness, we can choose to release it right then and there. We don't need to wait for more hard evidence, e.g., of people leaving us, that it's time we woke up from our hallucination.

Think of any fear that may underlie your limiting thoughts and behaviors. Can you see how it creates the result you fear the most when you give in to it? If you would like to contemplate this more, you can also look back in Chapter 4, where we described it as the Fear Paradox.

Notice that any fear has the potential to create endless struggle. We can never outdo or outrun our fears and yet our crocodiles feel compelled to do so. Like Don Quixote, we will fight the windmills in our minds— those fears that continuously lead us away from happiness—for as long as we believe them into existence. How do we take ourselves off this hamster wheel?

UNLEASHING THE POWER OF TRUTH

With an unflinching commitment to truth—*satyagraha*. Katie teaches us "The Work" as a method to apply truth to our most intransigent limiting beliefs and fears. Let's find out how.

The Work consists of four questions and a "turnaround." They are as follows:

1. Is it true?

2. Can you absolutely know that it's true?

3. How do you react when you believe that thought?

4. Who would you be without the thought? Turn the thought around.

Andrew Blum partners with Byron Katie and uses The Work all the time. He did an example with me. "If you were to ask me: 'What is one of the greatest challenges of growing a very high-end boutique firm, like Trium, where you really need incredibly skilled people?' I'd tell you: 'It's hard to find good people.'" Andrew paused for a second, then continued. "If I say that to you, you'd probably agree, right?" I affirmed. "We can create a lot of agreement on that," he said.

"Now, is it true? Is it true that it is hard to find good people? The first time I ask it, you'll probably agree with me," said Andrew. He asked me to think again. "Can you absolutely know that it is hard to find good people?" I realized that I was uncertain, and felt a bit unsettled by the question. Andrew continued: "Well, I have found a lot of good people. There are a lot of good people in all these big firms. So I can't absolutely know that it is hard to find good people."

Then it was time for the third question: How do I react, what happens, when I believe that thought, in this case, that it's hard to find good people? "Well, I get despondent," Andrew said. "I feel sort of hopeless, I start to settle for people that maybe are not a great fit. I feel a bit powerless. I feel resigned, let down. I feel a little angry. You know when I share with people that it is hard to find good people, I get a lot of agreement and some sympathy. I get to feel a little bit like a victim. With the thought 'It's hard to find good people' I have a resigned and negative experience.

"Next I go to question four, which is: 'How would I react as a leader if I didn't believe that it is hard to find good people?' Well, I'd be much more open, I'd be carefully looking at everyone without so many prejudgments. And I'd be much more neutral about the process of recruiting."

Relaxing a limiting belief yields clarity, freedom, possibilities, and the confidence that everything will work out in the end. If you'd like, take a moment for yourself and consider a potentially limiting belief or fear that you have about a challenge you are facing. Limiting beliefs and fears often include language like "It's hard . . . , I can't . . . , It's always . . . , They should/shouldn't . . . ," and "I should/shouldn't . . ." Once you have identified a limiting belief, ask yourself: "Is it true? Can you know it is absolutely true? How do you react when you believe that thought? Do you feel expansive and optimistic, or limited and resigned, or . . . ? Who would you be without the thought? What becomes possible for you?" Let these questions rest in your awareness for a little while. Some patience and thoughtfulness can pay off in a big way here, allowing you to see in new ways. Don't be discouraged if what you discover feels uncomfortable at first. That may be a sign you are in the process of transforming an old belief that has been limiting you and your team or organization. Your status quo crocodiles are protesting!

The last step in the inquiry process is called the "turnaround." Systematically Andrew explored the belief "It's hard to find good people" from multiple perspectives (self, opposite, other) and turned it on its head. As he shared his insights, I noticed there was a twinkle in his eye. "Well, yeah, I don't know that I'm being a very good interviewer," he said. "I'm not sure that I even have a good, clear picture of what I am actually looking for, or what attributes I don't want. So, is it hard to find good people? Or is it hard for me to find them? Given my skills as an interviewer, wow, it feels like it's harder for me to find them." He paused. "What's another turnaround? There are a lot of great people I didn't have to work that hard to find—I met them once or twice and they were great. So, it's also true that it's easy to find good people."

Andrew paused again, then added: "Here is a mind-blowing turnaround: 'It's hard for good people to find me.' I'm not marketing directly to potential employees. We haven't built an employee-focused brand. We haven't even decided where the place to find them is. So from that turnaround, the option set is blown open. I can do a million things to make it easy for good people to find us. Believing 'It's hard to find good people,' there is no movement at all, only validation of the limiting belief."

In his work, Andrew challenges widely held beliefs and fears and helps transform them into new views of reality that feel more accurate and help leaders and their organizations thrive. "I can collude with other leaders that it's so hard to find good people and we can talk about the challenges associated with millennials, how kids today don't really want to work for a living, blah, blah, blah. Those beliefs give me nothing but negativity and despair. If I go in search of the truth, everything opens. My journey has been a lot about challenging largely agreed-to beliefs. There are many aspects of reality that are unconsciously agreed to that we collude around. *The undercurrent of business is filled with widely held, rarely examined truths.* These are not truths, these are just sayings," Andrew concluded.

THE WORK OF TRUTH IN ACTION

Let's apply The Work to the pseudotruth that I uncovered doing my Tree practice: "I should produce to be loved." I should have tangible outcomes to show, before people can love me, and before I can love myself.

1. *Is it true that I should produce to be loved?*

Well, I know it feels good to get something done—that feels like love to me—and yet, no, I don't think it's true. But maybe it is.

2. *Is it absolutely true that I should produce to be loved?*

No. The people who love me don't love me because of what I produce, and they don't stop loving me when I don't produce. Even those people that withdraw don't stop loving me when they withdraw, as it's not possible to stop loving another person. We may not like another person, but that doesn't mean we don't love them. We are love, and connected. It's only our crocodilian beliefs and fears that have us experience otherwise.

Even if the previous paragraph doesn't resonate with you—they are my words only—go back to the question "Is it *absolutely* true that I should produce to be loved?" and check it out for yourself. The word "absolute" comes from Latin *absolvere*, which means "to set free, acquit, finish, complete," according to the Merriam-Webster dictionary. When we say something is absolutely true, it is completely true, for everyone, always. In that way, the "truth will set us free," as we can rely on it to liberate us from our self-limiting hallucinations, no matter what.

So, is it absolutely true that I should produce to be loved? I can't be sure, and I know it's not for some other people, so it can't be absolutely true. Also, it doesn't feel true to me when I sit back and feel into it, applying the truth litmus test Andrew taught me. No, it's not absolutely true. It's freeing to know that. I feel the grip of this thought becoming looser.

3.   *How do I react, what happens, when I believe that I should produce to be loved?*

I overwork, ignore the rest of my world, disconnect from presence, don't experience joy, think I have to do it all myself, and see life as one long to-do list. It's not much fun at best, and really painful at times when I am controlled by this belief.

4.   *Who would I be without the belief that I should produce to be loved?*

Well, I'd be free. I'd reflect more on my calling—why am I doing this beyond getting it done?—and I would feel inspired. Without this belief that I should produce to be loved, I feel the love that I am, and feel the inspiration to share that with others.

5.   *Turn the belief around.*

This is where we get to be creative—and brave, as it turns out, as we are invited not only to let go of our limiting thoughts but also to consider the opposite of beliefs we may have based (part of) our lives on. Byron Katie suggests we do at least three turnarounds:

1.   To the self;

2.   To the other;

3.   To the opposite;

and find evidence for each of those.

Let's practice this with my pseudo truth "I should produce to be loved."

One turnaround, to the self, is: "I should love myself no matter what I produce." The love I really want is unconditional, not dependent on circumstances. Turns out it's always here. The only thing I have to do is to be present to this moment. Conversely, when I let myself be distracted by fearful thoughts, frenetic actions, and attachment to outcomes, I am no longer here and disconnect from the love I have always been and always will be.

Continuing to turnaround #2—to the other. Here is what I found: "They love me, whether I produce or not." People don't love me for what I produce. They love me for who I am, no matter what. The other thing is not unconditional love, it's like or dislike, clinging or aversion—all conditional love. When people express or withhold love from me based on their agendas of what I can do for them, what I produce or who I should be (e.g., "the producer"), it's conditional love, which has nothing to do with the unconditional love I want.

Lastly, I did turnaround category #3—the opposite. I found quite a few helpful turnarounds here:

a. *I shouldn't produce to be loved.* Love in my life should come from other things, not from what I'm working on.

b. *I should produce not to be loved.* My motivation to producing can change and become about the work itself rather than about this specific result I want.

c. *I should produce to be unloved.* Would I still follow my passion for my work if it had the opposite result? Can I separate my work from the desire to be loved, and pursue my work for its own sake, whatever the consequences?

I am taking a moment to be with those turnarounds. Especially the turnaround "I shouldn't produce to be loved" feels a bit like an earthquake to me. I see that I have unconsciously spent a lot of my life working super hard, as it turns out, to gain love and approval. I now see it's based on a false belief system that has been in my family for many generations. Who will I be if I know I am loved irrespective of how hard I work? How will I do my work then? I let myself sit with this for a while and feel the ripples of this realization move through me.

Take a moment to practice this process yourself on a thought or belief that causes some contraction in your world:

1. Is it true?

2. Can you absolutely know that it's true?

3. How do you react when you believe that thought?

4. Who would you be without the thought? Turn the thought around—first to the self, then to the other, and finally to the opposite.

Do you experience greater freedom as you do this inquiry? How may this impact how you provide leadership differently, starting with to yourself?

———

Crocodiles are stubborn and crafty—they will come up with endless reasons why you should stay loyal to your limiting beliefs. *"Yes, hello, it's your crocodile speaking. You definitely should produce to be loved, be perfect, be liked, be like you, be shy, be a rescuer, have it all together, be the best, be the worst, be a failure, be a success, and stay the person I know so well. How else will I manage to stay safe?!"*

Resolutely applying the Work of truth, undeterred by the stubbornness of our crocodiles, sets us free to become more of who we really are—for most of us, one turnaround at a time. Yet sometimes we hit a cornerstone of our crocodilian house of cards and a big part of the veil obscuring truth—or maybe all of it at once—collapses. We can't control the pace of this process of unlearning who we are not. It's simply a matter of staying on the path of truth. Let life take care of the rest. Even on this part of our journey we stay unconditional—in our intention to be truthful. We don't tie ourselves to any outcome of when our process of inquiry should be done. As if it ever will be.

Chris Capossela, Chief Marketing Officer of Microsoft, taught me one powerful turnaround. He said: "It's easy to say: 'Oh, it looks like somebody here's perfect.' It's not, it's a mess. We're humans working together, competing with other companies with other human beings. It's a really messy system. The beautiful thing is that the job is so ridiculously vague and so completely impossible to do well that I've completely come to terms with the fact that any day could be the last day. That has made me really relaxed. Yeah, it could be the last day. And so, do you worry about it being the last day? Or do you say: 'I'm going to make this the best day I can possibly make it and maybe I'll get another one tomorrow.' That mental shift has been very important for me." One item on his Leadership

Learnings List reads: "Careers are unpredictable, enjoy the ride." Chris taught himself how. Challenged by Chris's turnaround that it's messy, I hear the old belief in me that "I should have it all together" creaking. Oh no, another crocodile bites the dust!

Many leaders' limiting beliefs are like this; they believe they shouldn't enjoy their work until things are solved. Then we can ask, "Is it true that things will ever be solved?" And we quickly see that issues, like love, are infinite. The more conscious, the more sensitive we become. As we grow our inner awareness, we grow in empathy with others. We must learn to enjoy the messiness, because we can only expect to experience more of it—rather than less—when we evolve. And as we grow through the messiness, inquiry into truth is our constant companion.

THE QUEST TO BE A TRUTHFUL LEADER

How did Andrew Blum get so deeply interested in truth and inquiry? When I asked him, Andrew quoted David Whyte, the poet, who wrote: "What are you tired of about yourself?" This is the question that got Andrew started on his exploration. "At some point you start feeling the weight of the unintended negative impact of your behavior. If you are a sensitive person, you are inspired to say: 'Okay, there must be something that I am doing.' There is a fundamental recognition of three things in this: one, that you are in a pattern; two, that you are the cause of your recurring pattern; and three, that somehow the way out of that pattern has to do with how you are thinking about and viewing yourself and the situation."

Andrew's first recognition came after he had served in the Marine Corps, earned his MBA, and been a management consultant for a while. "I think that was the first time I noticed how sick I was of myself and how burdensome it was to carry this egotistical identity of 'I'm an MBA; I'm a former marine officer; I'm a management consultant'—all these things that are very prestigious and institutionally validated. I became in touch with how dominant those identities were, how deeply attached I was to them, and how they created an image of invulnerability that actually kept people away from me. I think a very interesting thing is that people believe that if you are wealthy or have achieved certain successes or you have certain prestige, that that will attract people to you. I would meet people and quote my list of accomplishments and achievements at a young age, and I started to see that in fact it was not that people were attracted to me because of that, *they were attracted to me in spite of that.*"

Andrew's inquiry into himself and his world hasn't stopped since. It is a process that he continuously engages in, at all levels of his life. "After having been a marine officer, I'd participate in Iron Man triathlons—I went all the way down to work on the physical self. After that I did lots of intellectual self-improvement, with very strong academics.

"Eventually, you get to the other self-improvement rub, which is 'Wow, but how am I as a human being?' I first checked off the more traditional rubs. We live in a religion of weight loss . . . the highest good is to be thin or to be fit. Well, then you play that out, and the second-highest good is to be smart and accomplished and wealthy. Then you play that out, and then suddenly you are like 'wow, hang on, those didn't actually get me love, affection, or appreciation for myself.' At some point you have to say, 'Okay, but what else is there? How do I show up in the world? How kind am I? How connected am I? How patient am I?' That leads you down a different path of exploration."

Being truthful informs how we lead ourselves and others. Truth and love are two sides of the same coin. When we are truthful, we love what is, not what should be. We can only be loving when we let go of the veils that obscure our love for ourselves and others. This is a journey without end. We will always discover new vistas from which we can see ourselves and the people around us. New vistas give us new possibilities to extend love, as we discover new parts in ourselves that are confused and that may be ready to be restored to truth. *The more truthful we become, the more we will love ourselves.* The more we love ourselves, the more we will be able to share that love with others.

"Imagine you're visiting Earth from another planet," I asked Andrew. "Given your life experiences as Andrew to date, what would you tell us?"

"I'd say there seem to be a lot of people who are a little bit confused," he responded. "That it's all here now, except for the places where you're confused. And that's what Katie would say too. She's like: 'Look, there's no evil. There's just confusion. There's this misidentification.' And there's a belief that if I have a certain level of prestige or rank or success or wealth, that I would be happier than I am today. Every product in the world is sold with that premise, that everything in life is about getting, being in a higher ranking, having more money, having more prestige, having more acknowledgment, having more credibility. Most people's lives unfortunately are about the endless acquisition of those things, and anybody who's achieved some of them will tell you there's nothing in them."

Andrew's response summarizes the shift in consciousness Growth Leaders can create together, evolving ourselves and our world from Getting Leadership absorbed in having and accumulating (a dead end), to a journey of growing in our capacity to love, to serve, and to leave humankind in a more truthful and sustainable place than where we found it.

THE POWER OF TRUTHFUL LEADERSHIP

"What are *you* tired of about yourself?" What pseudotruths are you living and leading from that you are ready to question for truth? In what ways do you lead people based on beliefs you picked up somewhere a long time ago, that limit you and them? As you give more of yourself to this inquiry, you will create greater freedom for yourself and for the people you lead. Inquiry empowers you and others to be who you really are, disentangling from a web of untrue, crocodilian beliefs. When you are free from these limiting beliefs you no longer give them any attention. Instead, you can dedicate your energy to what you really value. The Work and self-empowerment go hand in hand.

Consider some of the great leaders that we admire. They were holding up the mirror of truth in their time. They were helping people take their power back from the false belief systems they had given their power to. As you let their examples marinate in your mind, reflect on these four questions:

1. What beliefs am I giving power to?

2. Which ones *am I willing to* question now?

3. Which ones *do I need to* question now given my role as a leader?

4. How will my inquiry empower me and others?

Lincoln challenged people to see the untruth in oppressing others through slavery. Unapologetic in his challenge, he said: "Although volume upon volume is written to prove slavery is a very good thing, we never hear of the man who wishes to take the good of it, by being a slave himself."

Martin Luther King was a living symbol of truth-seeking, echoing Lincoln's words in his famous speech: "Five score years ago, a great American, in whose symbolic shadow we stand today, signed the Emancipation Proclamation . . . But one hundred years later, the Negro still is not free. One hundred years later, the life of the Negro is still sadly crippled by the manacles of segregation and the chains of discrimination. One hundred years later, the Negro lives on a lonely island of poverty in the midst of a vast ocean of material prosperity. One hundred years later, the Negro is still languished in the corners of American society and finds himself an exile in his own land. And so we've come here today to dramatize a shameful condition."

Take a moment and reflect on Lincoln's and Dr. King's statements. What slaverylike beliefs may still disempower you and others today? Who (boss, celebrity, colleague . . .) or what (money, recognition, pleasure, safety . . .) do you put on a pedestal and give your power to? Who do you take power from, putting yourself on a pedestal? In what ways do you try to control your environment? What learned but untrue beliefs underlie these behaviors? How would you think, feel, and act if you freed yourself from these beliefs? Notice how your crocodiles really don't want you to look at this. Remember your crocodiles will fight for the status quo, however disempowering it may be to you and others.

Like Lincoln and King, Gandhi was relentless in his pursuit of truth, or *satyagraha*, which has another translation: "soul-force." Tremendous power unleashes when we stand in truth. Gandhi applied this power to let colonial oppression crumble, under its own falsehood. He inspired people to see the untruth in exploitation. His biographer, Easwaran, wrote: "As long as a people accept exploitation, both exploiter and exploited will be entangled in an injustice. But once the exploited refuse to accept the relationship, refuse to cooperate with it, they are already free." In March 1930, Gandhi wrote the British Viceroy, stating that he was about to launch nonviolent resistance by marching to the sea and making salt—breaking a statute that had made this a monopoly of the British government. His two-week march that started with a small band of volunteers attracted thousands by the time they reached the ocean, and made world news overnight. More importantly, India exploded in nonviolent disobedience to colonial law. Droves of people were put in jail at the time and yet, non-violence held. Many veterans recall these days in jail as the high point in their lives, as they "kept the pledge" and experienced "suffering for truth" as a badge of honor.

Consider for your own empowerment and that of those you lead: What beliefs am I willing to question, even if it means experiencing the discomfort of change for a while? How will this inquiry empower me and others?

When we take a stance for truth, questioning deeply held untruths, we may receive some beatings. First, the crocodiles in our nervous system may protest that it's not safe to let go of our tried and seemingly true beliefs and strategies—of needing to be perfect, pleasing, in control, all-knowing, indispensable, special and so on. Next, some people may disagree with us or even leave us, as they are not willing to evolve with us. In the midst of that battle with our internal and external crocodiles, we can remind ourselves of the great truth seekers, like Lincoln, King, and Gandhi, to give us strength and persistence.

Actively searching and standing for truth is empowering. Taking a stand for truth empowers us to tame our crocodiles, growing out of our limiting beliefs and behaviors. And it's a powerful shortcut in our growth journey. Either we find our truth, or eventually, after days, months, or years of living in our untruth, it will catch up to us, and force us to face it. This happened to me when I was faced with insomnia—it was my body's way of forcing me to look at a truth that I had been ignoring: that I was unhappy.

Life has funny ways of teaching us truth.

If we cling to our belief of having to be perfect and other people start reporting to us, we may experience distrust as our colleagues will want to appear beyond reproach to survive the culture we are creating, even if that means being disingenuous. If we pursue validation by others, we will hit a wall at some point in our careers. People will no longer value our words and guidance, as they know we're not authentic. If we insist on being in control, we will be left with disempowered colleagues who perform way below their potential. At some point reality will catch up with us.

If it's not external circumstances that sober us up, it will be our body and emotions. Living from untruths is stressful and at some point, our body will let us know. It's just a question when. *The whispers will become screams.* Life wants to empower us to step into our truth, even when we are still kicking and screaming. The beauty of actively searching for our truths—through The Tree and The Work—is that we can do so more on our own terms and in our own timing, cocreating a fascinating adventure of learning in partnership with life.

When the thought of uncovering your truths seems upsetting or frightening, look at what you see with the kind eyes of presence. Let yourself discover the underlying, overarching truth that *all is well. Satyam eva jayate.* "Truth ever conquers." Every time we unmask an untruth, we unlock greater power—of freedom and authenticity. With that knowledge, that all is well—infinitely more so than our puny brain can comprehend—are you willing to be a bit braver today and expand the scope of pseudotruths you are willing to question? Ask yourself:

What beliefs am I giving power to? Which ones am I willing to question now?

Which ones do I need to question now given my role as a leader?

How will this inquiry empower me and others?

Enjoy this part of the journey—taming your most intransigent crocodiles and getting to know the power of standing in the truth of who you are.

FIELDWORK

Think about a sticky belief that is in your system. Now take some time to do "The Work" on this belief, or pseudotruth, that you have been living as if it were true. You can practice this many times a day or throughout the week—whenever you come across a painful belief. You can use these four questions to workshop beliefs about yourself, or beliefs that you hold about others and how they should behave/perform. Today, try working with one deeply engrained belief that you have about yourself, maybe one you uncovered doing the Tree exercise in this chapter.

My belief is:

1. Is this true?

2. Can you absolutely know that this is true?

3. How do you react when you believe that thought?

4. Who would you be without that thought?

5. Turn the thought around, first to the self, then to the other, then define the opposite.

Bonus: Remember Andrew's turnaround? Emulate him by writing a genuine example showing how each turnaround is truer than the belief that you started with.

6. How does this inquiry empower you? How are you growing?

CHAPTER 7

Growing Owls in Conversation

"If you are honest and frank, people may cheat you;
Be honest and frank anyway." —Mother Teresa

O NCE WE'RE CLEAR on our purpose and more familiar with and thus possibly less constrained by our crocodilian fears, we're ready for our next growth challenge—bringing our newly found clarity into our relationships. This is a whole other level of learning. When we get into the grit of life, we find that a huge chunk of learning happens in conversation with others. The word *conversation* comes from Latin *conversari*, meaning to "turn together," or "change together." We can think of a true conversation as one where both people change a little bit or a lot through the course of it. We call such a true conversation a "Growth Conversation."

Learning together gives a positive feeling. We come out with any of the following from a Growth Conversation:

1. Feeling taller on the inside—with a bigger view of ourselves

2. Appreciating others more—with a bigger view of others, and more connected to them

3. Generating new possibilities for and commitment to action— with a bigger view of the task at hand

Think of the Growth Conversations that you have been part of. What made them Growth Conversations? It may have been a sense of authenticity; a sense of mutual respect, focus, joy, resoluteness, precision, honesty, learning, or maybe even awe. How often would you categorize a conversation as a Growth Conversation? Think about all the conversations we have that seem to be simply going through the motions—conversations where both people are talking but there is no real engagement. Conversations that don't go anywhere. Why? Because we are actually pretending rather than honestly communicating.

Kathryn Stockett illustrates one of these types of pseudoconversations in her book *The Help*, as follows: "I don't know what to say to her. All I know is, I ain't saying it. And I know she ain't saying what she wants to say either and it's a strange thing happening here cause nobody saying nothing and we still manage to have a conversation."

Remember our motivation to be in relationships and our fear of abandonment? These tend to play a huge role in how we navigate and construct our dialogues. Think about how often we say something affirmative, like "yes," or "that's great," when what we're really thinking is "I have no idea what he is talking about," or "That is never going to work!" In the grip of the fear of the loss of a relationship, we speak half our truth or less.

Although these pseudoconversations are held with the intention of keeping relationships alive, they lead to a decay in trust and connection over time, as both people involved sense that what needs to be said, well, isn't being said. We can see pseudoconversations as missed opportunities for our growth.

Paradoxically, speaking up actually tames our abandonment crocodiles, in part because it's a detachment practice. Here is how one teacher suggests we engage in relationship and in conversation: "I am great. You want some?" When we know that in essence, we are presence—unconditional love—we know that we are complete and feel free to speak our truth. Then we don't need the other to validate it, by appreciating or agreeing with it. When we speak our truth, which by definition is detached from outcomes—otherwise it would not be the whole truth—we practice freedom: *I am free and you are free*. I am free to see things my way and you are free to see things your way.

Also, when we speak up and share our truths, we implicitly encourage others to do the same. When we hear something that is truthful, our heart tends to open, and we become more ready to let the other's perspective in. Then we may feel called to share our truth as well. In the process, our heart matures and our capacity to see multiple perspectives, without being triggered by them—needing to be "right," or to be liked—expands.

Growth Conversations are truthful conversations. Being truthful with another takes effort and practice, and it turns out to be worth it—it's transformative and builds relationship. "You don't let me get away with anything," we may say to our friend who never holds back their truth. In a truthful conversation, there is a shared commitment to being mindful of what is true, and not let any energy be diverted to untruth: no excuses, half-truths, and other crocodilian diversions.

Having a truthful conversation can feel like it requires everything from us, like jumping out of an airplane. When we engage deeply in it, it can feel like an act of love. We may discover in these conversations that truth and love are two sides of the same coin. As we share truths, we reveal authentic parts of ourselves to each other. The more we do that without fear, the more love flows.

How can we have these Growth Conversations that are truthful without being brutal, and respectful without being wishy-washy or hiding parts of who we are? I have noticed five elements that help make Growth Conversations truthful and loving:

1. Conscious Unconditional Intention

2. Authentic Expression

3. Heart-based Inquiry

4. Resonant Cocreation

5. Courageous Commitment

Even though they are sequenced 1–5, you can apply elements 2–4 in any order. If you are not familiar with Growth Conversations, it may help to use this sequence for a while until you're Unconscious-Skilled in them. I use the acronym "COAX" to make the elements easier to remember: Center in Conscious Unconditional Intention, Open with Authentic Expression, Ask with Heart-based Inquiry, and eXchange through Resonant Cocreation and Courageous Commitment. Let's explore each of the elements of COAX now.

SETTING A CONSCIOUS UNCONDITIONAL INTENTION FOR OUR CONVERSATION

Growth Conversations start with Conscious Unconditional Intention, which reflects our purpose for the conversation. This can include being honest, respectful, and focused, and centering ourselves in that without dependency on what our conversation partner will and will not do. At this point, we start thinking about what we're going to say, what we want to inquire into, and how we can create something with the other person that is resonant for both people. How often do you end up in the middle of a conversation, thinking later: *Gosh, I wish I had said or asked that a little earlier?* or *I am not sure why we're having this conversation* . . . Setting an intention before a conversation helps avoid this.

Not too many years ago, I didn't know about this yet. In one typical conversation about to go off the rails, I was a partner in a consulting company and had just received an e-mail with my bonus allotment. It was a lot less than I thought I was going to get, and I wasn't happy about that. I had been working an entire year to create new products and services for the firm, which I felt was very important for the future relevance of our company's consulting offering. We had piloted a new product suite successfully with two clients already, and I thought I deserved three times the money that was written in the e-mail. I was angry. I was going to have a conversation with my boss about it and I was going to tell him my truth—"You are not fair!"

I was stressed out. And I didn't see how I was going to get to my desired bonus, so I requested an extra session with my coach to help me prepare for the conversation with my boss. *How could I get him to give me more?* She agreed to meet with me and we talked for about an hour. After I had told my story, she asked this question, which has stayed with me throughout the years: *"What is the highest intention you can have for this conversation?* Who do you aspire to be in this? Imagine the best possible outcome—who will you be and how will your boss be?" That stopped me in my tracks. I had started to think of my boss as a monster—as someone who was always unfair, who didn't really value me, and was short-sighted. My crocodilian momentum was going to have me act from my *unconscious intention* of being vengeful, greedy, manipulative, and judging. My boss was "doing this to me," so further, my unconscious intention was to punish him—an intention that was actually quite aggressive. But who did I aspire to be? I didn't want to be my crocodile. But what then? I scrambled. I also didn't want to be just honest and kind— that didn't feel like it could get me what I wanted. My coach let me rant. "My boss should have treated me better! If he is going to play hardball, I am going to do that too! Maybe I can get him to change his mind if I make a case he can't refute!"

She listened for a while. Then she added a new layer to her question: "Who do you aspire to be, *regardless* of the outcome?"

What does she mean? I thought. *I care about the outcome very much! That is why I want to talk with my boss!* My coach read my mind.

"Yes, I know this may be challenging to think about—you clearly care about the result, and you know you don't control the result, yes?" she said. Yes, I could see that. "So if you want to have a robust intention you can fall back on, it helps if it's not susceptible to your boss giving you more money or not . . . We can call this having an *unconditional* intention." I could see that as well.

She asked again: "Who do you aspire to be, *regardless* of the outcome?" I let the question sink in. I took a few deep breaths and started to relax—some space opened inside of me.

"I will be honest, caring, and visionary," is what came. I repeated that a few times to myself. I felt a bit more relieved. Anxiety was ebbing away and I started to feel some enthusiasm to have a really good conversation, motivated by my new conscious, unconditional intention. My new intention may sound a bit abstract, but compare to where I started: combative and focused on punishing my boss and "winning." My internal shift opened up a new space of possibility to reach the result I wanted. I felt energized to share what I really cared about: why this bonus was important to me, and how much of myself I had invested in this project. For a moment, I also appreciated my boss's side of the table. I saw this must also be challenging for him—I knew he cared about me and about doing the right thing. And I sensed there might be other ways to solve this that I hadn't thought about yet. Maybe we could find an alternative solution *together*?

If you like, reflect on an upcoming conversation that you dread having. What happens when you root yourself in a conscious, unconditional intention? What do you notice about how you may perceive yourself, the other person, and the topic at hand differently? Maybe this conversation can be a Growth Instant in which you become more conscious about what your heart really wants to see happen and what your fears are? Maybe you can use it to practice and strengthen your owl mind-sets?

To make sure that your Conscious Unconditional Intention takes care of the whole situation, check that it addresses each of the following elements:

- "I" (the self): awareness for my values, who I am, my fulfillment

- "We" (the other): impact on others, my relationships, our trust

- "It" (the task): my effectiveness with the task at hand.

Reflecting on these elements, I could see that my initial intention, "I will be honest, caring, and visionary," was incomplete. It was mostly about the "I" and the "We." What about the "It?" I completed my intention as follows: "I will be honest, caring, visionary, and focused." I trusted that by being focused on the issue at hand—my bonus—I was not going to let myself get sidetracked with niceties and jumping to other topics that were easier for us to discuss.

Another litmus test for your conscious, unconditional intention is Yin/Yang balance. Is it both connecting and purposeful? My initial intention had some Yang in it—being honest, but was mostly Yin—caring and visionary. Not surprising, given my relative Yin-strength. My opportunity was to add some Yang-focus in my intention.

It can be helpful to share your conscious, unconditional intention with your conversational partner at the outset of the conversation; it is a way to set the table and invite the other person to reflect on their intention as well. It's like inviting someone over to your house. If you had planned a pleasant evening hike with your guest, but your guest is not aware, you may very well end up with someone at your door who is dressed ready to go out to dinner, not for a hike. When you share your conscious intention up front, you implicitly invite the other person to join you. And it's an act of caring to check that the other is ready to go for a hike with you. It may be that they are having a challenging day or need some time by themselves to reflect on the topic at hand. Simply asking: "Are you willing to talk about this now? And if not now, when would be good?" can help that person, like you, bring their best to the conversation.

Check-ins

One tool that is a great way to set the table for any conversation is a "Check-in." A Check-in is a way to center in presence together and become clear about the collective intentions at the outset of a conversation. It's based on that age-old tradition of people sitting around the table or fire, where each person speaks for a short while about what is true for them while the rest listen *without interrupting or reacting*. People have practiced this custom for ages. They pass a talking stick around, either literally or in their mind. The person speaking holds the stick until they are done and passes it on, typically to the person sitting next to them. Then it is the next person's turn to speak, and so on, until everyone who wants to has spoken.

Starting a conversation this way helps everyone become present and sets a common purpose and atmosphere for the meeting. Check-ins typically center around a few key questions that help people become intentional and connected with each other. For example, people might be asked to reflect on any or all of the following prompts:

- How are you feeling?

- How are you growing?

- What is your intention for this meeting?

Bringing everyone onto the same page allows a discussion to start off from a place of shared intentionality. Gandhi was famously masterful in setting up conversations on this plane of higher consciousness by bringing the energy of love into any conversation he entered, without saying much. His energy was so powerful that it transformed almost everyone he met. According to his biographer, Eknath Easwaran, new British administrators were warned: "Don't go near Gandhi; he'll get you" when they assumed their duties in India. Even at the most challenging moments in the fight for India's independence, Gandhi managed to cultivate deep and lasting friendships with his British opponents—partly because of his ability to stay loving even with those on the other side of the divide. He exuded his intention of love—specifically nonviolence—which helped disarm even his fiercest of opponents. When we are as centered in our conscious, unconditional intention as Gandhi was in his, we transform potentially antagonistic conversations into Growth Conversations, before either person has said a single word.

Next time you are heading into a challenging conversation, it may be helpful to reflect on how Gandhi or someone else you admire would approach the conversation. Or take on the question from my coach and ask yourself about your highest intention. One intention I remind myself of at the beginning of a challenging conversation is "STANDS": Speak Truthfully, Ask Nonjudgmentally, and Dare to be Still.

Once I was anchored in my intention, I ended up starting off the conversation with my boss by saying, "Harry, I'd like to have a beautiful, constructive conversation with you about my bonus. I know this may not be the easiest conversation and I want it to be the best possible one we can have. I intend to be honest ("I"), deeply appreciative of your perspective and reasoning ("We"), and to work creatively to find a solution with you ("It")." Harry smiled and just said: "Ditto." We were off to a great start—both of us were smiling and I sensed our hearts had opened up a bit.

These were my words—you will need to find yours. How you say your intention is up to you. It depends on what you feel comfortable with and what you sense the other person can hear. I liken it to choosing a language to speak in. "Als ik dit in't Nederlands vertel, begrijp je me waarschijnlijk niet." Okay, that was Dutch, in case you wondered. My guess is that you probably don't speak Dutch, so I write to you in English. The same goes for translating your conscious, unconditional intention into a language that the person you speak with understands. What words will you use that reflect your intention authentically *and* can be understood by the other? Notice that I wrote "*can*" here. It's not that they *will* understand—we don't control that; it's that we do our best to make that possible. I used the word *beautiful* with my boss, as we both have a love for Italy and its emphasis on beauty. Food is beautiful there; even financial statements are called beautiful at times! My boss and I had had many conversations about the beauty in Italian culture, so that's why I felt comfortable using a word like that. We shared a common context. Reflect on the common language you share with your conversation partner. Given that, what words can you choose to say your conscious, unconditional intention?

TRANSFORMING OUR AGGRESSIVE AND AVOIDANT CROCODILES INTO AUTHENTIC TRUTH

Once you've set your intention within yourself and as conversation partners, it's time to get into the conversation. Being anchored in a clear unconditional intention isn't all that's needed to get the next part right—you also have to be open in expressing your truth, instead of falling back on an ineffective pseudoconversation routine. No matter how committed to saying your piece you may be, there is always the fear of alienating by being honest about your feelings or opinions. Sure enough, when I approached my boss about my bonus, my desire to please almost led me to chicken out and soft-pedal what was true for me. This happens easily when we get caught in the crocodilian belief that we can only be honest *or* kind. How can we be both?

Practicing a role play, especially before high-stakes conversations, can help us become aware beforehand how our crocodile may tempt us to either brutal honesty or inauthentic niceness.

Before the conversation with my boss, my coach and I imagined an "Avoidant Crocodile Exchange" playing out, where I avoided the hard stuff by giving in to my desire to please. This exchange would have gone something as follows:

Me: "Hey, I want to speak with you about my bonus."
Harry: "Okay, sounds good."
Me: "It's a little bit less than I hoped for. Can you give me some more money?"
Harry: "Not sure, let me think about it."
Me: "Great, thanks so much, I'm so glad you're my boss."

This is all that would be said. Sounds good, no? Not so fast. Let's see what my "Aggressive Crocodile" had to say:

AGGRESSIVE CROCODILE TALK (What I'd think and feel, but wouldn't say.)	AVOIDANT CROCODILE EXCHANGE (What we'd actually say.)
This is going to be tough . . .	Me: Hey, I want to speak with you about my bonus.
You f–ed me over, cheap B..rd! @%*&%!*&*!	Harry: Okay, sounds good.
I have been slaving away to save the firm and this is all you can say! You're a terrible, bottom-line-obsessed leader!!	Me: It's a little bit less than I hoped for. Can you give me some more money?
There we go again, vague promises again. I am going to talk to your boss and get you fired! That will show you!!	Harry: Not sure, let me think about it.
You're beyond help. You are a waste of my time!!	Me: Great, thanks so much, I'm glad you're my boss.

Talk about a pseudoconversation!

When we look at conversations from either our aggressive or our avoidant crocodile, we may feel discouraged. *Stuck if we do and stuck if we don't.*

If you suppress your honest feelings in order to people-please you might as well not have the conversation. You'll have a *The Help*-like "nobody saying nothing and we still manage to have a conversation . . ." exchange. You are tiptoeing around your real opinions. This consumes a lot of energy. Yet many conversations end up being the avoidant type despite how unsatisfying it feels. Why? We are afraid of conflict. *Will our relationship survive our conflict?* our crocodiles worry.

In the end, our crocodiles will want to vent our feelings somewhere, so we start to gossip behind our boss or colleague's back, where, unfortunately, it has no chance of being productive. Have you ever noticed that the "real meeting" often happens after the meeting—in the hallway, or behind closed doors, one-on-one? The intention behind avoidance is innocent—we just want to be kind to the other person and to not hurt each other. Yet it's a dead-end road.

If we just blurt out our aggressive crocodile thinking instead, the results are possibly worse: we brutally damage our relationship with the other person (We), and chances are that any satisfaction that we gain is short-lived (I). By the time we've had time to reflect, we're probably not proud of what we did (I), and we realize that the outcome was a combination of ineffectiveness (It), distrust (We), and more anxiety (I). Our aggressive crocodiles are mean and reactive.

You may notice that both the avoidant and aggressive styles are driven by the first three fear families—scarcity, abandonment, and failure. They're both different strategies to cover up our fear. Either we don't say what we mean to protect a relationship or not expose our insecurities, or we aggressively blurt out our thoughts and feelings to defend ourselves, harming our relationship and ultimately ourselves.

Come to think of it, doesn't our conversational partner have an aggressive and an avoidant crocodile as well? Of course, they do. Fred Kofman, author of *Conscious Business*, taught me that this means we're stuck in a quatrilemma—a dilemma with four horns. We both have some not-so-pleasant thoughts that we don't want to share, and we both know the other person does too.

The Quatrilemma

What's in my Aggressive Crocodile column?	WHAT WILL HAPPEN IF I...		What about their Aggressive Crocodile column?
	...say my Avoidant Crocodile?	...say my Aggressive Crocodile?	
Judgment Aggression Desperation Fear Manipulation It's toxic.	I—Frustrated, anxious We—Distrust It—Ineffectiveness	I—Momentary relief, then regret We—Break It—Ineffectiveness	They have one. They know I have one.

Adapted from "Conscious Business" by Fred Kofman.

Stuck between these two unproductive modes of conversational style on each side, we may give up. Our crocodile concludes: *That's just the way it is around here. You can't talk about the real stuff.* It might even tell you, *and that's okay, because it's only work after all.* But is it okay? How many hours of our lives do we spend communicating at work? Probably the majority of it. Do we really want to throw all that time away, instead of devoting it to growth? It's up to us.

Luckily, Fred also taught a way to grow out of this bind through a story of three wise elders. The three wise elders are walking in the woods and they come across a tree. As it turns out, it's a poisonous tree. Says the first wise one: "Let's cut the poisonous tree down, so it can't hurt our children." The others think that's pretty wise, until the second wise one says: "Yes, but the tree is also beautiful, it's part of the forest and provides shade and nutrients to many creatures—let's not cut it down but put a fence around it, so we're protecting both our children and the tree." The other two think this is really clever until the third wise one says: "Yes, that's smart, however there are many of these trees here. If we put a fence around this one, we'll be spending the rest of our days on earth putting fences around poisonous trees. Why don't we distill the poison of the fruit into a vaccine that will immunize our children from disease?"

We can resolve the dilemma of communicating with honesty *and* kindness like the three wise ones solved their tree issue. Too often, we use the first approach, cutting down the tree—blurting out our aggressive thoughts thinking we'll feel better after getting them off our chest. *Get rid of this yucky feeling!* yells our crocodile. Being brutally honest may provide some short-term relief, but it ultimately leads to long-term harm. Alternatively, we may try fencing in our aggressive crocodilian toxicity by putting on our avoidant crocodilian mask and pretending everything is all okay. Remember the Good Boy/Good Girl crocodile from Chapter 3? *Let's play nice and pretend,* mumbles this crocodile. The trouble is that we'll be wearing a mask, being untruthful and in the end not trustworthy, as what we're saying is not about our truth, but about what will keep us safe.

"Why don't we distill the poison of the fruit into a vaccine that will immunize our children from disease?" asked the third wise one. Similarly, why don't we distill the energy that is pent up in our Aggressive Crocodiles into an honest, respectful, and effective way of expressing ourselves?

How? We get to do some inner distillation distinguishing our motivations from our fears, just like we did in Chapter 4 (Fear Families). It's our fear that fuels our toxic thoughts and feelings. There is something that we're trying to protect, something we care about that lies underneath our aggressive, toxic crocodilian feelings.

Asking ourselves *"What do I really care about?"* and looking to our heart for a response leads us in the direction of a truth that helps us connect more deeply with ourselves and the other. We can call this truth our "Authentic Truth," meaning the deepest truth *for us.* When we speak our Authentic Truth, conversations become fuel for growth where we connect with each other from the heart by means of our authentic expression. We grow because we both get to know more about what is true, learning from each other. When we use words that our heart gives us, we give a piece of our heart to the other. Then our words are an expression of love. Truth and love are two parts of the same coin. As soon as we enter this space, there's no room for either aggressive or avoidant impulses to dominate.

As I reflected on what I really cared about in my conversation with my boss, Harry, I realized that it was not really about the money, but about something much deeper, that spanned the three dimensions of consciousness, the "I," "We," and "It." I had given my all to creating new products and services for the firm, spending nights and weekends, and I had a deep desire to continue that work (the "I" dimension). I interpreted my small bonus as a sign that what I was doing wasn't really valued and therefore I wouldn't be able to do it with our firm for much longer. Also, I was concerned that Harry and I hadn't communicated expectations clearly (the "We" dimension). And lastly I believed that creating a new business for our firm was important for its longevity, and so I felt we needed to incentivize ourselves to pursue it (the "It" dimension).

Looking at different dimensions of consciousness—the self ("I"), our relationships with others ("We"), and effectiveness with our tasks ("It")—helps to distill an Authentic Truth that is inclusive and whole. Deeply looking into these three dimensions helps us grow in our awareness of what our heart longs for and ultimately what we really are about, which is always something bigger than our aggressive crocodile is focused on.

How do we know we have found our Authentic Truth? We can do a litmus test: is it honest, kind, and effective? It's honest when it resonates deeply within our heart, without crocodilian reactivity. Peace comes over us as we find honesty. It's kind when we can see the perspective of the other person, while we think of ours and feel appreciation and care for them. And it's effective if it opens the door for new possibilities to be, think, and act together differently.

One way to help purify our Authentic Truth is to hold it both firmly and lightly, with Yang and Yin energy in equal amounts. Firmly in Yang assertiveness, as it is the deepest truth we have realized, and lightly in Yin care, appreciating the other person may have an entirely different perspective that is equally valid.

To scrub our Authentic Truth from any crocodilian judgments, we want to be aware of the difference between mutually observable facts and our interpretations and opinions about them. For example "The bonus is low," was my interpretation, while saying "the bonus was $15,000," is speaking about mutually observable facts. We can consciously differentiate our observations and interpretations in our expression by using a simple formula:

"I saw X, that's why I thought Y; what do you think?"

Putting it all together, I ended up sharing my Authentic Truth with my boss by telling him the following: "Harry, what I really care about is our relationship, doing the work I love, and doing work that serves the success of our firm. When I saw the bonus of $15,000, I thought, 'wow, that's low—does Harry value what we're doing?' The low bonus makes me question that. Does that make sense to you?" Harry responded that it did. I continued. "I also remembered a conversation we had on January 10 of last year about incentives. Looking at my notes from then, I understood that three new projects sold for this new service would give me $60,000 in bonus. Did I misunderstand?" Harry responded this time that he had a different recollection from that conversation—that it was a conversation where I had proposed the incentive structure and he had suggested we keep it open. At first when I heard this I was shocked. I distinctly remembered an agreement of sorts. Then, when I thought about it more, I realized that I had never made a firm request to agree on the incentive structure. This was a huge growth opportunity to assert myself with more Yang energy in the future. I let Harry know that I was beginning to realize where the disconnect was.

The combination of my setting a clear intention for our conversation and then moving beyond my aggressive and avoidant selves into a more authentic truth had freed me to make new discoveries about what our conflict was really about. Suddenly Harry wasn't the enemy, he was just someone I had had a miscommunication with.

LEAD WITH HEART-BASED INQUIRY

Harry didn't need any prompting to share his Authentic Truth. He shared it right after I had shared mine and he clearly had thought about it. This often happens; when we become truthful while staying caring, it magnetizes the owl in the other person to come forward. And our care calms any crocodiles that may want to hijack our partner's mind.

Harry told me, "Hylke, I also care about you and our relationship. And I value what you have done and how important it is for the firm and for your career. My concern is that I haven't seen you create buy-in from the team, so the new business is you for the most part at this point. And, yes, I also realize we haven't been clear with each other. I know I wasn't because I wanted to be nice. What do you think?"

I saw that Harry did have a point. I had avoided the tough conversation about accountability just as he had. And I had assumed others wouldn't be interested in what I was doing, so I worked independently—an old croc pattern of mine.

Not all our conversation partners will share their Authentic Truth so readily. Staying in presence, in touch with our conscious, unconditional intention, will help us to stay accepting of where the other person is— especially when they do not share as much as we would like them to. If we have expectations for how much the other person shares in return for our honesty, we are coercing them, implicitly or explicitly. And we unconsciously put blocks on our own share by doing so. "I only share if you share" leads to more pseudoconversation. Instead, we resolve to stay true to our unconditional intention. We're not there to convince, control, cajole, or manipulate— these are Lower Yang and Yin strategies. When we notice these crocodiles, we can see it as our next Growth Instant. Communicating Authentic Truth with Conscious, Unconditional Intention doesn't prevent us from running into those defensive or protective crocodiles again in the course of our conversation. When we notice them, we simply recommit to our intention and not give in to these urges. Instead of letting our crocodiles do the talking, we can respond with care and open our hearts to our conversation partner's truth. The more we practice this, the easier it becomes over time.

This type of opening, which we call Heart-based Inquiry, is an art. We empty ourselves completely from our expectations, our fears, and other mental patterns, staying supremely disinterested in them, being fully present to what the other person has to say. We keep our questions simple: *"what do you think?"* and *"how does that land with you?"* and *"what do you really care about?"* can help deepen the exchange. Questions like "don't you think that . . . ?" or "If you look at the facts, what do you conclude?" can lead to needless drama and combativeness.

Truth sharing is just that—it's not about convincing the other person of our point of view or enlisting them to validate our experience. When I give myself the freedom to be who I am and express that, I am only completely free when I also see the other person as completely free to be and express who they are. During such an unconditional sharing of truth, we often notice resonance with each other and find a deeper connection.

When Gandhi visited Britain in 1931, he spoke with the textile millworkers in Lancashire, thousands of whom had been thrown out of work after a downturn in demand after Gandhi led a boycott of foreign textiles in favor of home-spun cloth as a way to oppose British rule. British officials warned Gandhi not to go, fearful of the violence he might face from the masses. Gandhi spoke his Authentic Truth to them as follows:

"Please, listen to me for just a few minutes. Give me a chance to present our point of view, and then, if you like, condemn me and my people. You tell me that three million people are out of employment here, have been out of employment for several months. In my country, three hundred million people are unemployed at least six months in every year. You say there are days when you get only bread and butter for your dinner. But these people often go for days on end without any food at all."

The millworkers' authentic response to Gandhi's firm, fearless yet caring sharing of his truth astounded the British officials. Instead of attacking him, the workers expressed their full support and cheered him on—the very leader who had brought about their unemployment.

When we share our truth authentically and open our hearts to another's, completely detached from outcomes, we grow in self-respect and may inspire others to do the same. And yet the conversation is not complete with sharing only, even though it can be seen as the most important and daring part.

MOVING FROM SHARING TO RESONANT COCREATION

Once all parties in a conversation have spoken their Authentic Truth and are rooted in heart-based inquiry, the ball really gets rolling. As we share our truths, we enter the world of possibility, exploring: "What if we are both right? Then what can we create together?"

Harry and I entered this part of the conversation by moving the question of the bonus to the side in order to have a broader discussion around my role. We concluded that given my passion there was a space for me to give the new business 100 percent and also, that I needed to start thinking about what I really wanted to do. As I did, I discovered that my interest in newness in business was driven primarily by my interest in transformation in general, and more specifically personal transformation. In the end, this conversation was one of the whispers besides my insomnia that helped me realize I had to change course—that's how powerful these moments of joint reflection can become.

This part of the conversation can energize us as we grow out of defensiveness (the aggressive crocodile) and appeasement (the avoidant croc) to a place of truth and cocreation of new possibilities. This means change!

Our status quo–seeking crocodiles will, of course, try to sabotage: by being aggressive about it, *I want to change you* (so I don't have to), or by being avoidant, *I don't want change.* Grounded in the owl of our conscious, unconditional intention, we practice instead, *I have the heart to share my truth* and *I am willing to listen to your truth.* Then we enter a space where we both are *willing to grow together, through relating truthfully.* Cocreation questions like the ones below can help us to stay in this place of truthfulness and cocreativity:

- What if we are both right?

- Which goals do we have in common? How can we work on those? What creative solutions can we imagine?

- What if we both grew from this; then how would we see each other? Then, how would we approach this?

- What if there is no conflict?

- What are some of the ways we can express care for each other and for the issue at hand?

- How would people we both admire approach this conversation?

Gandhi learned about heart-based cocreation early on in his career when he was still a barrister in South Africa. Working on his first major case, he persuaded both parties to settle out of court. Looking back later, Gandhi reflected: "I had learnt the true practice of law, I had learnt to find out the better side of human nature and to enter men's hearts. I realized that the true function of a lawyer was to unite parties riven asunder." We can all make this our main goal.

MAKE A COURAGEOUS COMMITMENT

For there to be both inner and outer growth from a conversation, we need an awareness of the possibilities for cocreation, and we need to do something about it too.

It's like that old riddle: Four frogs sat on a log and three decided to jump into the lake. How many are in the water? Sounds easy, but it's a trick question. We're not sure, as just making the decision doesn't mean that any of them have jumped yet. Similarly, we need to get to a place of jumping into life at the end of our conversation. At this point, the fears of failure, uncertainty, abandonment, and hurt may kick in again. This is why, instead of giving in to crocodilian fixes like *let's come back to this later* or *let's leave it open,* we can look for something to commit to now, however small that next step is. Helpful questions we can use to elicit commitment, in ourselves first, are:

- How do I intend to grow?
- What request do I make?
- What do I promise?
- If I became twice as courageous, what would I commit to?
- What is the smallest yet most powerful next step I can agree to now?

Courage and commitment are closely related. When we commit to something, we step into the unknown. Our crocodilian minds tend to resist this, coming up with countless reasons to not do something new in order to stay in our comfort zones. Yet our heart often knows when it's time to act. It nudges us to commit fearlessly.

In my conversation with my boss, I grew in self-awareness. I found out that what I really cared about was not my bonus but my fulfillment in life: doing the work of transformation and growth. Harry grew in discovering his freedom to hold me and others accountable more firmly. He learned that he did not need to hold back in fear of damaging a relationship. I requested from Harry that we have monthly one-on-ones to build our alignment. And I promised to do a deep inner inquiry about my life's calling and share the results with him.

I stayed true to my promise—three months later I chose to transition careers, left the firm, and moved from consulting into culture, team, and executive development.

Now looking back, I realize that my concern about others not valuing my pursuit of new frontiers for the company pointed to my own longing and doubt about how I was spending my life's energy. But just this realization wouldn't have been enough if I hadn't taken the step of investigating my goals and then acting to make changes. Conversation opens up space for us to discover new possibilities; next, it's up to us to act on it.

THE TRUE PURPOSE OF CONVERSATION

When every conversation is held in an atmosphere of growth, there are no "good" or "bad" conversations, only conversations that may be more or less effective. When we keep our heart open, we are bound to discover more commonality with the other—how we are one in presence. This may be the ultimate purpose of every conversation that ever was and will ever be. In true conversations we grow together—first and foremost in our capacity to love. As others share themselves, it's our opportunity to accept all of it, even when it's uncomfortable. Our unconditional acceptance of the other is presence in action, as presence includes everything that simply "is," including our likes and dislikes.

Through this acceptance comes understanding; with understanding, every conversation turns into a gathering of the hearts in truth, where we get to take care of each other and cocreate our world in the best possible ways we know how to.

FIELDWORK

1. What is your weakest link? Select one.

   A. Conscious Intention

   B. Authentic Expression

   C. Heart-based Inquiry

   D. Resonant Cocreation

   E. Courageous Commitment

2. Think of the greatest conversations you've ever had. What made them great? Choose as many elements from the list below that resonate with you. Also add other elements that are not listed here. How can you practice the elements you picked more in conversations you have upcoming?

   A. Honesty

   B. Respect

   C. Lightness

   D. Focus

   E. Presence

   F. Precision

   G. Commitment

   H. Progress

   I. Provocative

   J. Challenging

   K. Compassionate

3. Think of a conversation that you need to have with someone but have postponed, dread happening, or feel anxiety around. The more juice it has, the more feelings you have about this conversation, the more learning will happen once you finally go through with it.

   Who is this conversation with?

   What is it about?

4. Why might you not want this conversation to happen? What is the crocodile saying about the conversation?

5. Write down all of the judgments that the crocodilian mind comes up with when you think about the person that you need to have this conversation with. Write down all the pettiness that you notice in your thoughts about that person, and how they "make you feel" about yourself.

6. What is your conscious or unconscious crocodilian goal for this conversation?

7. Play out this conversation in your mind, and write out your Avoidant Crocodile words and your Aggressive-Reactive Crocodile thoughts and feelings.

AGGRESSIVE CROCODILE TALK (What I'd think and feel, but wouldn't say.)	AVOIDANT CROCODILE EXCHANGE (What we'd actually say.)

8. What is your highest intention for this conversation? Remember to address the "I," (self) "We," (other/relationship) and "It," (task/effectiveness) as you create your intention. Who do you aspire to be, no matter the outcome?

9. Think deeply, past the issue at hand. Deep down, what do you really care about? What is your Authentic Truth?

10. What will you say to the other person that expresses your intentions and your Authentic Truth?

11. Which of your crocodilian judgments and expectations can get in your way, as you open your heart to deeply listen to your conversation partner?

12. What is something that you can anticipate committing to?

13. How are you growing?

CHAPTER 8

Growing Others—Coaching One-on-One

*"We should not hurry, we should not be impatient, but
we should confidently obey the eternal rhythm."*
—Nikos Kazantzakis, *"Zorba the Greek"*

GIVING BACK—COACHING OTHERS

THINK OF A PERSON who has helped you grow significantly in your life. This person can be a formal coach, or an informal one—a colleague, a family member, significant other, friend, teacher, or anyone else who has helped you on your way. What do you feel when you think about them? Maybe gratitude, love, inspiration, peace, or even awe? Most of us deeply value those who have helped us grow. Now think about how you have helped others grow. For which people are you a formal or informal coach? Go sit in their seat for a moment. They probably really value your help as well. And you may have found helping them fulfilling as well. We value learning with others.

Even if you've never had a professional coach or even an athletic coach, your life is filled with people who have nevertheless been coaches in some way. This chapter is dedicated to all the men and women who have ever coached me. It's a long and incomplete list, and some people I only have a vague recollection of. First there were my parents, my siblings, then my music teacher, my elementary school principal, my teacher in Classical Languages, my teacher in Dutch, my physical education teachers, my economics teacher, my first landlady, my consulting mentor, my vocal coach, my opera coach, my executive coaches, my therapists, my colleagues at Towers Perrin, SDG, Co-Creation Partners, Axialent, Constancee, and Growth Leaders Network, countless clients, my friends, my partner, and last but not least my spiritual teachers for the last fifteen years. And I could easily list another one thousand people who have crossed my path and taught me something that has made me who I am today.

We all have lists like this, spanning across the course of our lives. It's not only people who can show us how to grow, either. All of the places that have hosted me around the world have played a part too, as they may have for you. Each place has taught me something different. From Dutch resilience to Australian lightness; from Italian beauty to Argentine fire; from English ritual to Icelandic vastness; and from New York efficiency to Seattle self-honesty.

We help each other grow constantly, whether we are aware of it or not. Sometimes it can simply be our presence, or a passing glance, that can stir something in someone else. Whether you'd realized it or not, the world is a deeply connected field of coaches and coachees. We are surrounded by people and places that help us grow.

When are we helping others grow? Maybe the better question to ask is *when are we not?* When we are around others our mind-sets and behaviors will impact them, whether we are aware of it or not. If we are leading an organization or team, this may be even more apparent—we are always helping others grow: giving them feedback, mentoring, setting an example, working on challenging projects together, and directly sitting down to have a coaching conversation.

We may find ourselves more and more drawn to the idea of coaching others explicitly as we experience the benefits of growth ourselves. At some point, we may feel compelled to give back. On the path of growing more into who we really are, we come naturally to a place of wanting to share our path with others—helping them grow. At least that has been my experience. I loved mentoring people before I had ever received any formal coaching. Once I saw how my work, and the rest of my life, started to shift working with executive coaches, it wasn't long before I wanted to help others in the same way, applying some of the coaching tools I was learning. For example, I still remember how excited I was about discovering the power of being conscious of my intentions. It wasn't long before I started discussing with my colleagues, *What is the highest intention we can have for this conversation?*

In the preceding chapters, we have focused on our own growth. Now we are shifting our attention to helping others grow—coaching them to grow more into who they really are, unlearning their crocodiles. We will explore how we can do so skillfully. To begin, let's first define more clearly what we mean by coaching.

DEFINING GROWTH LEADERSHIP COACHING

The word *coaching* comes from the Hungarian word *kocsi*, which means carriage—the vehicle that was drawn by horses to transport you to your destination. Similarly, as a coach, we help others move toward their goal. *Growth Leadership* coaching is a particular style of coaching. As a Growth Leadership coach, we focus on helping people on their journey of self-discovery. Our destination is a moving target—it's about helping others find out more about who they really are, which is an endless journey. And it's about helping people to find ways to act and serve from that more authentic place. Most importantly, as a Growth Leadership coach, we help people discover their fire for learning about themselves, so they will continue their growth journeys long after we have crossed paths with them. In the rest of this book, when we speak about a coach, we are referring to a Growth Leadership coach. A few more words to define coaching follow.

Coaching, Mentoring, and Holding Accountable

Coaching is different from mentoring, giving feedback, and holding accountable, even though all of these roles are about helping others grow. When we mentor we share our experience with our mentee, having walked the path before them. We give them advice, and share stories and perspective relevant to their challenges and goals. When we give someone feedback, we share data about their behavior and our interpretations of their impact on their environment. *When I saw you do X, the impact was Y on me, and I think Z on others, does that make sense to you?* we may say. Lastly, when we hold someone accountable, we share our standards for performance and let people know how they are doing compared to that standard.

Remember the Stages of Growth we discussed in Chapter 1: Unconscious-Unskilled, Conscious-Unskilled, Conscious-Skilled, and

Unconscious-Skilled? As a mentor, we help people along all four stages; when we give feedback, we help a person become more aware, moving from Unconscious-Skilled to Conscious-Skilled. When we hold someone accountable, we first help a person become aware, moving from Unconscious-Unskilled to Conscious-Unskilled, and second, we help them consider their choices to become Conscious-Skilled in an area where they are not yet performing. *Are you willing to change some things to improve your performance and meet this standard?* is one question we can ask to encourage accountability.

In the coaching role, we help the person through all four stages, like mentoring. The difference with mentoring is that we help the person find their *own* answers, not giving them any advice. In its purest form, when we coach, we also don't give the person feedback or hold them accountable. We may share feedback from others, but we will not share our own. That way we make sure the coaching is about the coachee's process, not our own.

Consider the difference between holding a person accountable and coaching. Holding a person accountable can lead to letting the person go from the team if the standards are not being met. In coaching, we remain engaged with the coachee, whether they are improving or not. Remember that the coachee likely is making progress—we may just not have the eyes to see it. Who knows what journey the coachee needs to go through to really get to know their crocodiles before they can tame them? I am grateful to my coaches for not forcing me to let go of my crocodilian attachments—e.g., to money, status, or relationship—before I was ready for that. Yes, they kept asking me who I really wanted to be and what my values were, but they never told me what to do—to quit a job, project, or relationship. I had to find out for myself that money and status ultimately weren't fulfilling for me and that there was something else I really wanted to prioritize. Had I been forced to change before I was ready, I likely would still have doubts about having made the right choice of leaving money and status behind, because I hadn't allowed myself to fully see through their illusory nature. By experiencing both the euphoria and the emptiness associated with these attachments, I came to my own conclusions. I came to see something about these two that I have never been able to unsee: that they really weren't my values, but that they were borrowed ones—ideas I had copied from my environment.

Before you continue reading this chapter, think about a person you are coaching, formally or informally. What is their name? This can be yourself. What is their challenge? What may they be thinking and feeling? Hold your coachee in mind as you learn about the coaching tools that follow. When you apply the tools, you will likely absorb them much more deeply.

How can we be as effective as possible as a coach? It starts with the *conditio sine qua non* (indispensable condition) of coaching—safety. No safety, no coaching.

UNCONDITIONAL LOVE AS THE GROUND OF COACHING

What do we mean when we say we must create a safe space for our coachee? We are speaking about being with the coachee in the energy of unconditional love. The rest follows. This is a tall order that seems simple and yet, as it turns out, is challenging to implement at times.

It's easier to describe what unconditional love is not than what it is. The opposite of unconditional love, or "nonlove" in a coaching setting, is the coach trying to obtain something from the coachee, whether it is a result, approval, or a good feeling. On the other hand, coaching with unconditional love is about selfless giving, without agenda. Where unconditionality helps to have more truthful conversations, it's the precondition for a coaching relationship.

As coaches, we must disconnect from the ups and downs that come up inside of us during a coaching session. By doing this, we put ourselves in a mental space where we can empathize with but not judge the ups and downs of the coachee. It's a rare person who provides such a service to another individual—great therapists or spiritual guides come to mind. And yet, providing another with the environment to be exactly who they are without our interference is an absolute requirement for coaching. A coaching session is a meditation on the self. The coachee gains familiarity with herself by giving undivided attention to herself in the coaching session.

The primary function of the Growth Leadership coach is to be a clean mirror, and to question the beliefs and ideas coachees have that might stand in the way of their aspirations. The coach honors the coachee's learning process by not forcing answers and insights. The coachee sets the intention and the agenda, and the coach guides.

Unconditional love is also about never trying to change or rush a coachee—this would go against the natural rhythm of learning and may hinder someone's progress. If the coachee is not interested in learning, then no learning needs to occur. If the coachee wants to work at a different pace, then that will be the pace. Growth can't be forced.

Take a moment to read this excerpt from Nikos Kazantzakis's *Zorba the Greek*:

> "One morning . . . I discovered a cocoon in a bark of a tree. Just as the butterfly was making a hole in the case preparing to come out. I waited a while, but it was too long to appearing and I was impatient. I bent over and breathed on it to warm it. I warmed it as quickly as I could and the miracle began to happen in front of my eyes, faster than life. The case opened, the butterfly started slowly crawling out and I shall never forget my horror when I saw how its wings were folded back and crumpled; the wretched butterfly tried with its whole body to unfold them. Bending over I tried to help it with my breath. In vain.
>
> It needed to be hatched out patiently and the unfolding of the wings should be a gradual process in the sun. Now it was too late. My breath had forced the butterfly to appear all crumpled, before its time. It struggled desperately and, a few seconds later, died in the palm of my hand.
>
> That little body is, I do believe, the greatest weight I have on my conscience. For I realize today that it is a mortal sin to violate the great laws of nature. We should not hurry, we should not be impatient, but we should confidently obey the eternal rhythm."

As coaches, we remind ourselves that we are already whole. We all are presence, love, peace, and joy in our essence. Our life's journey is about discovering that—each person at their own pace, on their own path, with their own approach. It's not up to us to fix someone else, because there is nothing to fix. The only thing we are there to do is to hold up the clean mirror of presence. Then we guide and watch the coachee move through the four stages of growth, over and over again, sometimes multiple times in one session—becoming aware (moving from Unconscious- to Conscious-Unskilled), making a commitment (becoming Conscious-Skilled), and practicing the new consciousness with courage and humility (steadily working toward Unconscious-Skilled).

Coaching to LOVE or to FINISH?

To remind us to practice unconditional love in coaching, we can repeat a mantra to ourselves: *"Letting Others Voluntarily Evolve"*—in short, L.O.V.E. That is our intention as we coach someone. To coach someone with LOVE is to honor who they are now, where they are now, and how they are moving through their journey. It's about their journey, not ours.

Our crocodile has a very different idea about coaching. It wants to rescue, fix, manipulate, and convince the other. *"Fixing It Now, I, Super Hero"*—in short, FINISH—is its mantra. *I fix you so I feel better about myself,* it thinks.

Think again about someone you are coaching, formally or informally. What would it be like to step even more into a *Letting Others Voluntarily Evolve* mind-set? How will this help you coach them more effectively? Without the burden of having to fix them, you may find yourself daring to ask more challenging questions—undeterred by the prospect of not knowing their answers. You may have more patience, no longer needing to rush toward an outcome. And you may have greater ability to empathize, no longer worried that their feelings are problems you should fix. A LOVE-mind-set can be challenging, patient, and kind, all at the same time. A LOVE-mind-set is both Yang fierce and Yin empathizing.

Now ask yourself: What *Fixing It Now, I, Super Hero* crocodilian attachments do I have? How much am I trying to fix others? How much am I in a hurry to show results, so that I look good as a coach? How much is coaching about satisfying my needs for money, approval, and self-esteem? What questions am I not asking because my FiNISH-crocodile thinks it too risky? How am I pushing the coachee to satisfy my FiNISH-agenda? It's completely understandable that we have some FiNISH-crocodiles swimming in our system. It's just that it becomes that much more important that we name and tame them, as they now also directly impact the people we are coaching.

Reflect again on the great mentors and coaches—whether formal or not—that have guided you. What were their primary qualities? Chances are that they made you feel safe, and that they practiced nonjudgment as one of their core qualities. They were holding the intention of unconditional love for you. No safety means no coaching. Once we have established safety, we have created the conditions for greater self-honesty and self-care, to help the coachee grow more into who they really are—the primary intention of Growth Leadership coaching.

5QS OF GROWTH LEADERSHIP COACHING

Safety, unconditional love, is one of what I like to call the 5Qs, or the five quotients of great coaching. We honed these Qs together when I was working at Co-Creation Partners. Each of these elements are qualities that I have found helpful in developing my own coaching capacities, and those of others. Think of them as the meters on your internal coaching dashboard. Take a look at them and ask, How am I doing on this dimension? What is my opportunity to improve? Where do I see a red light that tells me I need to pay attention—and take some time for inner maintenance now?

Reflect again on the person you are coaching, as you look at this 5Q coaching dashboard. Where is your strength as a coach? Where are your opportunities to evolve the quality of your being so you can be of even greater service?

MQ—Meaning Quotient

Meaning Quotient (MQ) is the first of our quotients, and is about having the capacity to inspire the other to see the greater meaning of their current station in life. Purpose and meaning, besides unconditional love, can be seen as the greatest sources of energy within us.

We help coachees access their sense of meaning by inquiring how they intend to apply the unconditional love that they are in the world. We can ask *How will you serve from your station now?* as Yvonne Higgins Leach, the former PR director for Boeing, would ask herself at the beginning of every work day. It's about applying the essence that we are—presence, unconditional love—to the service of others. Another way to say that is, we help coachees discover their authentic contribution in life—what Gene White might call her purpose. To help infuse their journey with authentic meaning, we can ask them any of the following questions:

- What would you really like to see happen?
- How do you intend to contribute to yourself, your family, your team, your organization, your customers and partners, and society at large?
- Taking a step back, what is the gift of this challenge in your life's journey?
- How can you approach this challenge in a way that reflects your essence, your values, what you really stand for?
- How will you respond to this challenge in ways that will help you feel fulfilled and proud?

Inspiring questions help a person step out of the box of their habitual thinking. They help us move from the head to the heart, from where we can see meaning. In the head, we may be too boxed in by crocodilian fear to see clearly. From the heart, we see possibilities.

Then a challenging sales goal turns into an opportunity to share the benefits of our product more widely, to access more of our inner resourcefulness, and to create a higher performing team. The conflict with a colleague becomes an opportunity to become more clear about what we really stand for and develop our Yang-muscle, and to find out more what the other really wants—extending our Yin. A sense of being overwhelmed is transformed into an opportunity to create clarity about priorities, and to learn to say no (Yang). And a budget crunch turns into an opportunity to streamline activities and become even more focused on what matters to us (Yang).

With the eyes of meaning, we discover the bigger context and how each challenge is really an opportunity to grow and give more. When we stay in our limited crocodilian frame, we miss out on the adventure and the inspiration that larger meaning provides us.

EQ—Emotional Quotient

The second quotient, our Emotional Quotient (EQ), refers to our capacity as a coach to work skillfully with feelings, ours and theirs, by:

1.   Regulating our own emotions during a coaching session (so they don't get in the way, but rather encourage the coachee if needed);

2.   Empathizing with the coachee's emotions, without getting entangled;

3.   Helping them to gain mastery over their emotions.

Often, a vast portion of the energies of unconditional love and meaning get chewed up by reactive emotions in a coachee, like anger, anxiety, or shame. As a coach, we first must make sure we don't collude with our coachee. When the coachee is upset about something and blames someone else or themselves, we don't help them by also getting upset and placing blame. That is putting kerosene on the fire thinking we put it out. We are simply distracting the coachee from their inner work. We are joining them in their fruitless downward spiral of thinking and feeling *Why is this happening to me?* With emotional detachment, we are able to stay in a Growth Leadership mind-set and ask *How is this happening for you? How are you growing through this?* We don't provide the coachee with an ally for any crocodilian emotional state. Remember we want to remain a *clean* mirror.

This doesn't mean we ignore the coachee's emotions. We do empathize with them, without getting lost in them. "Emotions are terrible masters and great advisors," taught Fred Kofman. The coach taps into the emotions of the coachee to understand their inner landscape. Then, the coach helps the coachee gain awareness and subsequent control over their response to their emotions.

When Mary Jane showed up for our coaching call, she looked very stressed out. Her face was ashen, her eyes hard, and her jaw was clenched. She had just been told that her colleague Steve was leaving the company because he no longer wanted to work there with her leading the team. I asked her how she was feeling. She said she was angry at Steve and blamed herself for not being a better manager. When we explored where these feelings were in her body, she found that her chest felt very tight and that she felt a knot in her belly. I asked her to get in touch with the contractions in her chest and her belly and inquire more deeply, staying focused on the energy in the chest. We ended up applying the questions of The Tree (see Chapter 6). What is this painful feeling in the chest saying? What may be a belief that underlies these thoughts? What is the underlying fear? It turned out that underneath the anger lay a lot of sadness, and shame. Mary Jane was sad about not having managed to create a better relationship with Steve and felt shame and fear that she had done something wrong, that she had failed. *Ah, this may be the underlying crocodile that makes this so hard for her,* I remember thinking. When looking at this fear a bit more, we found that Mary Jane had been deeply afraid of failing her whole life. She came from a poor family that was evicted from their apartment multiple times. The first time they had ended up on the street with all of their belongings, Mary Jane was still a little girl. She still remembered going to school the next day and how ashamed she felt. Her classmates had completed the nightmare by mocking her for being homeless. Mary Jane learned that failure, in this case of not paying the rent on time, has severe consequences and is something to be ashamed of. Forty years later, her self-shaming crocodile took over when she heard that Steve was quitting. It paralyzed her. When we looked at this together, Mary Jane learned that the shame she was feeling now had nothing to do with Steve, but was an old tape replaying, of the anxious little girl who had to show up for school after having spent her first night on the street as a homeless person. *Is it absolutely true that you should feel ashamed that Steve is leaving?* we explored, doing The Work (see Chapter 6). "No," responded Mary Jane. She exhaled. *How do you react when you believe the thought that you should feel ashamed that Steve is leaving?* "I become paralyzed, keep going through my mind all that I did wrong, am unable to talk to Steve or my other colleagues, because I am afraid of what they will think of me, and I am totally unable to get any work done," reflected Mary Jane. When she did the "turnarounds" her eyes lit up. "I should be ashamed that I leave me" was the first one. Mary Jane saw that she was abandoning herself by listening to her "shame crocodile," which didn't leave her any mental capacity to take care of her own well-being and that of the team. "I should be happy for Steve that he is leaving" was a second one. Mary Jane saw that it was not her job to know what's best for Steve—that was Steve's. Steve was taking care of Steve. That was something to be happy about. The third turnaround was "I should be happy for me that Steve is leaving." Steve taking care of Steve was a reminder for Mary Jane to do so, as well, for herself and for the rest of her team.

Had I given in to her anxiety and anger crocodiles—giving them control over our coaching conversation—no real learning could have taken place. Staying firmly grounded in unconditional love, detached from any emotional turbulence, we empathize with the coachee's emotions without getting entangled in them. We inquire into them and discover together what crocodilian beliefs are behind these reactive feelings and thoughts, and we help the coachee find out more of who they really are when they free themselves from these "monsters underneath the bed."

We want to be able to clearly sense the coachee's emotions—they are "advisors" that point to valuable growth opportunities. Author Stephen Covey paraphrased Viktor Frankl (the psychiatrist and Holocaust survivor we met in Chapter 2), saying that "Between stimulus and response lies the freedom to choose." As coaches, we help coachees access that freedom by being a reflective surface, which the coachee can choose to look into or look away from. When coachees look into our clean mirror, they may discover what emotions they are running from, and how these emotions can be a valuable doorway to releasing crocodilian beliefs that limit their freedom and inspiration.

IQ—Intelligence Quotient

Besides MQ and EQ, we will need to have high IQ, or Intelligence Quotient, to be impactful. For a coach, IQ is about having a process that draws on precision, practicality, and clarity.

Coaching is a craft, like all else. To cook a good meal, we must be familiar with our ingredients and recipe. A high coaching IQ provides the coachee with a sense of comfort that they are in expert hands. A coaching session has a beginning, middle, and end. A great coach knows how to help a coachee go through these stages in one session without forcing anything. We will learn a process to do this, called GROW, later in this chapter.

One great way to create precision and clarity is to ask the coachee for specific examples. When I am in a coaching session with my coach, she will ask me, "Okay, so tell me about a challenge that is happening right now. You say you're feeling anxious. What specifically are you anxious about?"

Whatever I am anxious about points to a crocodilian belief I am holding. As soon as I have my hands on this crocodile, it becomes possible to release it. To tame the crocodile, we have to name it first. When we ask questions probing into the reality that the coachee perceives, we work like carvers, slowly freeing the statue from the stone, the owl from the crocodiles.

And to keep it practical, we help the coachee apply their learnings right then and there. *What are three ways you will practice this?* we may ask at the end of our coaching session. *What do you commit to doing differently now?*

NQ—Intuition Quotient

Another core quality of coaching is our NQ, or Intuition Quotient— our ability to provoke introspection that helps the coachee make new connections and uncover patterns that they didn't see before. We do so by being very tuned in to the coachee, knowing intuitively what questions to ask. Intuition helps the coach guide the conversation; in our gut we will be able to feel out which of the many topics that the coachee may have brought up will provide the richest field for learning now. Then, through intuition, we form our questions.

Highly intuitive coaches will sometimes begin a question without knowing the end of it, simply based on the feeling that is coming through. When a coach has high NQ, she can help the coachee access his NQ as well. One thing that my coach Jonelle Reynolds does very well is intuit what is going on with me. She provides a nonjudgmental space in which I can share my story. She doesn't have any questions prepared as we start our session. After she has listened for a while, she'll ask me a question that goes right to the heart of the matter. "On a scale from one to ten, how much do you love yourself?" was the first thing she ever asked me. Lack of self-love lay at the heart of the challenge I was facing at the time, and the journey to love myself more fully is one I continue to be on every day.

A great way to start developing our intuition is by contemplating *what does this moment say?* Or, if that doesn't resonate, *what does my heart say?* Remember that intuition is associated with lower brain frequencies theta and delta. If we want to develop our intuition, we need to slow down; and we can use meditation, conscious breathing, contemplation, and being in nature to do so. Softening the gaze, looking with soft eyes, can also help access more of our intuitive wisdom.

A teacher of mine once said, "It's difficult to be simple and it's simple to be difficult." When we access intuition, we start seeing the essence of things easily and effortlessly—and we discover that often, it's simple. Our crocodilian minds complicate. The crocodiles worry *But what about this and what about that?* to make sure we have covered all our bases and won't be surprised. While the crocodiles scurry around, our owls sit back, and ask *What is at the core of the issue?* and let the insights emerge naturally. Crocodiles force, while owls focus and observe.

CQ—Contentment Quotient

The last quotient we call CQ, or Contentment Quotient, to remind us that we are unconditional love at heart and that we can extend that to the coachee, no matter what. We manifest unconditional love in a coaching conversation by creating a safe space, where we LOVE—Let Others Voluntarily Evolve. When we rest in unconditional love, we are naturally confident, content, and cheerful, as we are resting in our owl essence away from any crocodilian interference. In that place we extend, by sheer presence, a field of acceptance and love that will naturally nourish our coachees and help them grow. We are content, because deep down we know that *all is well,* we all are unconditional love, no matter what is happening and how our crocodiles feel about it. We have all experienced people who light up the room in this way.

We cultivate CQ by being mindful, letting our hearts fill with the love and beauty of the present moment, staying supremely disinterested in all the crocodilian movements on the screen of our awareness—our own and others' mental and emotional stories. Paradoxically, as we stay supremely disinterested, a great intimacy with our surroundings emerges. The boundary between you and me stops being so hard—it softens and we start seeing the oneness in all things.

According to Gandhi's biographer, Eknath Easwaran: "When Gandhi succeeded in taking off his mask and 'making himself zero' through many years of living for others rather than himself, he found that what he had eliminated from his personality was only his separateness, his selfishness, his fear. What remained was the love and fearlessness that had been hidden there all the time." Coaching is a great way to practice the way of zero, the way of unconditional love.

Another way we can practice unconditional love is by seeing the sweet, innocent child in each and every person. Think about the people you are working with. Imagine them at age one. See their little faces, their eyes, their innocence, their wonder, and also maybe the beginnings of fear as they were getting concerned with *"Will I get fed on time?"* and *"Will someone be there when I wake up?"* See how they, just like you, deep down just want to be happy. See how you and they are very similar. Contemplate this for a few minutes and notice how your feelings toward others may become gentler. Your heart may be opening to them, and you may touch into a deeper sense that *all is well*. By doing this practice, we can learn to feel love for colleagues, even those that irk us; for strangers that we see walking down the street; for people who have hurt us; and for anyone and everyone else that we look at in this innocent light. When we see that everyone is innocent, and that every person and creature is doing the best that they know how, our hearts open to love all beings without condition. In that space, it's easy to stay a clean mirror, to LOVE, detached from our agendas.

50 Quality of Our Being

Our Quality of Being—consisting of the five quotients combined—is the biggest lever we have to transform a coaching session into a Growth Instant. Imagine walking into a coaching session where you are inspired (MQ)— even the twinkle in your eyes may help the coachee see their challenge as an invitation to grow. Now think about someone you coach who is anxious. Notice how they may relax as you meet them with the equanimity of emotional detachment (EQ). Or what about that person who is in the midst of a confusing situation, being pulled in different directions? Do you see how your focus on this moment helps to bring about clarity (IQ)? And how your patience in letting insights intuitively show the way is a great benefit to them (NQ)? And what about you exuding the energy of contentment, knowing that all is well (CQ)? Will that not help them find their way more easily?

Even though we could have a coaching session without ever exchanging words, relying entirely on the quality of our being in the moment—that can work well, as a joint silent meditation—we will want to know what to say and when. Having a clear process in mind helps, especially when we are starting out as coaches.

Where do we begin the conversation? Where do we focus? How do we end the session? We will now explore a simple coaching process that was developed in the late 1980s in the United Kingdom and is used extensively in corporate coaching. It's called the GROW process, shorthand for Goal, Reality, Options, and Wrap-up. Think of this process as the chapter headings in a coaching conversation. You can apply any and all of the tools you learned in this book, like crocodile and owl, I-We-It Awareness, Fear Families, SUCCESS Intentions and Personas, Yang and Yin Balance, The Tree, and The Work, as tools you write the chapters with. And of course, there are many other tools you can use as well. Just apply what works and let the GROW process take care of the rest. Let's see how this works in practice.

GROW COACHING PROCESS

Our coachee is showing up in five minutes. It's the first time we're meeting them. What will we do?

First tune into the present moment and activate our CQ, so we are a clean and safe mirror from the moment of our first interaction with the coachee, not putting our day, our needs, our desires, or our fears on the coachee. *This is their time.* We are only here to guide them as they are ready to be guided. Before we say anything, we can remind ourselves to stay grounded in our Conscious Unconditional Intention: *Who do I intend to be no matter what happens in this conversation?*

Then they walk into our office. We get to know them a bit, maybe we share something about ourselves and invite them to share something about themselves.

Before we proceed further, we establish our coaching relationship. This is what the first part is all about: contracting our relationship, or setting the boundaries that make it clear that this conversation is safe and that it is about coaching. It will help both the coach and the coachee feel more purposeful and secure. We may need to re-contract several times during one conversation if we sense the relationship needs to be re-established.

To create the coaching relationship we can simply ask, "Are you willing to be coached by me?" If they say yes, we may share a bit about what that can mean and check in with them as to whether they are comfortable proceeding. We might say something like: "Everything in this coaching conversation is for your growth. I will give my best to help you. I will listen and sometimes challenge you if I see that may be helpful. And occasionally I may point something out to you. In all cases *you remain the expert on you*—nothing I ask or say is true, unless something within you tells you that it is. You can throw the rest out. I won't be offended. Also, I will ask you questions, not provide you with answers. I will help you find your own answers. Does this work for you? What else would you like to put in place to create an optimal learning environment for you?"

Goal

Then we are ready to go into the G, the goal exploration stage of the GROW process. We can start with an open question: "What is happening? What would you like to talk about today?" Some coachees will dive into the deep end right away and talk about a fear they are unable to manage. Yet most people start with a practical challenge. Remember the Tree (see Chapter 6)? Most people will talk first about what they can see aboveground—the results and actions; they are not focused on the inner landscape of beliefs, fears, and needs that underlies their external reality.

John, a product manager, began a coaching session by telling me, "We're not getting the traction with the engineering department we need to ensure an on-time launch of our product. And I would like to change that."

At this point, we could go with this goal or explore it a bit more. Most people don't give themselves time to think about what it is that they really want to see happen. In our society we have been conditioned to believe that we need to stay productive, and staying productive means that we don't have time to think about "impractical" things like what we really care about. In coaching sessions, we create space for this reflection. "What would you really like to see happen, John?" I asked. Such a simple question, and yet . . . try it on yourself. It may take you places you have not been before.

We help the coachee gain awareness of their bigger goals by asking about the "I" (self), "We" (relationship with others), and "It" (effectiveness in accomplishing their tasks). Often coachees start with the "It." In our conditioned training to survive, most of our attention goes there—and John's initial response was about that. He primarily cared about the on-time launch of the product, or so it seemed. When asked about what he really wanted to see happen to his relationship with the engineering department he said, "I want them to prioritize our product completion over all others." Another "It" answer.

We always respect the coachee's answers. Each of us interprets reality our own way; the coachee's responses reflect the lens through which they see their world. And there is no problem with that. We are only here to help them discover opportunities to grow their perspective to the extent that they are interested. I asked John the same question about what he really wanted to see happen a few more times in different ways, and John's response stayed the same—that the engineering department had to change their ways.

With that clarity and focus, we know it's time to move on. We may come back to the goal later, once we have taken a closer look at the reality the coachee is perceiving.

Reality

Looking at Reality, the R in the GROW process, may be the most important part of the coaching session. We gain freedom the more we discern what is true from the illusions that we have *believed* to be true. Courage in coaching is to dare to look reality in the face and say, "I am here for you, 100 percent. It's safe to show yourself 100 percent to me."

"What is happening?" is the R-question I asked John.

"We have had several delays with our product and I don't trust they will get this one done on time," he told me. Another response on the "It" dimension. I followed up with an "I" question:

"How do you feel about this, John?" At this point in the coaching conversation, we're helping the coachee become aware of the lenses through which they currently perceive reality, their consciousness, moving from Unconscious-Unskilled to Conscious-Unskilled. As Einstein wrote, "problems cannot be resolved from the same consciousness that created them."

"They should do what they promised to us. They know better," John responded. Many coachees, like John, respond to a feeling question with thoughts. This is understandable, as for many of us, thoughts are closer to the surface of our experience than feelings are. For a person who is unfamiliar with introspection, naming feelings may be a foreign concept. So I helped John a bit.

"And how do you feel about this, John? Frustrated, anxious, miffed, sad, curious?"

"Well, obviously I am frustrated," John told me. "And I have been for a while!"

At this point, there are many great ways to proceed. We could start to identify the underlying crocodilian belief systems that fuel John's anxiety; we could look at his balance in Yin and Yang so far, we could go straight to coaching him to have a Growth Conversation with the engineering department—we could even propose the Abiding in Presence Meditation to help John experience the underlying okay-ness of himself, the engineering department, and the situation, and awaken a sense of unconditional love in him. And yet, these approaches were probably not suitable for what John was asking and where he was at. We can't force someone to go deep, who is deeply curious about the surface. Remember the story of the butterfly that came out of the cocoon before its time.

Two Perspectives: Victim and Self-mastery

So what to do? For coachees like John—and many people live from this perspective—*the world is doing things to them.* It's not fair and they feel powerless in the face of it. Their interest in growth is in learning to protect themselves from the world, or control it the best way that they know how. We may recognize this as being in a Contraction or Crocodilian mind-set, but for a person who lives in this perception of reality, that distinction may not yet be helpful. Then, what is?

For a person who feels powerless, the idea of becoming self-empowered is an attractive one. And self-empowerment is a stepping stone toward growth. As we start taking responsibility for ourselves, we awaken the curiosity about who we are in relation to what is happening around us. We shift from being primarily interested in the physical reality and move our attention to the mental reality, leading the way to eventually explore the third, transcendental reality (see Chapter 5 for a description of these three realities).

Notice, though, how prevalent the energy of victimhood, of powerless-ness, is in most of us, regardless of our stage of development. What do we say when we're late for a meeting? "It was traffic," "I was stuck in another meeting," or "my boss kept me." We say this because one of our crocodiles—remember the Good Boy/Good Girl?—is hijacking our attention. We blame our external circumstances, like traffic, to maintain our sense of innocence, at least temporarily.

The downside of blame is powerlessness and stagnation. What is the likelihood that we'll be on time the next time for a meeting if we keep thinking about how traffic "makes" us late? Zero. Our mind simply won't allow space to consider new possibilities for action if we are in the grip of blame thinking.

How can we grow out of this? First, by becoming aware that we're stuck in victim thinking and by choosing a different mind-set. We can call this the mind-set of Self-mastery, as opposed to staying in Victimhood. From a place of Self-mastery, we look at being late as something we played a part in. "Given traffic, I left late," may be our revised response to the question "Why were you late for the meeting?" This gives us insight into our own actions, and opens the door to deeper introspection into the beliefs and fears underlying our ineffective action. This is how every *upset* becomes a *setup* for learning. We become curious about our part in it.

Of course, the downside of taking self-responsibility is anxiety, as we shift our attention from out there to in here. We may not like what we are seeing when we first take a close look at ourselves. We may not like the idea that we have contributed to being late, for example. We may not like that we haven't learned our lessons in an area of our lives yet.

As we take the hot seat in our lives fully, the *only* person we can look to change is ourselves. If we are living in a worldview of having to be a good person who has everything figured out and never makes a mistake—remember Fear Family #3, the fear of failure—this can be a very painful place to be, because we judge ourselves for being imperfect. This is why Self-mastery without unconditional love hurts. We must see simultaneously our part in the issue at hand, and the absolute innocence in every thought and action we've ever had.

To help John move toward greater awareness and Self-mastery, I asked him a series of questions that Fred Kofman and others taught me as a useful template to help create the shift from Victimhood to Self-mastery:

1. What is the challenge for you on the "I," "We," and "It" dimension?

2. How have you responded so far?

3. What has been the impact of your response so far on the "I," "We," and "It" dimension?

4. Who has the greatest incentive to make change happen now?

John responded to the first question as follows: "I feel stressed about this all the time. I am actually not sleeping well. And you know what really bothers me is that Sigmund and I—we used to be good friends, and we're not even hanging out anymore since he became the head of the engineering department. I guess we don't trust each other anymore. And it gets worse as time goes on. We already had three launch delays because Sigmund and his crew didn't deliver and now we're about to have our fourth one. This is not acceptable!"

The cat was out of the bag. Now we could take a good look at her, with the eyes of unconditional love. "So, John, since this clearly is bothering you, how have you responded so far? What have *you* done to mitigate the risk of a fourth launch delay?" I asked.

"Well, I have explained the situation to them numerous times and I have sent numerous e-mails. And you know, there has been no response. They are just ignoring me!" Despite his deflective, victim response to my question, a feeling of awareness was slowly building in him.

"John," I asked, "what has been the impact of your response so far—telling them and sending them e-mails—on reducing your stress, rebuilding the relationship with Sigmund, and getting what you need for timely launch?"

John looked down despondently and said, "Zero. Nada. Nothing. Every day that goes by things are getting tenser and we seem to be falling further and further behind . . . There is nothing I can do." Once we reach the *I can't* awareness, the opportunity to grow toward mastery comes in full view. It's a beautiful part of the coaching journey.

Next, I asked, "Who has the greatest incentive to make change happen now?"

At first John reacted. "Well, Sigmund should know better! He knows our company's growth depends on this product shipping out on time!"

"Yes," I responded. "But *who, in this moment, has the awareness that something needs to change now?*"

John sighed. "Well, that's me I guess. No . . . I mean, of course, I am. I know that, but what can I do?" John's energy had shifted from frustrated to somewhat curious. Sometimes it takes coachees a while to embrace Self-mastery. It requires courage to take the hot seat in our lives.

Options

Taking the seat of Self-mastery in any challenge is turning the corner from reactivity to creativity. Once John had taken his Self-mastery seat, awareness and insights started to flow more easily. I could now ask:

1. What would you *really* like to see happen on the "I," "We," and "It" dimensions?

2. How could you respond in a way that will make you feel proud and increase your effectiveness?

"What would you really like to see happen, John, for your own fulfillment, in your relationship with Sigmund and his team and in your effectiveness?"

John responded, "I'd like to feel confident that we are working together to launch this product with quality. And I'd like Sigmund and I to be friends again." He smiled as he said this. It all sounded so simple. And yet this new goal was very different from the one John had come in with: have the engineering department get their act together. Notice the different energy in these two goals:

- I want them to change.

- I'd like to feel confident we're working together to a common goal.

Notice that the second goal offers more possibilities for action than the first one. The first one leads to blame, waiting, and self-pity. The second one opens up proactiveness, care, and focus.

Our meticulous exploration of John's perception of reality had unlocked new options for learning and effectiveness for him, going from blame to Self-mastery and going from separation to relationship building.

"How could you respond in a way that will make you feel proud and increase your effectiveness?" I asked next.

"What I really need to do is sit down with Sigmund and have a conversation with him, to ask what is happening on his side that leads him to act this way. He is not a bad guy, you know. And I need to share with him what my concern is," John said.

"How does it feel saying that?" I asked.

"Well, good," said John. "And you know, I also need to create a backup plan in case Sigmund is not able to deliver. There are some other engineering teams in the company that may be able to lend a hand." When we open our awareness to what is true, possibilities start to flow abundantly.

To further expand our perception of what is possible, it helps to reflect on people we admire. We can ask the coachee: "Who do you admire? And why?" And then, "Be them for a few minutes; how would they respond to your challenge?" Amazing insights come from linking our consciousness with a great leader. When we think like them, we become them for a while, and start seeing possibilities they would see if they were in our shoes.

Wrap-up

We aren't done yet when we have only defined our possibilities for action. "So, John, *what will you do, and when?*" John sat up straight. "Well, I will schedule a meeting with Sigmund right away ... today ... and start working on a backup plan with my team tomorrow."

To help John reap growth from this situation beyond short-term problem resolution, I asked John a question to kindle the fire for growth in us: "*How are you growing* through this experience, John?" He grew silent for a moment, then responded.

"Well, I feel so much better now that I can see what I can do about this. I see that staying in a place of blame didn't help me and simply putting my attention on what I can do makes me more powerful."

I asked John another question: "*How do you feel now?*" John said he felt optimistic and relieved now that he saw what he could learn from the situation and how he could resolve it.

We finish every coaching session combining Yang assertion and Yin reflection. We invite the coachee to assert their commitment for action and growth. And we nudge the coachee to stay open to the ongoing learnings. Life is our greatest teacher. The coachee will likely have their greatest breakthroughs living his or her life outside of the formal coaching setting. To help the coachee stay open to learning, we conclude the session by asking: *"How will you practice your learning?"*

After John and I discussed a few ways to practice his learnings, including writing, taking reflective walks, and pausing in the middle of his day to do a review, John shared his growth commitment: "I will practice by reflecting at the end of every day for two minutes about where I transformed my thinking from a victim to a self-mastery mind-set. Also, I will think about the situations during the day where my Victim-thinking got the better of me, and how I could approach it differently next time."

GROW Summary

GROW offers a clear path for coaches and coachees. The steps in this process are presented here in a linear fashion, although conversations are often nonlinear. When we first start coaching others, it may be helpful to stay with this flow of the basic GROW questions:

Goal: What would you really like to see happen?

Reality: What is happening?

Options: What could you do?

Wrap-up: How are you growing? What will you do?

A GROWTH LEADER AS A COACH

Eknath Easwaran wrote that "As human beings, Gandhi pointed out, our greatness lies not so much in being able to remake the world outside us—as most of us are led to believe—as in being able to remake ourselves on the highest model of human achievement we know of."

As Growth Leaders, we learn to appreciate the infinite potential of our human being–ness. As we grow in the realization of this potential, unavoidably selfless service follows. We are hardwired to help others. As we start to see our own infinite potential, we recognize it in others. We see that presence, infinite potential, love, unites us.

Coaching others, then, becomes a natural act of self-expression, as natural as the tree providing shade to its surroundings; as natural as the sun sharing its warmth. Some of us may discover it as a true life passion, while others might see it as one of many callings. Gandhi wasn't just a politician, spiritual leader, writer, father, husband, friend, activist, coach, counselor, jokester, vegetarian, barrister, or guru. He served in all of those roles, as they were needed, with inexhaustible energy. As he aged he became more energetic. In his seventies, he'd go to sleep around 11:00 p.m. and wake up around 3:00 a.m. or 4:00 a.m. to do his meditation, and then give the rest of the day to selfless service. He didn't start off that way; he grew into a being who mastered the capacity to embody infinite love, through unflinching devotion to his ideal and commitment to continuous self-transformation.

People would come to visit Gandhi with their problems night and day, including the political leaders of India and other countries. According to his biographer, "Usually it was only minutes before such visitors found themselves chuckling in spite of themselves at one of Gandhi's jokes, and when they left, by some alchemy of personality, they would be relaxed again, full of new enthusiasm and inspiration, ready to take on their problems with a clear perspective and deeper strength."

We can serve as coaches to ourselves and each other, selflessly reminding one another that we are sleeping giants who yearn to awaken, and be awakened, with the human care from another. In the end coaching is just that—unflinching devotion to the growth of another. It's like learning about a new country. Once we've visited and loved it, we want others to experience it as well. Once we get to know ourselves more—and discover more of our innate strength, love, wisdom, and compassion—we can't wait to help others to find the same.

FIELDWORK

1. Write down the name of the person who you might be able to coach, or who is asking for your help with a situation.

    That person is:

    Their situation is:

2. How do you feel at the thought of coaching this person?

3. What are some of the qualities of a great coach who has helped you grow? Circle as many as are applicable.

    A. Inspiring

    B. Challenging

    C. Empathetic

    D. Calm

    E. Precise

    F. Practical

    G. Intuitive

    H. Vast

    I. Safe

    J. Confident

4. Write out how your "Fixing-It-Now-I-Super-Hero" (FiNISH)-crocodile would approach this coaching conversation. What expectations does this crocodile have of you, the other, and the conversation? How would you coach (thoughts and behaviors) with the FiNISH-crocodile in the driver's seat of your mind?

5. Write down how you will approach the conversation with a "Letting-Others-Voluntarily-Evolve" (LOVE)-intention. What will you do? What will you *not* do?

6. What is your strongest quality as a coach?

    A.   MQ (my ability to inspire meaning)

    B.   EQ (my ability to stay centered in the storm of emotions)

    C.   IQ (my ability to precisely delineate a challenge and use robust coaching processes)

    D.   NQ (my ability to intuitively sense what's emerging and work with insights as they emerge mid-flight)

    E.   CQ (my ability for contentment, knowing everything is okay, staying true to LOVE, and being able to inspire that feeling)

7.   What is your weakest quality as a coach?

    A.   MQ (my ability to inspire meaning)

    B.   EQ (my ability to stay centered in the storm of emotions)

    C.   IQ (my ability to precisely delineate a challenge and use robust coaching processes)

    D.   NQ (my ability to intuitively sense what's emerging and work with insights as they emerge mid-flight)

    E.   CQ (my ability for contentment, knowing everything is okay, staying true to LOVE, and being able to inspire that feeling)

8.   What coaching qualities do you intend to apply in the conversation with your coachee? List them here. See how it feels to really commit to practicing them in the coaching conversation.

9.   Now practice a coaching conversation, with yourself first, then practice with the coachee you identified above. Practice GROW with the questions below:

- Goal

    – What is your intention? What would you really like to see happen?

- Reality

    – What is the challenge for you on the I (fulfillment), We (relationship), and It (effectiveness) dimension?

    – How have you responded so far?

- What has been the impact of your response so far on the I, We, and It dimension?

- Who has the greatest incentive to make change happen now?

- Options

  - What would you really like to see happen on the I, We, and It dimension?

  - Who do you admire? Why? Be them for a few minutes. How would they respond to your challenge?

  - How could you respond in a way that will make you feel proud and increase your effectiveness?

- Wrap-up

  - What will you do and when?

  - How are you growing?

  - How will you practice your learning?

10.   How are you growing as a coach?

CHAPTER 9

Growing into the Owls We Are— Coaching One to Many

"We have to surprise them, with compassion, with restraint and generosity." —Nelson Mandela

S O FAR, WE have explored personal growth by ourselves and one-on-one. How does growth happen in larger settings, like a family, a team, or a whole organization? You may remember the SUCCESS Intentions we introduced in Chapter 2. What would happen if the collective you are part of worked together on shedding some of its crocodilian beliefs and fears, and operated more from owl SUCCESS Intentions—samurai-like courage, uniting through authentic and empathic relationships, centeredness in purpose, curiosity, extending contribution, sensitivity to the whole, and simplicity in service? You may think that vision is too big for us. Think again. Who's talking, the owl or the crocodile?

WHAT IS YOUR FIELD OF CARE?

We grow our capacity to love through inner work and service to the world. Then the question becomes: What part of the world are we called to care for? What is our "field of care"? Many of the great leaders we admire took whole nations into their care. And there are legions of lesser-known great leaders, who are taking care of their family, community, team, or organization with a similar commitment to growth, grounded in unconditional love. I think of my coach, Jonelle Reynolds, who has supported me for more than ten years now. She is selfless love embodied. She has been serving many clients for many years, without ever taking credit, or asking for big sums of money. You pay her what you want. When I asked her for a photo of her, she told me she didn't have one to share. Her service is purely selfless in my eyes. One of her fields of care is her coachees, including me.

Take a moment and reflect *what is my field of care?* What is the collective I am called to serve? This can be your family, organization, team, charity, or any other collective that you are part of. And you can have multiple fields of care as well.

A METHOD TO THE MADNESS: FIVE THINGS TO SHIFT A CULTURE

Many of us believe that the distance between us and the leaders we admire, like Mandela, Gandhi, and FDR, is huge—that we have ourselves no ability to positively influence our field of care that way. One thing we may think is: *Yes, but they ran a country. I am sitting in my office or at home or am on the road somewhere. What does my life have to do with theirs?* There is a method to how we can serve the world around us, whoever we are. Following the footsteps of the great leaders of history and also the great mentors and coaches in our lives, we can notice some patterns. Five things stand out in how leaders shift the culture of their fields of care to a new way of feeling, thinking, and acting that is less crocodilian reactive and more owl creative. Together we call these five things a "Growth Stewardship System":

1. They Define a Higher Purpose
2. They Model First, and Unflinchingly Create Critical Mass
3. They Equip Others with Language Markers
4. They Choose Symbols Wisely
5. They Communicate, Communicate, Communicate

McKinsey, the consulting company, first developed the basis for this understanding. Studying their research and applying it to culture change of organizations and teams over the years, I have found that these factors are all critical pieces to make sure the new way stays. If one piece is missing, the whole system starts to weaken and the new owl ways will not take root. This might mean that some people adopt the new ways of working while the majority of the system sticks to its old crocodilian ways, that the new owl way becomes the flavor of the month, or that the new owl way is never fully adopted.

So think about your field of care again, and how you could apply the Five Things approach there. You may wonder, will it work? If you apply all five of them consistently, practicing the growth tools we have discussed and others you already know, you can't fail. Why? Because you will set in motion a journey that is magnetic—*in the end, everyone wants to be themselves*. You are offering a path for that to become reality in your field of care.

One caveat is timing. If you do it with your family—be prepared that it may take a lifetime or even generations for the fruits of your work to become tangible. Resistance in family lineages can be particularly deeply entrenched and we are not going to force the butterfly to come out of its cocoon before its time. We practice LOVE—Letting Others Voluntarily Evolve.

If you introduce a Growth Stewardship System to your team or company you can agree together on a timeline that ensures the new culture is in place soon enough to meet business goals, and gradual enough so people have time to adjust. Establishing the new culture becomes a goal in itself, which will motivate people to work toward it and to hold each other accountable for growing into it. In some cases, people who stay very attached to their crocodiles will self-select out, or will be asked to leave over time.

Let's now explore how to establish each of the Five Things of a Growth Stewardship System in your field of care.

1. Define Your Higher Purpose to Inspire Others

Each year, students at the Greenwood School in Vermont—a school dedicated to awakening human potential in boys with learning differences and disabilities, such as dyslexia or attentional difficulties (ADD/ADHD)— are asked to learn to recite the Gettysburg Address by heart and deliver it at the annual Greenwood School celebration. Ken Burns made a moving documentary about them, *The Address*. In his documentary, we watch the students work hard for months to master the words, the pronunciation, the meaning, and the cadence—sometimes with great difficulty, and often with great perseverance. Their example reminds me of the human strength that comes online when we truly dedicate ourselves to something we value.

At the end of the documentary, we get to see the fruits of their dedication and hard work. At the festive Greenwood celebration, attended by parents, friends, teachers, and administrators, we watch thirty-four students, one after the other, go onstage and give their address. In his suit,

Geo, an eleven-year old student, who previously wasn't able to pronounce some of the consonants, now stands tall behind the lectern. With all eyes on him, he makes Abraham Lincoln's declaration slowly, musically, beautifully, by heart, and from his heart: "It is rather for us to be here dedicated to the great task remaining before us—that from these honored dead we take increased devotion to that cause for which they gave the last full measure of devotion . . ."

When the filmmakers interview Geo three months later on a school trip to the Gettysburg memorial in Pennsylvania, he shares that giving the Gettysburg Address in public "makes me feel I can do anything I want." Other speaker-students add: "It makes me feel like a new man," "When I'd done it, I felt I could fly," and "I felt like I recited a million things at once when I recited the Gettysburg Address."

Indeed, the Gettysburg address, written and delivered by Abraham Lincoln at the turning point of the Civil War, has become one of the most quoted and memorized speeches ever written. Lincoln started off reminding his listeners of the intent of the nation's founders: "Four score and seven years ago our fathers brought forth on this continent a new nation, conceived in liberty, and dedicated to the proposition that all men are created equal." He continued by addressing the current state of the country, which demanded action from the American people. "Now we are engaged in a great civil war, testing whether that nation, or any nation so conceived and so dedicated, can long endure." A minute later he concluded his speech: "It is rather for us to be here dedicated to the great task remaining before us—that from these honored dead we take increased devotion to that cause for which they gave the last full measure of devotion—that we here highly resolve that these dead shall not have died in vain—that this nation, under God, shall have a new birth of freedom—and that government of the people, by the people, for the people, shall not perish from the earth."

He asked his audience then—and we can hear his call to us now—to consider their dedication to devote themselves to something larger than their immediate concerns. Lincoln had learned from his own life, having faced many setbacks and overcome them, that dedication generates inspiration to grow taller in being, goals, and actions.

Lincoln dedicated the end of his life to union and freedom, inspiring us to be free and dedicate ourselves to something great; something that makes our heart sing; something that helps us grow and be fearlessly creative, whatever happens. The Greenwood School is dedicated to awakening human potential. By holding a vision of great possibilities for their students, the school fuels the dedication of its students to do what many of them think is impossible when they start. This includes reciting the Gettysburg Address. Their example touches people like us, who get to watch their human bravery and excellence with awe. One positive influence engenders another. *What will become possible when we all stand up and speak our own Gettysburg Address?*

This is where Growth Leaders start. Remember our discussion on finding our Authentic Calling in Chapter 2? Now we create a *collective* statement of purpose, together with other leaders in our field of care. This is what starts the fire and builds the inspiration to go for it as a team, unflinchingly.

Nelson Mandela gave his own Gettysburg-like speech when he advocated for the continuation of the South African rugby team, the Springboks, despite their associations with apartheid history. Here is his speech we looked at in Chapter 4, this time in full:

> "Brothers, sisters, comrades, I am here because I believe that you have made a decision with insufficient information and foresight. I am aware of your earlier vote. I am aware that it was unanimous. Nonetheless, I believe we should restore the Springboks. Restore their name, their emblem, and their colors immediately. Let me tell you why. On Robben Island, in Polsmoor Prison, all of my jailers were Afrikaners. For twenty-seven years, I studied them. I learned their language, read their books, their poetry. I had to know my enemy before I could prevail against him. And we did prevail, did we not? All of us here, we prevailed. Our enemy is no longer the Afrikaner. They are our fellow South Africans, our partners in democracy and they treasure Springbok rugby. If we take that away, we lose them. We prove that we are what they fear we would be. We have to be better than that. We have to surprise them, with compassion, with restraint and generosity. I know all of the things they denied us. But this is no time to celebrate petty revenge. This is the time to build our nation using every single brick available to us. Even if that brick comes wrapped in green and gold."

What can we learn from Lincoln and Mandela about leading a field of care to a higher purpose? Both leaders appealed to people's hearts: the source of inspiration. Think about a story or speech that has deeply touched you and that has helped you expand the vision you have for yourself. For me, *The Diary of a Young Girl* comes to mind. Anne Frank, a Jewish teenage girl, wrote most of the journal from 1942 to 1944 while hiding in a secret annex in Amsterdam with her family and a few friends, until they were discovered and deported to the concentration camps, where she and most of her family died (only her father Otto survived the camps). On August 1, 1944, three days before they were arrested, she comments: *"I know exactly how I'd like to be, how I am . . . inside . . . I am guided by the pure Anne within, but outside I'm nothing but a frolicsome little goat who's broken loose."* I remember Anne Frank for what becomes possible when I connect with who I truly am, the real Hylke, and the strength that comes online with that. Her story touches my heart and stirs my courage. Remember, *Courage* comes from the Latin word *cor*, which means heart. When we are coming from the heart, we become kinder and more unflinching—our heart keeps beating the steady drum of vitality, wisdom, and compassion. Compare that to trying to be courageous because it makes rational sense, relying more on our prefrontal cortices, particularly the left lobe, our logic center. As soon as it doesn't make sense anymore, we stop being courageous. From the rational mind, we can only be *conditionally courageous*, because it makes sense. From the heart, we choose courage, just because. That courage doesn't waver and is therefore unconditional. Meher Baba, a spiritual teacher, wrote it this way: "Do not listen to the voice of the mind. Listen to the voice of the heart. The mind wavers, the heart does not. The mind fears, the heart is undaunted."

How do we paint a collective picture that speaks to people's hearts and awakens unconditional courage? One important tool is to share a vision that inspires growth. Our hearts like to open to new possibility. Our hearts love to see us grow more into our potential, like parents delight in their children's progress.

All three leaders, Lincoln, Mandela, and Anne Frank, painted a picture of the current consciousness, its limitations, and what we can grow into if we listen to our higher collective wisdom. "I know exactly how I'd like to be," writes Anne Frank, in contrast to being a "frolicsome little goat."

These leaders described a *"from-to"*: they showed us the place we had been and the place we aspire to go to. We can summarize Lincoln's

Gettysburg *from* as "division and inequality" and Lincoln's *to* as "unity and equality." Lincoln's growth-oriented leadership helped unite the country, even though true unity and equality remain elusive to this day.

Like Lincoln, Mandela spelled out a new consciousness for South Africa, his field of care, in no uncertain terms: "We have to surprise them [the Afrikaners], with compassion, with restraint and generosity," instead of giving in to "petty revenge." Mandela urged his fellow countrymen to grow *from* retaliation *to* compassion as a necessary step toward uniting the nation. FDR used this playbook as well, whether in encouraging confidence in the banks or overcoming isolationist resistance to the Lend-Lease program.

How do we translate this type of growth-oriented leadership from a country to an organization or team? What about how it would apply to an individual's social circle and family? It may seem too idealistic and exalted to have anything to do with *us*. But there are always opportunities to lead with a great vision and unite people around a shared aspiration to grow into. In 2014, Satya Nadella, then the new CEO of Microsoft, declared a bold new vision for the company: the move to cloud computing with a Growth Mind-set culture. He coached an entire company to move from the incumbent mind-set that comes with arrogance, assuming you're the top dog, to taking a Growth Mind-set, where every moment is approached as an opportunity for learning. It's too early to tell the financial impact of this culture shift. Yet, if the atmosphere is any indication, things are looking bright for the company. Employees report feeling more empowered than before and supported in pioneering new approaches, both internally and with clients and partners. Even well-established cultures have the possibility of change if a leader can inspire people with their vision for growth.

You can inspire growth in your field of care by developing a Growth Stewardship Vision. This describes both the *from* and the *to*: where you want to go and where you are now. One way to get started is to look at the nature of the crocodiles in your field of care. Consider which of the seven Crocodilian SUCCESS Personas are most active now. Then consider what new consciousness—what new ways of feeling, thinking, and acting—you aspire to grow into together. You can draw examples from the personas and intentions listed below. To make this really compelling, communicate the practical reasons for wanting to evolve the consciousness of your field of care. For Microsoft, adopting a Growth Mind-set is critical to helping the company succeed in its shift to the cloud-first environment. For FDR, inspiring the country to move from fear to courage was essential to restoring financial and social stability in the country. What is the core aspiration or need you hope to address with the culture shift? What shifts in consciousness ("from-tos") will be most helpful?

FROM: Crocodilian SUCCESS Personas	TO: Owl SUCCESS Intentions
1. *Safe*: Overworking, victim, and short-term biased Driven by the fear of *scarcity*	1. *Samurai*—having the warrior-like courage and fortitude to take care of our basic needs and face our challenges resourcefully without being overwhelmed by them
2. *Us vs. Them*: Judging, complying, and siloed Driven by the fear of *abandonment*	2. *Uniting*—creating authentic, empathetic relationships that welcome everyone and go beyond tribal, us-vs.-them dynamics
3. *Controlling*: Perfectionism, manipulating, and micro-managing Driven by the fear of *failure*	3. *Centered in purpose*—being driven by our inner compass, pursuing our goals wholeheartedly and with focus; and seeing every "failure" as part of moving forward
4. *Certain*: Rigid, dramatic, and close-minded Driven by the fear of *uncertainty*	4. *Curious*—opening our hearts to life's teachings—the whispers—no matter what, and seeing every moment as an opportunity for discovery, bigger vision, and being innovative

5. *Essential*: Dominating, rescuing, and hiding Driven by the fear of *hurt*	5. *Extending*—expressing our gifts to others unapologetically and caringly
6. *Sapient*: Knower, paranoid, and advice-giving Driven by the fear of *complexity*	6. *Sensing*—looking for the connection between everything and everyone, integrating the seeming polarities in life; creating cohesion
7. *Special*: Pedestal, martyr, and ivory tower–oriented Driven by the fear of *losing identity*	7. *Simple*—seeing what is needed and doing it, letting go of all ego personas, simply being and contributing who we are

Creating "from-tos" for your field of care is more of an art than a science. Often it requires a bit of iteration and dialogue. What are the most limiting crocodiles you notice? What is the impact of these on your team's effectiveness? How could you describe those so that they resonate with others? What are some owl intentions you wish to grow into as a team?

After two intensive retreats to reflect on their new business model and the culture changes needed to support it, the leadership team of a financial services company came to the following "from-tos" to help them become more innovative and service-oriented (rather than product-centric). I added in parentheses the corresponding SUCCESS Personas and Identities.

FROM (Persona)	TO (Intention)
1. Talking about each other (#2: Us vs. them)	Working with each other (#2: Uniting)
2. Keeping the peace / pseudo-collaboration (#2: Us vs. them)	Passion (#3: Centered)
3. Indecisive (#3: Controlling)	Decisive (#3: Centered)

4. Victim (#1: Safety)	Mastery (#1: Samurai)
5. They (#1: Safety)	I (#1: Samurai)
6. Certainty—rigidity and drama (#4: Certainty)	Curiosity—open and creative (#4: Curiosity)

You'll notice how this team defined several "froms" related to SUCCESS Personas #1 and 2, indicating that these two personas were most prevalent in the organization and most standing in the way of what the organization aspired to become. Also, they found that one of the personas, #2, Us vs. them, could best be worked on by focusing on intention #3, being centered in purpose.

Take a moment and jot down the from-tos that you believe are most helpful for the growth of your field of care now. Think about your purpose together and then use your intuition to identify the most limiting crocodiles and the most empowering owl intentions. If you think you don't know, who is talking—your owl, or your crocodile?

2. Model Your Vision First and Unflinchingly; Create Critical Mass

We breathe life into our Growth Stewardship Vision by resolutely acting on it. We are role models for the change we want to see. This is a very Yang quality. We go first even if nobody else is willing to jump yet— we don't wait for others to get on the same page. If everyone around us is attached to crocodilian limitation, we can still move into owl wisdom on our own. Rather than wait for others to adopt the same mind-set as us so that we can all begin this journey together (this scenario sounds lovely, but is very unlikely), we can accept others as they are, while we are modeling our own aspired owl way. This may help others in our field of care move in a similar direction.

Nelson Mandela transformed his own crocodiles first. It wasn't something that he learned how to do overnight. When Mandela came into politics he was very aggressive and judgmental. It was during his twenty-seven years in prison that he became wiser, gentler, and more compassionate. On his last day of prison, he walked out and embraced his captors. It is a rare person who is so forgiving. President Bill Clinton asked Mandela about this when he was visiting the White House. This was during the time of the Monica Lewinsky affair, and there was a lot of mudslinging happening. Clinton became inspired by

Mandela's devotion to his Unconditional Intention—be free from aggression, no matter what. President Clinton reported after the visit:

"I asked him, 'How did you ever let go of your hatred? Didn't you hate those people when they let you go?' And he responded: 'Briefly I did. But when I was walking out of my compound for the last time I said to myself they have had you for twenty-seven years. If you hate them when you get through that door they will still have you. I wanted to be free and so I let it go.' And he looked at me and he grabbed my arm and said: 'So should you.'"

Nelson Mandela exemplifies an unrelenting, lived commitment to his vision for his field of care: compassion, restraint, and generosity. He role modeled letting go of resentment in harrowing circumstances, and chose freedom instead.

Marianne Williamson wrote: "People who profoundly achieve aren't necessarily people who do so much; they're people around whom things get done. Mahatma Gandhi and President John F. Kennedy were both examples of this. Their greatest achievements lay in all the energy they stirred in other people, the invisible forces that they unleashed around them. By touching their own depths, they touched the depths within others."

We create depth through deliberate continuous practice on ourselves. And to cultivate a shift in consciousness in our field of care, we create a critical mass of people who embody the new consciousness with us. How do we build critical mass?

Changing a way of being and behaving is a personal choice—it cannot be forced, and it can be demonstrated. When we start embodying our new owl consciousness, being more of who we are, others will follow. In addition to us being role models, we can build critical mass by inviting our field of care to join us in a deliberate journey of retreats and other group reflections that follow a path like the one laid out in this book:

1. Defining a *Growth Stewardship Vision*—Establishing our Collective Calling (chapters 2 and 9)

2. *Growing Self* to become role models, through (some of) the following practices:
    - Navigating the Stages of Growth (Chapter 1)
    - Moving from Contraction to Growth Leadership and from Crocodile to Owl Mind-sets (Chapter 3)

- Transforming Fear-based SUCCESS Personas into Owl-oriented SUCCESS Intentions (Chapter 4)
- Learning Yin-Yang Balance (Chapter 5)
- Conducting Truth Inquiry into Our Roots, Doing the Tree and the Work (Chapter 6)

3. *Growing with Others*, learning to use every conversation as an opportunity for growth:

- Practicing Growth Conversations (Chapter 7)

4. *Growing Others*, learning to coach others one-on-one:

- Adopting a 5Q-Coaching Mind-set and the GROW process (Chapter 8)

5. *Growing a System*, learning to inspire our field of care to evolve:

- Applying Five Things to Shift a Culture (this chapter)

Before attempting any full-fledged retraining or hoping that retreats will be enough to change your group's attitude, reflect on yourself. When those around you see you in action, do they see someone embodying the new goals, direction, and awareness you would like to embed? Make sure your actions speak for themselves—act the way you are asking people to act. The power of this type of role modeling is intense. If you aspire to greater trust in your team, are you able to let go of any crocodilian judgment toward others who are not "getting with the program" as quickly as you would like them to? If you envision greater courage, are you willing to speak up first to name the elephants in the room? If you wish to remove the pedestals, are you willing to listen equally deeply to others who are "junior" to you, and those who are not as popular? And are you willing to see yourself as a leader no matter what your job title says?

3. Lead through Language Markers

When you role model, you lead the way. Yet not everyone will recognize your new mind-sets and behaviors. To embed the new culture in your field of care, you can help others become aware of the new way and grow into it, if they choose to. We use *Language Markers* for this. Language

Markers are words or phrases we repeat to remind each other of the new way.

Language markers describe both the *why* and the *how* of the new way. Let's look at a part of Mandela's speech about the Springboks to see how he used both types of language markers. "They are our fellow South Africans, our partners in democracy and they treasure Springbok rugby. If we take that away, we lose them. We prove that we are what they fear we would be. We have to be better than that. We have to surprise them, with compassion, with restraint and generosity. I know all of the things they denied us. But this is no time to celebrate petty revenge. This is the time to build our nation using every single brick available to us . . ."

The *why* of Mandela's vision is captured by "If we take that away, we lose them," meaning the white minority who had previously ruled South Africa. Mandela's vision was *unity*; making sure that both races work together to build a great South Africa. He nudged his audience to "surprise them with compassion, restraint and generosity," giving the people the *hows* of compassion, restraint and generosity, to carry out the *why*.

Reflect for a minute on what the *why* and *how* Language Markers could be for your field of care. One family told me that their *why* was "to love" and their *how* included four principles they practice together: "Don't panic, Be kind, Play, and Be honest."

In Satya's Microsoft, the *why* is "Helping people achieve more with technology," and one of their *hows* is practicing a Growth Mind-set. At Adobe they use words like "Burning the Boats" and "Revenue Addicts" to create a mind-set that supports their move to a cloud-based business.

In my organization, the Growth Leadership Network, the *why* is "shifting leadership consciousness"; and our master tool is "Growth Leadership," which includes tools like the Owl, the Crocodile, and Yin and Yang.

We keep repeating our *why* and our *hows*, so they come to stand out in the mind's eye, as trail markers do on a hike we are on. And we give them the power to shift consciousness by applying them deliberately, like in day-to-day conversations. The word *crocodile* in itself has no power. But when people talk about their crocodiles before going into a difficult conversation and reflect on them in other dedicated spaces, like town halls and webinars, "crocodiles" become a commonly understood reference point for growth.

We can get creative with our language markers. One team adopted the song "Impossible Dream" as their meta reminder to never give up in standing up for their authentic purpose. They play it sometimes at team meetings.

4.   Choose Symbols Wisely

Creating a critical mass of people who commit to growing in owl mindsets and behaviors is a nonlinear project. We will need to creatively nurture the organism toward growth. We could compare building a movement to raising a child; it's an ongoing, challenging, and ultimately fulfilling project that takes time. At the start, parents have no clue what will be needed from them. Fortunately, they find out along the way. The same goes for building a movement. Whenever we are in doubt, we go back to the present moment and can ask our intuitive, nonlinear self: "Guide me to be an instrument of growth and well-being for the people who are in my care." Insights and actions follow. We can trust that. Let go and surprise your linear mind.

It was in a dream that Gandhi received the idea for the Salt March—the collective walk to the ocean where Indians harvested salt and defied the British salt laws that forbade this. The march became one of the most potent symbols on India's road to independence.

Symbols are great helpers in evolving the consciousness of a field of care irrevocably—they are tangible reminders that the new way is here to stay. In a family, tangible symbols can include setting aside a space in the house for meditation, or doing a group contemplation regularly. This can symbolize the importance of presence and unconditional love in family life. The practice of doing a check-in (see Chapter 7) where everyone gets to talk about how they are feeling and growing can be a symbol that reminds people, like prayer before the start of a meal, of the value in connecting to one another and to a higher power. Having a "no-technology day" can be a powerful symbol to emphasize spontaneity and direct interaction with one another.

In a larger organization, such as a company or nonprofit, similar symbols can be used. Because a large part of many people's motivation to come to work is related to money, relationships, and self-esteem, it's important to address these big three in our symbols.

For example, at Microsoft, people used to be graded on a scale from 1 to 5, from highest to lowest performer. Everyone was being compared against each other on a forced bell curve. This reinforced people's go-it-alone, perfectionistic mind-sets, creating a defensive culture weighed down by fear of failure and exclusion. If you got a "5," you would likely lose your job.

By 2014, the 1–5 rating system had outlived its usefulness, so Microsoft's Senior Leadership Team replaced it with a performance management system that is more team-based. This is not to say that the 1–5 system hadn't been a powerful and effective symbol that helped the company mature into a more performance-oriented organization a decade ago, when that was needed. But as we know, over time, any strength overused becomes a weakness. The change of the performance management system was a powerful symbol that Satya's talk about Growth Mind-set was in fact real, as it got translated into what many people value first: security in dollars and cents.

Here are some other examples. At LinkedIn, CEO Jeff Weiner's core values are wisdom and compassion. LinkedIn shows commitment to these values through their monthly all-company meetings, where you can ask any question to the senior leadership team. I see this all-company dialogue as a powerful indicator that Jeff and his team value wisdom. Wisdom is grounded in truth. Collective truth and wisdom can be discovered in group dialogues. *What is really happening?* tends to become clear quickly when you create a forum for it, like an all-company meeting, where the CEO and his team role model openness. And it's a gutsy concept, because anybody can say what's on their mind; the CEO is there and anything can be discussed. What I've heard from the people who work there is that they really appreciate this custom.

And the football team the Seattle Seahawks has a similar, symbolic practice called "Tell-the-Truth Mondays." It's basically where all the players get together and talk about their fears and their failures. Paradoxically, by sharing their insecurities, they gain confidence in themselves and each other.

Wisely choosing symbols, such as the Salt March; daily check-ins; a team-based performance system; and regularly sharing fears and failures with each other strongly contributes to the evolution of consciousness in a field of care. Part of what makes these symbols powerful is that they also have *practical* value. People harvested salt *and* helped India's independence; teammates talk about their fears *and* they create a cohesive, confident team; they adjusted the compensation model *and* cultivated a Growth Mind-set. We act in new, practical ways that become powerful symbols for the new culture.

Potent symbols are visible and somewhat risky; that's why we also call them "symbolic bets." They speak to people's hearts and invite them to grow and evolve in ways they may not have on their own. Our minds are partly set up to make predictions—we enjoy them. Making a bet (for instance, on a new process or act) where the outcome is uncertain engages the predictive part of the brain and energizes us, like reading the beginning of a great adventure story where we can't wait to read the next chapter.

In his book *Straight from the Gut*, CEO Jack Welch remembers the following: "I wanted GE to stay only in businesses that were No. 1 or No. 2 in their markets. We had to act faster and get the bureaucracy out of the way." Part of the GE bureaucracy was driven by the "good old boy" network that had developed in its culture over the years. Success at GE had become more about who you knew than what you contributed. Welch intended to change that, and had his eye on a particularly powerful symbol of the culture that needed to change. It was called the Elfun Society, an internal management club at GE. "It was a networking group for white collar types," wrote Jack. "I didn't have a lot of respect for what Elfun was doing—I thought it represented the height of superficial congeniality. Being an Elfun was considered a 'rite of passage' into management." Elfun, unlike the word it resembles (*elfin*, meaning "dainty," or "petite"), had become a colossus in GE's bureaucracy.

"As a new CEO, I was invited to speak before the group's annual leadership conference in the fall of 1981. It was supposed to be a nice meeting, one of those pat-on-the-back speeches from the new guy. I showed up at the Longshore Country Club in Westport, Connecticut, where some one hundred Elfun leaders from all the local chapters in the United States gathered. After dinner, I got up and delivered what one member still remembers as a classic 'stick-in-the-eye' speech ... 'Thank you for asking me to speak. Tonight I'd like to be candid, and I'll start by letting you reflect on the fact that I have serious reservations about your organization.' I described Elfun as an institution pursuing yesterday's agenda. I told them I could never identify with their recent activities. 'I can't find any value to what you're doing, ... You're a hierarchical social and political club. I'm not going to tell you what you should do or be. It's your job to figure out a role model that makes sense for you and GE.'"

Jack's calling the baby ugly at first caused upset, then reflection, then decisive action. Today, Elfun has grown into one of the more powerful symbols of the culture change Jack Welch led at GE. "Today [2001] Elfun has more than 42,000 members, including retirees. They volunteer their time and energy in communities where GE has plants and offices. They have mentoring programs for high school students . . . Elfun's self-engineered turnaround became a very important symbol [of reducing bureaucracy]. It was just what I was looking for," Jack reflects.

We remember symbols, often for the rest of our lives. Gandhi, Jack Welch, Nelson Mandela, FDR, and JFK were masters in creating symbols that inspired people to think and be bigger. What's a symbolic bet that you can introduce into your field of care that says that growth is here to stay?

5.   Communicate, Communicate, Communicate

We have established a vision, role models, language markers, and symbols— what's missing if we want to shift the culture of our field of care sustainably and powerfully?

How we behave day-to-day is shaped by our thinking, our self-talk. From this perspective, we can see culture as our *collective* self-talk—the stories we tell each other. When we shift culture, we evolve from one collective narrative to another one. Growth Leaders help to upgrade a collective crocodilian story to an owl one.

THE POWER OF GROWTH STORIES

People love stories—we are hungry for them. For many of us, listening to a bedtime story is one of our favorite childhood memories. In the dictionary we find under *story* a reference from Anglo-Latin, saying, "perhaps originally denoting a tier of painted windows or sculptures on the front of a building representing a historical subject." When we tell a story, we share a piece of our mental landscape with others in a way they can relate to and remember: a symbol in words. When we tell a Growth Story, we share a verbal symbol that inspires us to keep growing, individually and together. Growth Stories are powerful. Let's learn from Abraham Lincoln just how powerful.

Lincoln became a great storyteller during his presidency. He started off mainly as a great listener. He'd allow throngs of people weekly into his office to hear and address their concerns, and to learn what was going on in the country. During his election campaign in 1860, he received a letter from Grace Bedell, an eleven-year-old girl from Westfield, NY, that read: "I have got 4 brother's and part of them will vote for you anyway and if you will let your whiskers grow I will try and get the rest of them to vote for you; you would look a great deal better for your face is so thin." He wrote back four days later: "As to the whiskers, having never worn any, do you not think people would call it a piece of silly affection if I were to begin it now?" While he didn't make any promises, he wore a full beard as President-elect when he stopped in Westfield on February 16, 1861, and met his young correspondent. Lincoln knew how to listen and act on it, no matter who the messenger was.

Only later on in his presidency did Lincoln become masterful in *assertively sharing* his story with the nation. Until Lincoln took office, presidents, once elected, had no direct contact with the public. Their job was to run the government and only share their actions and wishes with Congress. They'd rarely leave the capital, except for vacations. Dramatically, Lincoln bid farewell to this tradition and stepped out of the convention-created isolation that was the White House.

In creating a new, direct relationship with the American public, Lincoln applied something he'd learned practicing foreign policy. Months before, Lincoln had directly corresponded with the people of Great Britain and averted a British attack on Union soil, which some of their leaders were advocating. The British economy had been hurt badly by the Civil War, as the cotton from US textile mills they relied on had stopped coming when the Union Army barricaded Confederate Southern ports.

Lincoln recognized the threat of this crisis to the Union cause and started writing public letters to British workers—explaining the reasons for the port closures and the Civil War. He appealed to them to join in the fight for freedom of their fellow human beings, the slaves of the South. Lincoln reminded people of a powerful purpose we have all in common—being humane. While met initially with resistance, Lincoln's letters led to mass demonstrations by mill workers in Manchester and London, expressing *support* for the President's struggle for the freedom of all mankind. We can see one element of Growth Story telling, *uniting people in a shared purpose*, at work here.

Seeing the impact the letters had on British public sentiment, Lincoln started a public letter-writing campaign in his own country, hoping to rally much-needed support for his policies there. People were tired of the Civil War, of the cost in human lives and the decline in the economy.

It worked. On June 12, he sent a letter to Erastus Corning, with a copy to the influential *New York Tribune* newspaper. Corning was president of the New York Central Railroad and leader of an Albany protest against the arrest and trial of Clement Vallandigham, a leading anti-war Democrat who had been convicted for expressing sentiments that aided, comforted, and encouraged those who were up in arms against the government. Quotes of Vallandigham include attacking the President for acting as "King Lincoln," and for starting "a war for the freedom of the blacks and the enslavement of the whites." In his letter, Lincoln explained why he had gradually become tougher with regard to holding people accountable, and predicted that "The time [was] not unlikely to come when I shall be blamed for having made too few arrests rather than too many." In what would widely be seen as his most effective paragraph, the President asked his Albany petitioners to see that it was his right and duty as President to punish incitement, writing, "Must I shoot a simpleminded soldier boy who deserts, while I must not touch a hair of a wiley agitator who induces him to desert?"

The victories of Lincoln's party in the fall election, which boosted Lincoln's effectiveness, were partially ascribed to his mastery in re-engaging public opinion through his writing campaign. The *Chicago Tribune*, often critical of Lincoln, now called him "The most popular man in the United States" and predicted: "Were an election for President to be held tomorrow, Old Abe would, without the special aid of any of his friends, walk over the course, without a competitor to dispute with him the great prize which his masterly ability no less than his undoubted patriotism and unimpeachable honesty, have won."

Lincoln knew how to pithily capture the crocodile narrative of the time, negativity and narrow-mindedness, and replace it with a new owl story that inspired growth—being decisive and seeing the bigger picture: appreciating that attacking the government and deserting the army were similar. And he didn't just write a new story, he also assertively shared it.

Lincoln expanded his job to include becoming one of the nation's most powerful storytellers—not just of any old tales, but of narratives that inspired people to grow in their consciousness. During his presidency, Lincoln emerged as a communicator of higher consciousness—we can call him a *Growth Communicator*. What growth story do you want to write and take a stand for to help your field of care grow?

THE 5QS OF GROWTH COMMUNICATION

Growth Communicators apply the 5Qs we explored when we discussed coaching one-on-one: MQ (meaning), EQ (emotion), IQ (intellect), NQ (intuition), and CQ (contentment). Repeatedly Growth Communicators ask themselves: "How can I shift the collective story today? What stories can I share?" "How do I want people to feel, think, and act differently by the end of the communication?" Let's explore how we communicate growth using the 5Qs.

Communicating Meaningfulness—MQ

Satya Nadella wrote in a letter to all employees of Microsoft on July 10, 2014, "The day I took on my new role I said that our industry does not respect tradition—it only respects innovation. I also said that in order to accelerate our innovation, we must rediscover our soul—our unique core."

Growth Communicators appreciate the state of consciousness of the audience they are speaking with. Satya didn't lead with the word *soul*, but with *innovation*. Most engineers relate easily to innovation; and seeing it written alongside "soul," a less common word in business, helps them to relate to the *meaning* of what they are doing in a deeper way.

"What are you here to contribute?" is a core question we can pose to invoke meaning. We challenge our audience to consider their contribution to expanding circles of care—themselves, their team, their organization, their customers, their partners, and society. This can help expand their perception of their individual *why*, and the *why* behind the journey to higher collective consciousness. As we widen our circles of care, we increase our capacity to love, accessing the infinite energy of unconditional love. Satya challenges people to think about the unique contribution they can make to innovate their collective—Microsoft, and by extension customers, partners, and society. His challenge energizes—it asks people to think bigger.

Growth Communicators stay focused on the contribution they wish to make and elicit in every communication they have; this purpose drives their words. They are not led astray by the crocodilian draws of being liked, or of staying safe. When Satya wrote, "We must rediscover our soul," he took a risk of being unconventional, not fitting the mold of corporate-speak. He boldly invited a Growth Mind-set in tens of thousands of employees. It inspired them to reflect: *What is this company really about? What am I doing here? What is my purpose? And what will be fulfilling?*

We will only know that the new consciousness has landed when we see people be and act differently. Every great communication, whether it's a speech, a blog post, or a dialogue, invites personal choice. "How will you respond differently, with your new awareness?" we ask implicitly or explicitly.

"When we have the courage to transform individually, we will collectively transform this company and seize the great opportunity ahead," concludes Satya in his letter to employees. His implicit message seems to say, "Do you choose to be a leader in our courageous undertaking?"

Communicating with Emotional Maturity—EQ

The biggest obstacle to any evolution of consciousness is the attachment people have to their old identities—who they thought they were, what made them survive and thrive previously, how they thought they were appreciated, and who they thought they could rely on and how—or in one word: ego. Any components of the crocodilian identity can be triggered when the collective consciousness begins to shift. *But I thought I was the top dog here?* a person may think. Or, *I have always won by focusing on my team first and letting the rest take care of itself.* Another might say, "I don't trust this new leadership group—why would I follow them in their quest for transformation. It's too risky, I have a family to feed."

This is where emotional maturity comes in. We must have the wherewithal to stay open in dialogue with both advocates and detractors of the new way, giving each *equal* interest and empathy. People have innocent reasons for their crocodilian thinking, if that's what is holding them back. To tame the crocodiles in an organization, we apply the same approach as we use with our inner landscape. We invite the fearful crocodiles to tea. To tame them, we befriend them without giving in to them. We inquire into and acknowledge their concerns, and together we see what new ways can be found to see the challenge at hand differently, as an opportunity for growth. When a person with an active crocodile is acting out, we can see it as a call for love.

The most reactive crocodiles can become the most powerful symbols for the transformation to the new consciousness. Elfun, formerly a self-aggrandizing crocodilian collective, grew into a generous, inclusive organization that became a symbol for simplicity and less bureaucracy at GE. That transformation started with a frank exchange that triggered growth. Emotional maturity doesn't mean softness, it's about integrating empathy *and* firmness. Each leader finds their own way to stir growth. The most emotionally mature communications are grounded in presence, firm truthfulness, and deep empathy.

Communicating Intelligently—IQ

Many people in business are trained to be Yang/left brain-oriented, and are not comfortable with ambiguity. Yet the evolution of culture is more of an art than an exact science. To make it understandable and exciting for Yang-oriented people, it helps to have a clear process of milestones that lays out a rhythm of business for the journey: when will we work on what, why, and how.

And it's important to be precise in our dialogues—always bring it back to the simple grounded facts we can all observe. The facts themselves become motivators for greater consciousness. One leader in an all-company culture call said, "Gallup suggests that employee engagement is around 30 percent in the United States . . . in our organization we're at 27 percent. That tells me we have so much untapped potential. Our culture journey is about understanding what disengages us and working together to make this company once again a place where we all want to be, wholeheartedly . . . To make this happen, we will make a significant investment in time and money to support our transformation, which includes Growing Self, Growing Others, and Growing System workshops . . . I want us to stand here next year saying: 'We're at 60 percent.' Let's work together to make that happen." High-IQ communications call out the challenge and aspiration with as much precision as possible—in this case, moving from 27 percent to 60 percent—and lay out the process that will be used, with a clear beginning ("understanding what disengages us"), middle ("workshops"), and end (achieving the goal of 60 percent).

Precise dialogue also means we look at both sides of progress. We openly share what is not working, and celebrate what is, both with specific examples—describing setbacks and highlighting forerunners and success stories.

Communicating Intuitively—NQ

Often our greatest breakthroughs in communication are not scripted but happen in the moment, or just before. Martin Luther King completed his "I Have a Dream" speech early the same morning he was delivering it, as did Lincoln with his Gettysburg Address. As Gandhi built *satyagraha*, his insights into what to say and what to do next came at the eleventh hour; often when addressing a crowd of thousands, he wouldn't know what to say until a few minutes prior. And in company meetings, I have witnessed the most memorable words being spoken in a spontaneous dialogue. Do we have the courage to let our deeper wisdom speak in the moment? Our owl is always ready if we allow it space. The only thing we need to watch out for is to not let our controlling crocodile steal the show.

One way to cultivate intuition in communication is to create safe spaces for it. The crocodile will feel compelled to perform and say the right and rational thing when it feels it is being judged. That's why we often start meetings with a Check-in, a sequential monologue that allows everyone to address one to three questions we pose up front (see also Chapter 7). We also conduct "Fishbowls" in meetings, where we invite one or more people from the group, often including the leader, to come to the front of the room and have a conversation with each other as if they were in their own living room with nobody else watching. One client organization calls these "Living room conversations." Speaking off-script, from the gut, has led to some of the most transformative moments in meetings I have seen.

When people are truthful with others in ways they may never have been, they inspire others to do the same. That level of truthfulness can feel like a confession. "What I really believe is . . . ," "My biggest concern about this is . . . ," "My growth opportunity I see here is . . . ," and "I sense . . ." are some phrases that have prompted these "confessions."

When we create a safe space for intuition, it blossoms. We need to foster environments where it is okay to speak from a place that is deeply truthful and from beyond the limitations of our rational mind. Intuition tends to make things simple, fast. In the end, what we all deeply care about is quite similar. And one person pointing out what they see as truth helps others do the same—making the *undiscussable* discussable. One way to inspire people to speak from their intuition is to be deeply truthful ourselves first, and exude an energy of mindfulness. When we throw out the rulebook of what we think we should say, we open the door to deeper and more spontaneous expression and connection.

Communicating Contentment—CQ

No matter how well we communicate, life happens. We hit a snag. Someone says or does something upsetting and all of a sudden we're feeling as if the world is crashing down on us. Our crocodiles are out in full force and we're feeling stressed out, reactive, and upset. And even worse, people in our field of care are too.

Growth Leaders may find themselves in the eye of a storm frequently, as growing consciousness means constant change in the inner and external world. Most people don't like change, and when people don't like something and they are operating on an unconscious level, they tend to become reactive, often causing harm to themselves and others around them.

How do we communicate contentment and confidence, even when we're not feeling it at all? When we're feeling hijacked while in the midst of guiding others—in a meeting, at a dinner table, or anywhere—it helps to remember that our primary concern is not us feeling good. As with coaching one-on-one, our first and foremost intention is to be present, like the sky. When we become mindful of the stillness of the current moment (taking a few deep breaths in the belly can help calm our crocodiles) we may feel some space emerging around the heat and heaviness of our raging crocodiles. Once we have done this, it helps to ask ourselves some questions to further reclaim our sanity:

- What is upsetting me?

- What do I believe that is upsetting me?

- Is that true?

- What if I release this thought altogether, knowing that no thought is absolutely true?

- How can I grow from this?

- What if I became twice as kind to myself now, then how would I see myself and others?

- How can I lead from my higher purpose now?

Contemplate any of these questions, or any other that brings you back to presence. Perhaps try a brief meditation exercise. Sometimes this requires digging deep. The good news is that when we dig deep, we find the resources within ourselves to address any situation we face—unconditional love never fails. With the eyes of presence, unconditional love, *everything becomes an opportunity for growth and service*. I remember being in a workshop where a participant asked me why I thought I was qualified to lead the workshop, even though I didn't have a degree in psychology. My crocodile wanted me to share my credentials. I didn't. Instead, I took a breath and let myself become still inside. Then I remembered why I was there: to help evolve consciousness. The question came: "For this workshop to be helpful to you, what would you like to get out of it?" After I had heard her response, I said "I don't know whether I will be the right person to help you with that. And to find out, do you want to stay for the afternoon session and make your decision then whether this is working for you?" Being in presence helped me to see the underlying concern, which was not about my qualifications but about her needs. Being in presence helped me detach from outcomes. Whether the participant stayed was not my concern. From presence, I was able to see what was needed and act on that.

When others around us are upset, we can choose mindfulness and kindness. We communicate through our gentle yet firm mind-set that upsets are not the end of the world, simply parts of the growth process. This can help disarm the crocodiles that are controlling others, as they are receiving signals that all is well. Please note that it is wise not to probe into others' crocodiles unless specifically given permission. When people are under the influence of crocodiles, they are unlikely to experience any help as helpful—a crocodile perceives everything as a threat, even someone trying to be helpful.

We remind ourselves that everyone is on their own journey. We are not here to fix; we are here to be present to ourselves and others, and to extend a helping hand when asked. We are here to be present and LOVE—Letting Others Voluntarily Evolve.

FIVE ELEMENTS OF A GROWTH STORY

Lots and lots of communication will need to happen when you start actively working on the culture of your field of care. One way to keep it simple is to write your Growth Story, and have it permeate all your communications. As you write it, keep in mind these five elements. A Growth Story:

1. Unites people in a powerful collective purpose.
2. Names the collective crocodiles.
3. Points to the aspired owl mind-sets.
4. Elicits unflinching commitment to think and act differently.
5. Communicating all 5Qs (MQ, EQ, IQ, NQ, and CQ).

Or, to put it simply, a Growth Story answers the question:

How do you want people to think, feel, and act differently?

GROW YOUR FIELD OF CARE TODAY

All right, enough said. We have explored how to steward our field of care with the Five Things that Shift Culture: Vision, Role Modeling, Language Markers, Symbols, and Communication. And we have learned how to share a Growth Story and communicate Growth through the 5Qs. Are you ready to get started and dive in?

The first step in becoming a Growth Leader is to commit to our own growth. Once we have made this courageous resolution and have practiced it for a while, we can start working with others, one-on-one and one-to-many. I noticed in myself and others hesitation to becoming a Growth Leader, as opposed to just growing myself. We may believe we need to be fully evolved, to have completely seen through all our fears, or to always be in balance, before we can get started. This is not true. By engaging in the world with a Growth Leadership mind-set, we find our internal growth accelerating. The external world provides valuable triggers that surface the crocodilian parts of ourselves that we haven't seen through yet. Moreover, when we enter the world intending to serve it the best way we know how, we are bound to benefit it in some way—however imperfectly.

Growth Leadership is not about perfection, it's about progress. Do we dare to share ourselves as we are now, accepting our own and others' unconscious parts? We can enter the world, even steward it, without being delayed by our anxieties about being imperfect.

Where to start with serving others? Select your field of care. This can be your family, your group of friends, your organization, your team, or another community—whatever group you feel called to serve. Then start talking to others about your interest to evolve consciousness and see who this resonates with. These will be the people that may become your first partners in growth. And with them, you can architect an approach that will help shift the culture in your field of care more broadly.

Be patient. It takes time for mind-sets to evolve. Don't get discouraged. Martin Luther King said that "we cannot afford the luxury of despair." Know that there are many people around the world working on similar journeys. Imagine you're sitting with them and sharing your stories. Feel unity in purpose. In the end, everyone is on a journey to grow their consciousness. It's just that you may have decided to become a more conscious steward for that.

Gandhi's mantra was: "Renounce and enjoy." To steward a field of care, we intend to be at zero—zero attachment to outcome, zero attachment to personal gain, and zero attachment to our agenda. Renounce any fruits your crocodile decided it wants to get from your stewardship. Do it because you feel called to. And enjoy the stewardship itself. That *is* the reward.

With that zero-attachment mind-set, are you ready to dive in? There is a powerful Growth Story waiting to be written and lived by you. Are you ready to put pen to paper, take a stand, and serve the evolution of your field of care wholeheartedly?

FIELDWORK

1. What is your field of care? What is the organization that you would like to influence? Is it your team? Is it your family? Is it your friends? Is it your community?

2. Who is someone that inspires you? How would he or she use the Five Things that shift Culture described in this chapter?

3. What is your Growth Stewardship Vision for your field of care? What are two or three crocodiles that have a grip on your field of care right now? And what are two or three owls that you would like your field of care to move toward? What is the underlying purpose, *the why*, that this will serve?

FROM: Crocodiles	TO: Owls

Purpose:

4. What are some language markers you can use to help people follow?

5. What is a symbolic bet that you can make to inspire your field of care? What is a symbol that you can put in place to show that this change in consciousness is here to stay?

6. What are some things that you can do to ensure effective communication within your field of care? How will you communicate with each of the 5Qs?

   I will communicate meaningfulness by . . .

   I will communicate with emotional maturity by . . .

   I will communicate intelligently by . . .

   I will communicate intuitively by . . .

   I will communicate contentment by . . .

7. Now write your Growth Story, addressing the following questions:

    •   What do you stand for as a leader?

        a. What mind-sets and behaviors are you committed to growing in yourself? FROM (croc) → TO (owl)?

        b. What is your underlying purpose?

    •   What is your vision for your field of care?

        a. What mind-sets and behaviors of your field of care do you intend to grow? FROM (croc) → TO (owl)?

        b. What specific outcomes do you aspire to? What contributions do you intend your field of care to make to themselves, the organization, customers, partners, and the world? (If your field of care is not a team in an organization, think about other stakeholders instead of the ones listed here.)

    •   What choices, however small, do you make now to make progress?

    •   What choices do you invite others to make now?

    First write the story in a few paragraphs . . .

        . . . then in one sentence

        . . . then in one word

        . . . then in a symbol.

8. How are you growing?

What Is Your Priority?

"Don't be satisfied with stories, how things have gone with others. Unfold your own myth." —Rumi

N
O ONE CAN DECIDE your priorities for you. Yet, what you place priority on has a defining impact on your life experience.

How do you know what your priorities are? They are where you put your time, attention, and other resources.

If you are prioritizing money, you may be spending a lot of your thinking energy on worrying about and delighting in money—having too little, just enough, a lot, more than others, enough to last you and your loved ones a lifetime, a charity to help others, and the list goes on. You can build your whole life around money. Many people have done it in the past and even more people are doing it today.

If you are putting relationships first, you may have meaningful connections, or be overwhelmed by relationship ups and downs, be very sensitive to others, be very protective of the people closest to you, exclude others, include everyone, or whatever other experience you may have.

If you put yourself first, you may develop yourself, you may be very successful, you may despair when you aren't, you may become very important, you may create very self-nourishing places to work and live, you may struggle to do so, and so on.

What if you put growing into who you really are first? Then what would your experience be? First, you may discover that who you really are is not separate from others. It's like a limitless energy of presence, unconditional love, joy, and peace. Words can't describe it. It has no opposite. It's been described as the observer. We have also called it the sky in this book. It's unopposed, yet all-embracing, firm and gentle, clear and open, focused and sensitive, and still and dynamic. The more we grow into who we really are, the more we embody this presence—peace, joy, love—this dynamic stillness. We become that.

Then *everything* else becomes an opportunity to learn, serve, and play—with effortless effort. Money may become a teacher that helps us understand and release some of our fears of not having enough, uncertainty, and so on. Once we release these fears, we may become even clearer about who we really are—presence, unconditional love, joy. Money becomes an energy we learn to work with skillfully. From presence, we have a natural concern with balancing resources for all of us. *Is it true that I need this money?* we may ask. We learn to surrender to our intuition that, just like a river, knows which way to turn. We know what to do. Working with money changes from watching it speed past you and becomes like driving a car on the highway. We can't possibly anticipate all the twists and turns beforehand—if we tried to figure it out beforehand, we'd go mad—but somehow we know when to switch lanes, how to give space to an oncoming car, and when to turn. And there are plenty of signs along the way. The more we let go of the fear of money, of our clinging and aversion to it, the more we enter a natural flow. In flow, we may see that we are caretakers of money and that we are called to use it to what serves most in that moment.

What about relationships? When we prioritize growing into who we really are, relationships are no longer an end unto themselves, something we need to get and keep, but they become something we learn through, play in, and serve from. We are students of and caregivers in relationships. Relationships teach us about the fear of abandonment, about boundaries, about staying true to our purpose, about integrating seeming opposites in conflicts, about helping someone, and about allowing things to flow as they are. There are so many lessons to be found in the relationship syllabus. When relationships are not about getting or keeping them, but instead about growing through them and caring, they become like the plants in our garden. We water them. We learn about ourselves and our own growth as we watch the relationship evolve. We learn about human intimacy as we taste the fruits, and we learn to let go as things change. Relationships, by their changing nature, are excellent teachers about that which is constant within us, by showing us the contrast between unopposed presence, unconditional love—our essence—and the fleeting things of our world: being in a relationship and experiencing joy, longing, warmth, appreciation, sadness, anger, envy, frustration, awe, and all the other human emotions that come up so strongly when we engage deeply with others.

And what about me and my place in the world, my self-esteem, my worth, who I am as a person? We may come to see ourselves as a collection of roles that presence takes on, like changing costumes, some of which we wear for quite a while. Our identity can be a great teacher about standing in the power of presence. There is a paradox here. The more we let go of our identity as a person—e.g., a good, nice, competent, wise, generous, or special one—the more we can connect with the timeless presence that we really are beyond surface attributes. The more we rest in this timeless presence that we are, the more we can be of service in the world, contributing to safety, intimacy, achievements, learning, charity, cohesion, and wisdom. Our persona, which is always about protecting a seemingly separate "me," is no longer in the way. Instead we may come to see ourselves as an empty vessel through which the power of presence flows freely.

When we make true self-discovery our top priority, life becomes an endlessly inspiring adventure. Whatever we encounter on our path, we recognize as our next doorway into who we really are. This attitude empowers us with a fire for learning that gives us peace, calm, warmth, and tremendous strength to transform everything in our lives into an opportunity to grow more into who we really are—presence, joy, peace, unconditional love—and embody that more in our lives, a little bit more every day.

This is not a journey that you or I control. We can choose to grow consciously. And we can surrender to life, trusting it will guide us the way it will. We can't force insights; we let them come to us. We listen to the whispers. We don't control events and what they teach us; they simply appear. We don't control when and what we will learn; we honor the flow of things.

Are you ready to become this open? This outrageous? This playful? This fierce? This forgiving? This caring? This trusting? I hope reading this book and spending time with yourself has fueled your resolve to grow more into who you truly are and let go of the fears, doubts, and other distractions that may have kept you from decisively walking up the endless mountain of self-discovery.

When I go on hikes, I often see people stop at the souvenir stand at the bottom of the mountain. Many stay there and never venture out into the backcountry. We love our comfortable, controlled surroundings. If we don't leave the souvenir stand in our lives, we don't give ourselves permission to get to know our true selves.

The more we know ourselves, the more we come to appreciate the gift that we are. The more we appreciate the gift we are, the more we will share it. Will you allow yourself to discover and share your gift a bit more every day?

Leave the souvenir stand you know so well. Take a small, bold step outside of it now. Give yourself that gift. Today. Why wait?

Thank you for traveling with me on this journey of discovering who we truly are.

Acknowledgments

I WISH TO ACKNOWLEDGE everyone I have ever met. You have helped me find out more of who I really am. Your stories have become this book. Even though I don't remember all your names, I will mention a few of you here.

Thank you, Mom and Dad, Hanny and Bertus Faber. You have taught me so much. Your countless examples of perseverance helped me complete this book. A big thanks to my siblings, Douwe, Janneke, and Trude. You taught me about relating to and growing with others, each in our own way. Douwe, I admire your courage; Janneke, I celebrate your warmth; and Trude, I honor your wisdom. I thank Adrie van der Veen. You taught me about staying in the moment and appreciating my innate talents. Thank you, Mr. Brouwer and Japke Wiersema—you taught me about loving language. Thank you, David Kat, for teaching me about real friendship and always being there for each other. Thank you, Maarten Dirk van der Heijden. You helped me understand what it means to stand on my own two feet. Thank you, Paul Hansen, for helping me appreciate Frank Sinatra-like ease. Thank you, Jerry Cacciotti, for teaching me that I have a choice to be happy no matter what. Thank you, Pamela Kucenic, for helping me uncover my authentic voice. Thank you, Jonelle Reynolds, for coaching me all these years and teaching me about the power of love. Thank you, Karen Aberle, for helping me jump into the amazing field of coaching. Thank you, Theresa Visser, for helping me accept myself as I am. Thank you, Monique Wise—you taught me about relating intimately to myself and another. Thank you, Christina Leijonhufvud, for teaching me about friendship and fortitude. Thank you to all the clients I have ever worked with. You have taught me everything I know. You are a gigantic mirror to help me understand myself. Thank you to all my colleagues at Towers Perrin, Strategic Decisions Group, Axialent, and Co-Creation Partners—you all helped to understand more deeply how to be myself and be of service. Thank you, Maria Sofia van Dooijeweert, for teaching me how to love myself. Thank you, Ricardo Gil, for coaching me to always keep a question on my heart. Thank you, Sharon Ting, for encouraging me and helping me appreciate what coaching truly is about. Thank you, Kay Crista, for introducing me to heart-opening poetry. Thank you, Gaurav Bhatnagar, for helping me believe in my strength and introducing me to the Qs. Thank you, Shobha Nayar, for helping me to express myself authentically and clearly. Thank you, Fred Kofman, for providing me with the foundation from which to work in this field. Thank you, Julio Olalla, for coaching me to let go of my pedestals. Thank you, Patricio Campiani, for teaching me about being purposeful, introducing me to yin-yang balance and not giving up. Thank you, Patrick Connor, for all your coaching and providing incredible depth and warmth to help me rekindle the fire for this journey and for introducing me to many of the tools that are in this book, including cultivating fascination, also with our fears, the eyes of love, good girl/good boy mind-sets, yin-yang strategies, staying supremely disinterested with our thoughts and feelings to connect with presence, and taking an attitude of mutual learning in conversation. Thank you to everyone at the Sharmadã Foundation for providing a community with whom I get to grow. Thank you, Cindy Rowe, for helping me to discover myself with resoluteness and warmth. Thank you to my colleagues and cofounders at the Growth Leaders Network to help me trust others at a completely new level: Debbie Lynd, David Tunnah, Gary Keil, Gene White, Yvonne Higgins Leach, Ramu Iyer, Daniel Richmond, Mieke Bouwens, Nienke Schaap, Amanda Voogd, Marjolijn Bunicich, Goska Sixma, Fred Kok, Jannes Schuiling, and Mascha Perquin-Sarneel. Thank you, Seymour Boorstein, for introducing me to the symbols of the owl and the crocodile. Your guidance and these icons have been deeply inspiring on my path and in my work. Thank you, Nicolas Blaiotta, for teaching me about real empathy and the art of the long view. Thank you, Hitendra Wadhwa, for teaching me how to support Columbia students. Thank you, Holly Wright, for having the confidence to stand with me as we piloted this work at Columbia Business School Executive Education. Thank you, Rita Cortez, for helping me apply the Work on myself, especially when I didn't want to. Thank you, Byron Katie and Vijay Govindarajan, for providing powerful tools that taught me about self-renewal. Thank you, Jahon Mikal Brown, for teaching me about truthfulness, play, and awe. Thank you, Toni Townes-Whitley, for teaching me about fearlessness and forgiveness. Thank you, Chris Capossela, for teaching me about kindness under pressure. Thank you, Robert Tarkoff, for helping me appreciate interdependence. Thank you, Andrew Blum, for kindling my fascination for truth. Thank you, Adyashanti, for showing me how to embody love.

Thank you, Isabella Steele, for doing an amazing edit on this book. Without you this book would not exist. Thank you, Nora Rawn, for having the courage and wisdom to help me understand what this book is really about as you helped me refine it.

And thank you all, the millions of people who came before us. Thank you for paving the way on which we walk.

Three Realities Meditation
(To Be Recorded by Yourself)

TAKE TEN TO FIFTEEN MINUTES daily to do this practice. Set a gentle timer so you know when the time is up. Prerecord it so you can listen to this text.

Please sit comfortably, easily, in a chair with your legs uncrossed, or on the floor with your legs crossed. Rest your palms on your thighs. Take a deep breath into your belly, and another one. And one more. When you are ready, please close your eyes.

Start noticing the breath, going in and out, the chest going up and down, up and down, as the breath is going in and out, in and out.

Notice where there is tension in your body; allow the tension to be there fully. Now allow it to expand to as much tension as it wants to be. Allow it fully. Yes, that's it. Allow it a bit more and a bit more and a bit more.

Now ... please open your eyes, halfway, looking down (five seconds silence) ... now, please close your eyes (thirty seconds silence).

Now ... please open your eyes, quarter of the way, looking down (5 seconds silence), now, please close your eyes, and ... start noticing the rise and fall of the breath in the chest. No concentration, no control, just an easy effortless focus on the breath. Just like watching clouds in the sky. The breath goes in and out and the chest rises and falls again.

You may notice some thoughts or outside noises. When this happens, very easily and effortlessly bring your attention back to the breath as the breath goes in and out and the chest is rising and falling as the breath goes in and out. We're at the second reality, thinking, and the first reality, breathing.

Notice your thinking about what you just heard and very easily and effortlessly return to watching the breath, until you hear this voice again.

Silence (five minutes)

Now, very easily, notice any tension in the body, let it become stronger and even stronger . . .

Become supremely disinterested in it, lose all interest in the body sensations, the first reality. It's there and you're becoming supremely disinterested in it. You allow yourself to relax and let the body sensations, pleasurable or painful, be what they are.

Choose over and over again being supremely disinterested in the body sensations. Now notice any thinking and other feelings. Become supremely disinterested in those as well. Choose losing all interest in those. Notice any resistance, and lose all interest in that as well.

There is nothing you need to pay attention to. The only thing you're being asked to do is to relax into a space that is beyond your body, thoughts, and feelings.

Start noticing what is beyond the thoughts and feelings. And notice the mind trying to understand it, or label it. Also let go of that. Become supremely disinterested in all thoughts and feelings and let yourself fall, deeper and deeper, and deeper and deeper, into the beyond. And beyond, and beyond that, and beyond that.

You may notice body sensations, feelings, thoughts come up, just let them pass through you. You are supremely disinterested in them.

Notice what is opening up for you. Rest in that, more and more deeply. Rest as presence, awareness, nothing to do, nothing to fix, only rest as presence. And stay supremely disinterested in everything that comes up in the body and mind. Come back to resting as presence, awareness, peace.

Silence (five minutes)

When you are ready, please open your eyes.

Three Realities Meditation (To Be Read)

M AKE YOURSELF REALLY comfortable. Find an even more comfortable place to sit in your chair. Rest. Become really at ease, even if your body is not feeling good today. That has nothing to do with it. Allow yourself just to be in this chair. For the next five to seven minutes we're going to do the Three Realities meditation. And for that, I'm going to invite you to read slowly, breathing deeply into the spaces. We want to move awareness through the body, to begin to really feel the physical reality. If you find that you are reading too quickly, try putting five seconds between each line of text.

Start by feeling the sensation of your feet. If your feet aren't already on the floor, maybe place them on the floor.

Feel your ankles.

Feel your thighs.

Feel your sit bones.

Feel your stomach.

Feel your chest.

Feel your heart area.

Feel your shoulders.

Feel your arms.

Feel your hands.

Feel your fingers.

Feel your neck.

Feel your throat.

Feel your chin.

Relax the jaw.

It may feel like it unhinges.

Relax the tongue.

It may feel like it shortens.

Relax the eye sockets.

The eyes might feel like they're softening.

Relax the forehead.

It may feel like it opens.

Relax the top of the head.

It may feel like it's melting.

Relax the ears.

They may feel like they're softening.

Start to become aware of the rise

and fall

of the

breath

in the

chest.

Now, when you're ready.

Please close your eyes halfway, looking down. You should still be able to read this text.

Keep your awareness on the rise

    and fall

        of the

            breath

        in the

    chest.

You may wander into some, or many, thoughts or feelings. Just notice these. Do not try to change them. Notice how they just come, stay a little bit, and leave. Like clouds blowing through an open sky, they always go. Notice the thoughts and feelings. Any thoughts and feelings.

Start to become aware.

    Deeper.

        Loosely.

            Of the rise

    and fall

        of the

            breath

        in the

    chest.

No concentration.
No control.

Just easy,

effortless

breathing.

Allow yourself, over these next few minutes, to become sincerely disinterested in all thoughts, feelings, and sensations.

Allow yourself to rest like you may never have before.

Anything that you notice.

Become sincerely disinterested.

Don't push it away. Don't study it.

Just stay supremely disinterested.

And allow yourself to go deeper,

  and deeper,

    and deeper,

      into space.

        Into the space.

And even become supremely disinterested in the space.

Rest here.

Be here.

Rest in silence.

Stay supremely disinterested.

Allow yourself to rest deeper.

Please close your eyes for a few minutes. And then when you're ready, please come back, into this room.

What did you notice, about these three realities (physical, mental, and transcendental)? What did you notice in these last minutes? Give yourself some time to reflect on this question.

Growth Leadership Summary Worksheet

Y OU'LL FIND BELOW a summary of the core Growth Leadership tools presented in this book. Please practice any of these tools whenever you find it useful. If you don't understand an exercise, it may be helpful to consult the corresponding chapter, or simply skip it for now. You can always come back to it later. We have included the chapter numbers for easy reference.

To help accelerate your learning, focus your practice on a challenge you are currently facing. Take a moment to think about it.

- What is it about?
- Who is it with?
- What will be a fulfilling outcome?

Browse the tools below and pick a few that may help you grow through this challenge. Make sure you pick at least one of the Growing Self tools.

GROWING SELF

Introduction

1. *Crocodile and Owl*—What reactive fear-based crocodilian mindsets and behaviors might I fall into? How would my wiser owl respond?

2. *How Are You Growing?*—What are you learning about yourself today? It doesn't matter how big or small, just take note of it and acknowledge that you are growing. What are you discovering about who you truly are? What about who you are not?

Chapter 1: Cultivating an Attitude of Growth

3. *Growth Instant*—What if I saw this moment as a moment of learning? Then how would I feel? What would I discover about myself?

4. *I-We-It Whisper Awareness*—What feedback am I getting about what my growth opportunities may be? What growth opportunities might I have in becoming more effective (It), having stronger relationships (We), and/or feeling more fulfilled (I)?

5. *Stillness Practice*—What happens when I allow myself a moment of doing nothing now? What if I stop paying attention to my busy thinking? What if I allow myself to rest? What am I discovering in stillness?

6. *Unflinching Fascination*—What area of learning do I not want to address in my life and leadership? How do I judge myself for not being masterful in this area yet? What if I saw every part of the challenge at hand as my teacher for this area of learning? What if I became a bit more gentle with myself? Then what might I learn? How can I be grateful for this station in life?

Chapter 2: Finding Our Fearless Calling

7. *Owl SUCCESS Intentions*—Which of these seven intentions am I most drawn to: *Samurai*-like courage and resourcefulness, *Uniting* with others through authenticity and empathy, *Centering* in my purpose, being *Curious* about possibilities, *Extending* my gift, *Sensing* cohesion, and *Simple* in service? Which of my core intentions do I intend to apply even more in this challenge to stretch myself?

8. *Growth Vision*—Who do I intend to be and become, no matter what (*unconditional intention*)? What do I intend to contribute to my world?

Chapter 3: Growing through Challenge— Transforming Crocodiles into Owls

9. *Growth Leadership Mind-set*—What if I approach this challenge with a Growth Leadership Mind-set, where I see it as an opportunity for *presence, self-discovery, contribution, and excellence*—how will I see and lead through it then?

10. *Twelve-Breath Presence Practice*—What if I took twelve conscious deep breaths now, resting my attention on the breath and the movement of my belly, and letting all thoughts and emotions just pass through me? How present would I be then?

11. *Owl Growth Leadership Coaching*—What is my challenge? What assumptions have I made about it? Who is talking now, the owl or the crocodile? How have I responded thus far? What has been the impact? How would my owl respond? How will I respond? How am I growing?

Chapter 4: Learning from Our Seven Fear Families— Befriending Seven Crocodiles

12. *The Fear Paradox*—How does my fear create the result I fear the most when I give in to my fear?

13. *Fear Families*—What may be some of the major fears driving my crocodiles (scarcity, abandonment, failure, uncertainty, hurt, complexity, loss of identity)? How would I lead without these fears?

14. *Crocodilian SUCCESS Personas*—Which of these seven masks do I wear to make up for my crocodilian fears? The *Safe* one who overworks, and goes into victimhood and short-term bias; the *Us vs. Them* one who judges, complies, and works in siloes; the *Controlling* one who is a perfectionist, manipulates, and micro-manages; the *Certain* one who is rigid, dramatic, and close-minded; the *Essential* one who is dominating, rescuing, and sometimes hides; the *Sapient* one who knows, is paranoid, and gives advice; or the *Special* one who puts himself on a pedestal, is a martyr, and lives in an ivory tower? How would I lead differently without these masks?

Chapter 5: Balancing All of Ourselves

15. *Yin-Yang Balance*—Which is my strongest leadership style, Yang (purposeful) or Yin (connected)? What is my weakest? How can I rebalance them to lead more effectively through this challenge?

16. *Abiding in Presence Meditation*—What would happen if I could rest more as the observer, as presence, as unopposed unconditional love; then what would become possible for me? How could I be in balance continuously?

Chapter 6: Truth Inquiry into Our Crocodilian Roots

17. *The Tree*—What is a recurring result in my relationships, in my effectiveness, and in my fulfillment that I don't like? What actions or behaviors are contributing to this unwanted result? What thoughts and feelings are associated with this action, and may be driving it? What history of beliefs may be driving these thoughts, feelings, and actions? What is the primary need at stake here? What is the underlying fear? How does the fear paradoxically create the result it fears the most?

18. *The Work*—Is it true? Can I absolutely know that it's true? How do I react when I believe that thought? Who would I be without the thought? Turn the thought around.

GROWING WITH OTHERS

Chapter 7: Growing Owls in Conversation

19. *COAX Growth Conversations*—Which of the four elements of a COAX conversation is my weakest link? Center in Conscious Unconditional Intention, Open with Authentic Expression, Ask with Heart-based Inquiry, and eXchange through Resonant Cocreation and Courageous Commitment.

20. *Center in Unconditional Intention*—Think of a conversation I need to have to make progress with this challenge. What is my Unconditional Intention for the conversation, detached from how the other person may respond? Consider *STANDS*: Speak Truthfully, Ask Non judgmentally, and Dare to be Still.

21. *Check-in*—What if, before a meeting, I created a space for a sequential monologue where everyone speaks in turn without interrupting, responding to a few simple questions, like: How are you feeling? How are you growing? What is your intention for this meeting?

22. *Open with Authentic Expression*—What is the *Authentic Message* I intend to convey? What is it, deep down, that I really care about?

23. *Ask with Heart-based Inquiry*—What expectations do I have of my conversation partner? Step into their shoes for a few minutes— what is it that they may want to share with me? Now imagine the conversation with them where I am completely free from expectations of them—how will I listen differently?

24. *eXchange through Resonant Co-creation and Courageous Commitment*— Imagine the heart of the conversation. What if we are both right? What if we both grew from this; then how would we see each other? Then, how would we approach this? What are some of the infinite ways we can express care for each other and for the issue at hand? What requests and promises will I make? What is the smallest yet most powerful next step I can agree to now?

GROWING OTHERS

Chapter 8: Growing Others—Coaching One-on-One

25. *FINISH "Coaching"*—How would my "Fixing-It-Now-I-Super-Hero" (FINISH) crocodile approach a coaching conversation with someone involved in my challenge?

26. *LOVE Coaching*—How I will approach the conversation with a "Letting-Others-Voluntarily-Evolve" (LOVE) intention? What will I do? What will I not do?

27. *5Q Coaching Mind-set* (MQ Meaning, EQ Emotion, IQ Intellect, NQ Intuition, and CQ Contentment)—Which of the 5Qs of the quality of my being as a coach is my strongest? Weakest? What is my growth opportunity?

28. *Coaching for Mastery*—Where may I go into victimhood leading through this challenge (blaming myself/others)? How can I respond more from my values?

29. *GROW Coaching*—Who of my stakeholders may be interested and benefit from coaching? Which of the four GROW elements is most important to focus on (Goal, Reality, Options, Wrap-up)?

Chapter 9: Growing into the Owls We Are— Coaching One to Many

30. *Growth Stewardship System*—Given my challenge, what is the Field of Care (e.g., organization, team, or family) that I would like to coach to evolve its mind-sets and behaviors? Build a Growth Stewardship System for this Field of Care addressing:

    a. What is my *Growth Stewardship Vision* for my Field of Care? What mind-sets would I like us to let go of that no longer serve us ("Froms")? What mind-set would I like us to adopt that will help us grow to our next level of excellence ("Tos")? What is the underlying purpose for doing so (the Why)?

    b. How do I intend to *role model* my Growth Stewardship Vision? What old mind-sets will I let go of? Which new ones will I practice?

    c. What *Language Markers* will I use to help people ractice the new mind-sets and behaviors? Language Markers are words and/or phrases I use repeatedly to point to the new intended ways of working.

d. What *Symbolic Bets* will I make to let people know the new way is here to stay? Symbolic bets are inspiring, visible, and gutsy investments of time, attention, and, often, money that make the new way tangible.

e. In what ways will I *communicate* the new way over and over again? How will I communicate all 5Qs (meaning, emotional maturity, intelligence, intuition, contentment)?

31. *Growth Story*—What new narrative do I intend to communicate that will help me lead through the challenge? How do I want people to feel, think, and act by the end of my communication? What do I stand for as a leader? What is my vision for my field of care? What crocodile-to-owl shifts do I aspire to? Why? What choices do I make now to make progress? What choices do I invite others to make now?

Bibliography

Introduction

Seymour Boorstein, M.D., *Who's Talking Now: The Owl Or The Crocodile*, AuthorHouse, 2011

Gallup research was quoted in: Marcus Buckingham and Curt Coffman, *First, Break All the Rules: What the World's Greatest Managers Do Differently* (New York: Simon & Schuster, 1999)

Chapter 1

Eknath Easwaran, *Gandhi The Man: How One Man Changed Himself To Change The World*, Nilgiri Press, 1972.

Henri J.M. Nouwen, *Making All Things New,* Harper Collins, 1981

Chapter 2

Viktor E. Frankl, *Man's Search For Meaning*, Rider Books, 1946

Nelson Mandela, *Long Walk To Freedom*, Little Brown & Co., 1994

Chapter 3

William L. Silber, "Why Did FDR's Bank Holiday Succeed?" *FRBNY Economic Policy Review*, July 2009

Ken Burns, *The Roosevelts: An Intimate History*, PBS, 2014

Jean Edward Smith, *FDR*, Random House, 2007

Daniel Goleman, *Emotional Intelligence: Why It Can Matter More Than IQ*, Bantam, 1995

———, *The Brain and Emotional Intelligence: New Insights*, More Than Sound (1601), 2011

Judy Willis, *Research-Based Strategies to Ignite Student Learning: Insights from a Neurologist/Classroom Teacher*, ASCD, 2006

Chapter 4

Vijay Govindarajan, *The Three-Box Solution: A Strategy for Leading Innovation*, Harvard Business School Press, 2016

"Adobe's Bold Embrace of the Computing Cloud Should Inspire Others," *The Economist*, March 22, 2014

Clint Eastwood, *Invictus*, 2009

Richard Waters, Monday interview: Shantanu Narayen, Adobe CEO, *Financial Times*, February 22, 2015, 6:30 PM

Judy Willis, *Research-Based Strategies to Ignite Student Learning: Insights from a Neurologist/Classroom Teacher*, ASCD, 2006

Chapter 5

Jill Bolte Taylor, *My Stroke Of Insight: A Brain Scientist's Personal Journey*, Viking, 2008

Anna Wise, *The High-Performance Mind: Mastering Brainwaves for Insight, Healing, and Creativity*, TarcherPerigee, 1997

Chapter 6

Byron Katie, Stephen Mitchell, *Loving What Is: Four Questions That Can Change Your Life*, Random House USA Inc., 2002

Chapter 7

Fred Kofman, *Conscious Business: How to Build Value Through Values*, Sounds True, 2006

Chapter 8

Max Landsberg, *The Tao of Coaching*, Profile Books, 1996

Chapter 9

Tessa Basford and Bill Schaninger, The four building blocks of change, *McKinsey Quarterly*, April 2016

Ken Burns, *The Address*, PBS, 2014

David Herbert Donald, *Lincoln*, Simon & Schuster, 1995

YouTube: Clinton on lessons learned from Mandela, December 9, 2006, https://www.youtube.com/watch?v=KZneBcyGEkk

About the Author

HYLKE FABER serves as a leadership coach and facilitator and leads the coaching organizations, Constancee and the Growth Leaders Network. He sings kirtan (East Indian meditative practice), loves the outdoors, and lives with his partner in Seattle, Washington.

Hylke received his Bachelor of Business Administration from Nijenrode the Netherlands Business School and a Master of Arts in International Relations from Johns Hopkins University. He served as a Partner at Co-Creation Partners and Strategic Decisions Group and as a consultant at Axialent and Towers Perrin, supporting leaders across multiple industries globally on strategy, organization, and culture development programs. He teaches the "Leader As Coach" courses at Columbia Business School Executive Education and has contributed to *Harvard Business Review*, including the article "What FDR Knew about Fear in Times of Change."

Hylke's mission is to realize his essence and help others do the same. He shares *Taming Your Crocodiles* to help all of us, including himself, take the next step in our endless journey to become more of who we truly are.